Lawrence S. Cunningham, editor

THE CATHOLIC FAITH: A READER

PAULIST PRESS
New York / Mahwah

Library of Congress Cataloging-in-Publication Data

The Catholic faith : a reader / Lawrence S. Cunningham, editor.
    p. cm.
    Companion vol. to: The Catholic faith : an introduction / Lawrence S.
Cunningham. c1987.
    Includes bibliographies
    ISBN 0-8091-3020-3 (pbk.) : $8.95 (est.)
    1. Catholic Church—Doctrines.   I. Cunningham, Lawrence.
BX1751.2.C3464 1988
282—dc19   88-21745
                                                    CIP

Published by Paulist Press
997 Macarthur Boulevard
Mahwah, New Jersey 07430

Printed and bound in the
United States of America

Acknowledgements:
The articles reprinted in *The Catholic Faith: A Reader* first appeared in the following publications and are reprinted with permission: "Scripture and Dogma Today" from *America* by Raymond E. Brown; "Christian Marriage: Basic Sacrament" from *Sacraments and Sacramentality*, by Bernard Cooke, Twenty-Third Publications; "Vatican II Reform: The Basic Principles" by Avery Dulles, *Church*, Summer 1985; "The Church as a Eucharistic Community" by Tad Guzie, *Chicago Studies* XXII, 1983; "Christian Initiation: Gate to Salvation" by Monika Hellwig, *Chicago Studies* XXIII, 1983; "The Marian Tradition and the Reality of Women" by Elizabeth A. Johnson from *Horizons* XII, 1985; "The Eucharist and Social Justice" by Roger Mahony from *Worship*, 1983; "Catholicism: A Synthesis" by Richard McBrien from *Catholicism*, Vol. 2, Chapter XXX, Winston Press, 1980; "The Community Called Parish" by Philip Murnion, from *Church*, Winter 1985; "A Theology of Sin" by Timothy O'Connell from *Chicago Studies* XXI, 1982; "Theology and Spirituality: Strangers, Rivals or Partners?" by Sandra Schneiders, *Horizons* XIII, 1986; "A Commitment to the Future," U.S. Bishops from *Economic Justice for All: Pastoral Letter on Catholic Social Teaching and the U.S. Economy*, Chapter 5, Washington, D.C.: United States Catholic Conference, © 1986; "Why Am I a Christian Today? by Karl Rahner from *The Practice of Faith: A Handbook of Contemporary Spirituality*, Crossroad.

Contents

iv

Introduction

The Catholic Faith: An Introduction (1987) is a basic approach to the Catholic faith. No one more than the author realizes how sketchy that introduction is. In the space of a very few pages the author attempted to lead the willing reader into a first encounter with that complex reality which is called the Roman Catholic Church. It was the hope of the publisher that this book might find some use in the classroom, and that hope has been realized. At the same time it is a fair guess that both teacher and student might wish a fuller discussion of some of the issues which are mentioned only in a short page or two. The editors at Paulist Press suggested an accompanying reader to flesh out the skeleton of the text. This volume attempts to fulfill that need.

Anthologies of essays by different hands on a given topic are always problematic as those who attempt to sell them well know. Such collections tend to be idiosyncratic, and this one is no exception. After much searching, for example, I failed to find a satisfactory short essay on Christology that would be broad enough for inclusion in this collection although fine books on that topic could fill a hefty bookshelf.

Much is left out that could be included; a certain ruthlessness impelled me to excise favorite essays simply because they did not meet the criteria which I set out at the beginning of the selection process.

What are those criteria?

In the first instance, I decided to omit articles which are too strenuously scholarly because the readings are meant for the beginning student more than for the professor. Twenty years in the classroom has convinced me that profound erudition might please the professor but only manages to bewilder the undergraduate. I looked for articles which were relatively unadorned with footnotes, technical vocabulary, and arcane historical discussions. That does not mean that these articles will not stretch the abilities of the student (as a reading of the article by Rahner will show) but that, by and large, the articles chosen do not presuppose a vast store of learning in order to gain something from them. I also tried to find non-scholarly articles which had a kind of survey quality to them so that one might find the current state of the question on a given topic.

Next, I tried to search out articles which had a strong pastoral orientation. It is one of the convictions of my book that Catholicism should be viewed not as a system to be studied but as a way of life into which one enters. With that in mind, I have tried to keep my remarks close to the experience (or possible experiences) of the putative ordinary Catholic who experiences the Church in the setting of North America. Many of the authors in this collection have devoted a goodly part of their professional lives speaking to such audiences. Their particular gift is the ability to absorb the fruits of scholarship in order to mediate it to a broader constituency.

Finally, I have made no attempt to be inclusive. To reproduce studies which touch on all aspects of Catholic life and worship is simply too daunting a task for such a beginning text. I felt no need to reproduce the very rich panorama of a book like Richard McBrien's *Catholicism* although I did include an excerpt from it.

In my first effort at getting an anthology together I tried to key the selections to the chapters in *The Catholic Faith*. Further reflection caused me to change my mind about that strategy. Such an organization presumes that the teacher is going to march through the text from beginning to end. Teachers do not always operate in that fashion. For that reason this collection is not organized along thematic lines. It follows the much more pedestrian strategy of listing the articles in alphabetical order so that the reader/teacher might use them *ad libitum*. Such an arrangement makes for a rather loosely constructed volume, but that was my intention. This reader should be seen as a resource for the teacher and not a ready-made lesson plan for a course.

The selections which are offered here should be seen as only a "second step" beyond the basic text itself. My hope would be that the interested student will understand that some fine theological minds grapple seriously with basic theological themes in order to deepen their own faith and, in that process, to pass the fruits of their study on to others. If students can see that, they will have learned how theology functions in the Church and how profound the issues are when reflected upon in a serious fashion. All of the articles reflect the passion and intelligence of people who are Church people; they are theologians in the sense that Saint Anselm defined theologians: persons who attempt to clarify and deepen their faith by sustained reflection.

Being in the "middle of the road" is not always seen as the best place to be. A populist politician in Texas once remarked that the middle of the road contains only yellow streaks and dead opposums. Nonetheless, I will unabashedly claim that position, however risky it is to remain there. Much of my personal and professional life has been spent trying to navigate between the Right (who brazenly arrogate to themselves the adjective "orthodox Catholic") and the self-congratulatory Left who see themselves alone as "progressive." It is my hope that this anthology reflects that middle path, which is to say, a respectful awareness of the traditional character of Catholicism and an openness to that process by which we continue the great task of reaching up to the revelation of Jesus who is the Christ.

Douglas Fisher of Paulist Press suggested that I do a reader. To him, and to Father Kevin Lynch, publisher of Paulist Press, I owe a debt of thanks. Much of the reading and research for this volume was done in the fall term of 1987 when I enjoyed the hospitality of the University of Notre Dame while serving as John A. O'Brien visiting professor of theology. I would like to thank the Department of Theology and its chair, Rev. Prof. Richard McBrien, for many kindnesses during my sojourn. Finally, much of the legwork for this reader was done by my assistant at Notre Dame, Brother Donal Leader of the Irish Christian Brothers. He is living proof that the Emerald Isle still produces saints and scholars.

A List of Contributors

RAYMOND E. BROWN is Auburn Distinguished Professor of New Testament at Union Theological Seminary in New York City.

JOHN A. COLEMAN is professor of theology at the Jesuit School of Theology in Berkeley, California.

BERNARD COOKE is professor of theology at Holy Cross College, Worcester, Massachusetts.

AVERY DULLES is emeritus professor of systematic theology at the Catholic University of America in Washington, D.C.

TAD GUZIE is a noted sacramental theologian.

MONIKA K. HELLWIG is professor of theology at Georgetown University.

ELIZABETH A. JOHNSON is a member of the theology faculty at the Catholic University of America.

PHILIP S. KEANE teaches moral theology at Saint Mary's Seminary in Baltimore.

ROGER MAHONY is the archbishop of Los Angeles, California.

RICHARD MC BRIEN chairs the theology department of the University of Notre Dame.

PHILIP J. MURNION heads the National Pastoral Life Center in New York City.

TIMOTHY E. O'CONNELL, a moral theologian, is one of the associate editors of *Chicago Studies*.

KARL RAHNER was one of this century's most distinguished theologians.

SANDRA M. SCHNEIDERS teaches theology and spirituality at the Jesuit School of Theology and the Graduate Theological Union in Berkeley, California.

Raymond E. Brown

Scripture and Dogma Today

I have been asked to contribute some observations on the relation of the current approach to Scripture to the understanding of Catholic dogma. One must be careful about speaking too simply of "the current approach to Scripture" as if there were only one. To the contrary, as with automobiles, each year produces a new model for studying the Bible or, to use the language of the guild of scholars, a new model of biblical criticism. But, if I may be permitted to cut beneath luxuriant theorizing, I think there is an element in our approach to the Bible today that is especially essential to the question of the relation between Scripture and dogma. This element is sometimes called "historical criticism," as heir to a form of biblical study developed in the 18th and 19th centuries often by scholars of rationalist background. However, the approach today has lost a rationalist tone for most Protestant practitioners, and probably never had it for Catholics who began to use the method in the 20th century.

The core element in a historical-critical approach to the Bible, if I may simplify, is to take seriously the human authors of the Scriptures as people living in history whose views were affected by the conditions and limitations of their time, by their backgrounds and by the sources of knowledge to which they had access. Before the advent of historical criticism, all issues could be solved by affirming that God was the author of the Bible, that God knew all truth and was addressing the current reader who lived thousands of years after the Bible was first written. In its rationalist origins, historical criticism was first thought to refute such affirmations about God; but a more moderate approach has sought to combine both positions. The human authors of the Bible were people of their times, and yet the infinite God communicated through their writings in a unique way (inspiration). These authors wrote for their contemporaries, but what they wrote is still uniquely effective in God's communicating to us. A balanced use of historical criticism does not pretend to give access to the entire meaning of the Bible but to a basic component in interpretation.

In Catholicism, after a long period of resistance, historical criticism in its basic direction was affirmed by Pope Pius XII in the encyclical *Divino Afflante Spiritu* in 1943. Since there had been little transitional preparation for this change, the affirmation of such criticism was resisted and only partially comprehended by the beginning of the Second Vatican Council. A major battle over the implications of biblical criticism marked the beginning of the council in November 1962, and the victory of the supporters of a modern approach to Scripture set the direction of the council toward openness to change in many areas. Thus the most fundamental contribution of biblical criticism to Catholic dogma and doctrine may be the general direction opened for Catholic development by Vatican II. A strong component in this has been ecumenical cooperation; for Catholic biblical scholars learned biblical criticism in the 1940's to the 1960's from Protestants, and thus much progress in the study of the Bible has been an ecumenical venture.

Before I turn to more specific relationships between Scripture and dogma, a word about "dogma" and "doctrine." I wish to discuss here specifically what the Roman Catholic Church teaches infallibly as an interpretation of divine revelation. Such infallible teaching includes not only what has been taught in an exceptional or *extraordinary* way (e.g., creeds, condemnatory statements of ecumenical councils, papally defined teachings)—doctrines to which the term "dogma" is often applied—but also a wider body of truths flowing from revelation that have been taught and believed as part of the *ordinary* essentials of Catholicism. In some ways, this ordinary teaching is more important for Catholic life and practice, even if more difficult to define.

In confining myself to the impact of scriptural research on infallible church teaching, extraordinary and ordinary, I recognize that I am avoiding a difficulty. Too many Catholics assume that whatever they were taught in religion by parents or schoolteachers is unchangeable and infallible Catholic doctrine, whereas in fact their religious beliefs are an amalgam ranging from what theologians would regard as infallible teaching to pious opinions. I can still remember the anger of one woman at my discussions of the Gospel infancy narratives because she thought they undermined Catholic doctrine that Jesus was born on Dec. 25. Yet a discussion of the impact of scriptural research on pious opinions that have never been taught by the church as infallible interpretations of revelation would take us too far afield. Let me concentrate on two contributions of biblical criticism to the contemporary understanding of doctrine infallibly taught.

The first contribution has been a growing understanding of the limitation of human perception of divine truth. For example, Old Testament study has shown that the author of Genesis had no scientific knowledge of the origin of the world or of human beings but shared the legendary views of his time. This has led to greater precision in the Catholic doctrine of creation. At one time, the doctrine might have been phrased in terms not only of the *fact* of creation (all things have been brought into being by God) but also of the *manner* of creation described in Genesis (a work of six days without a hint of evolution). Biblical study has enabled us to regard the latter as nonessential phrasing in the limited perceptions of a millennium before Christ, and now we can distinguish ourselves from fundamentalists who regard the *manner* of creation as divinely revealed.

More difficult has been the application of biblical critical insights to doctrine based on the New Testament. For instance, Vatican II ("The Dogmatic Constitution on the Church," No. 18) repeated the Catholic doctrine that Christ willed that the successors of the apostles, namely the bishops, should be shepherds in His church to the consummation of the world, but supplied no guidance as to how the bishops became the successors of the apostles. Many Catholics would have read that statement with the simplified understanding that the Twelve Apostles chosen by Jesus picked successors to rule over churches they had founded so that each church in New Testament times was ruled by one bishop.

Biblical criticism of the New Testament shows that we know virtually nothing about members of the twelve founding churches or appointing successors. The letters of Timothy and Titus show that in some of the Pauline churches groups of presbyters had episcopal care. Throughout the second century, the custom of one bishop gradually became universal. These insights do not invalidate the doctrine that the bishops eventually became the pastoral successors of the apostles, but warn that the how of the process was more complicated than formerly thought and that many details cannot be recovered. The two examples given of increasing doctrinal precision as to what may be the core of revelation stem from what is taught by the extraordinary magisterium of the church as explained above (creeds, councils). This process will continue, and surely other instances of doctrinal clarification could be offered.

When one enters into the area of what is taught infallibly by the ordinary magisterium of the church, the process of doctrinal clarification becomes even more delicate. A recent work of mine, *Biblical Criticism and Church Doctrine*, was found by one Catholic theologian reviewer to be too conservatively generous in what I accept as taught infallibly by the ordinary magisterium. Unfortunately (but perhaps prudently), the reviewer did not specify the items that I wrongly thought to reflect infallible teaching, and so I shall have to guess at an example of what may have been meant. I refer to the virginal conception of Jesus—namely, that He was not engendered by a human father. That idea is found only in two places in the New Testament, the first chapter of Matthew and the first chapter of Luke. No other New Testament author clearly refers to it, and the accounts of Matthew and Luke differ from each other significantly. In terms of critical exegesis, I have contended that one cannot prove that Matthew and Luke preserve a historical memory, but that factuality is still a more plausible explanation than the nonfactual suggestions that have been offered (imitation of the births of pagan heroes, reflection on Is. 7:14, etc.).

I have also been careful to insist that the inability of critical exegesis to go beyond probability (at most) on this question does not mean that it is an open or undecided issue among Catholics, because I think the virginity of Mary in conceiving Jesus is infallibly taught by the ordinary magisterium of the church. Some Catholic scholars (more often theologians, but some biblical exegetes) disagree and claim that it is not infallibly taught by the church that Jesus did not have a human father. The Congregation for the Doctrine of the Faith (C.D.F.) in Rome or local bishops have acted adversely to such a claim of noninfallibility when it was made in Holland, Spain and most recently in Germany. Inevitably, this cautioning reaction by church authorities is dismissed by some as the unenlightened limitations of ecclesiastical understanding in our times.

A factor in such encounters is that in a 1973 document (*Mysterium Ecclesiae*) the C.D.F. itself admitted that the infallible doctrines of the church, while never wrong, are sometimes phrased in the changeable conceptions of a given epoch and may need to be rephrased. How far can that rephrasing go and what mechanism persuades church authorities that rephrasing is necessary? More adventurous theologians contend that only by their challenging past phrasing can the authorities be persuaded to look at a doctrine anew and determine what are nonessential elements. Church authorities contend that theologians may be wrong in the points they challenge and mislead ordinary Catholics toward a rephrasing that will never be acceptable. (It is difficult to imagine a church-accepted rephrasing of the virginal conception to include Jesus' having a human father or of the Resurrection to allow that Jesus' body corrupted to dust in the grave, for such rephrasing seems to negate an essential aspect of the doctrine.) To church authorities, the bold affirmations of some theologians clamoring for change respect neither the caution required by the uncertainty of the evidence nor the pastoral "domino effect" of creating doubts.

As for the contribution of Scripture to such issues, there may be agreement among exegetes, conservative and liberal, about the extent of the biblical evidence (assigning to it a shade of possibility or probability), combined with disagreement among theologians as to whether the church's teaching constitutes an infallible interpretation of divine revelation in relation to the matter concerned. In other words, the focus is shifting to the authority of the teaching church.

Those biblical scholars who know very well the limitations of the biblical evidence (and thus are sharply distinguished from a kind of Catholic fundamentalism that refuses to apply biblical criticism) and who nevertheless decide to be cautious in dismissing as misunderstanding what has normally been thought to be taught infallibly by the church may be acknowledging that, if all human perception is limited, so is the perception of the 20th century and that a future retrospection may have more appreciation for centuries of Christian wisdom than momentary reactions in the face of new knowledge.

If the first contribution of biblical criticism to greater precision in Catholic doctrine has concerned areas that are dealt with in the Scriptures, a second contribution has been to make us aware of the extent to which doctrine has gone beyond the Scriptures. If one reflects on the theological disputes of the 4th century or the 16th century (Reformation), the disputants on both sides often assumed that *their* views were clearly held in New Testament times and that their opponents had introduced novelties foreign to the New Testament. Often, however, biblical criticism has shown that the suppositions on both sides of the dispute involve issues beyond the detectable understanding of New Testament Christians.

The Reformation arguments about whether there are seven, three or two sacraments is a good example. The New Testament refers to sacred actions such as baptism, eucharist, forgiveness of sins and anointing of the sick; but we have no real evidence of whether the Christians of that period joined such actions in an "umbrella" category. The term "sacrament" is not found in the New Testament, and no other term is offered that would show how the early Christians interrelated what *we* call sacraments. That does not mean that the Reformation debate was foolish or irrelevant; but it does mean that more accurately the debate concerned developments after the New Testament (even in cataloging baptism and eucharist, which the Reformers assumed to be New Testament "sacraments").

The issue of lines of development going beyond the New Testament to doctrines that have been disputed in subsequent centuries has been expounded in two ecumenical books done by Catholics and Protestants together, *Peter in the New Testa-*

ment (1973) and *Mary in the New Testament* (1978). In those books, all the parties agreed that the clear conception of the papacy and some of the Marian doctrines go beyond the New Testament evidence. Interestingly, the parties also saw lines of development connecting such doctrines to strands of thought in the New Testament. The debated point, then, is not so much the New Testament evidence, but the validity of church developments related to the New Testament.

If often Protestants have been explicit about rejecting the validity of some of these doctrinal lines of development, there are now curious attempts by Catholics at both ends of the theological spectrum to confine dogma and infallible teaching to what was explicitly known in New Testament times. Ultraconservatives may do this as part of their rejection of a critical understanding of development; they want to read all Catholic dogma in or into the Scriptures. Ultraliberals may have another agenda—namely, the revival of a Christianity and a church less encumbered by the structures of authority. If moderates or centrists stress both the limitations of the scriptural insights into divine revelation and the validity of more-than-scriptural developments in later church teaching, they still must struggle with the fact that not every church development over the ages was necessarily a divinely guided insight into revelation. The very necessity for Catholic reforms such as those enacted at Vatican II suggests that. How to decide what is truly doctrinal and truly an infallible insight into God's revelation in the area of post-New Testament lines of development, as distinct from what is passing or even developing into a blind alley, is now a major problem in theology.

I have written this article with the goal of explaining some important elements in the relationship between biblical interpretation and church teaching. Inevitably the doctrinal examples chosen from Christology and ecclesiology reflect the concentrations of my own career. (Biblical exegesis does not come into such direct confrontation with some of the troubled sexual issues of modern ethics.) Allow me then to end on a personal note.

I received my knowledge of Catholic doctrine from my parents and from catechism, not from reading the Scriptures. Scriptural study came later in my life and has served to clarify and make precise doctrine that I already knew—much in the same way it has served the Catholic Church in the 20th century. That sequence has meant that personally I have never found critical interpretation of the Bible a threat to my faith. I know full well that some regard this admission as a sign that my interpretation of Scripture must necessarily be blinded or prejudiced or skewed. However, I do not think it irrational or dishonest to have a greater confidence in the guidance of God experienced in the church, the community of God's Son, than in my abilities as a scholar, which might theoretically lead me to other conclusions. (I am aware that "church" is wider than the church authorities of whom I have spoken above, but "church" must include those authorities as its official spokesmen.) I find divine guidance drawn from a living church an enabling, not a hindering, factor in the interpretation of the New Testament precisely because I think that those who wrote the books of that Testament drew their guidance about divine revelation from the living church of their times. They also made a contribution to shaping the church of their times (and future times) even as, I hope, interpreters of the biblical books are doing today. A lively dialogue about the import of critical biblical research for traditional Christian doctrine is a source of rejoicing, for it means that in the Roman Catholic Church both those elements are treated as very important—something not always true in other sections of Christendom.

John A. Coleman, S.J.

The Substance and Forms of American Religion and Culture

In a famous aphorism, the Protestant theologian Paul Tillich argued that "religion is the substance of culture and culture is the form of religion." Few commentators have since improved on his pithy formulation of the essential relation of culture and religion. Without a religious vision and substratum, a culture withers and loses creative vitality. But any vibrant religion will mirror the face of the culture it embraces. As Andrew Greeley notes, a culture-free faith is a contradiction in terms. And when explicitly religious myths wane, as Mircea Eliade has demonstrated, new quasi-religious-depth myths take their place in literature, the media and popular imagination.

Despite the shifting vagaries of reported religious statistics (e.g., data from a Gallup poll that in 1986, for the first time in decades, American public confidence in *institutional* religion has dramatically declined, or new evidence supplied by sociologist of religion David Roozen that the "baby boomers" have returned in large numbers to church as they start their own families), religion in America continues to be central to American self-definition.

The topic of American culture and religion is capacious. I want to state and expand two main theses about American culture and religion: (1) Religion continues to be crucially central to American self-definition; (2) The transpositions of religious terrain in the 1980s and beyond create some crisis of American religion and culture—a crisis of terrain adjustments rather than any withering away of religion as such. I want to suggest a brief map of these adjustments which will include the following main relief points on the map: (A) the breakdown of two earlier vital centers of American culture: liberal Protestantism and the secular myth of rational progress; (B) the emergence of what Harvard sociologist Daniel Bell calls Protestant evangelical moralism as culturally aggressive, and (C) a new Catholic moment in American culture.

THE PERSISTENCE OF RELIGION FOR AMERICAN SELF-DEFINITION

In a classic book, *The Denominational Society*, sociologist Andrew Greeley, following the earlier lead of Will Herberg, argues that religion provides a quasi-ethnic function in a pluralistic society such as America. Religion gives anchored identity and locates people on a map of belonging: who am I and to what story do I belong? More importantly, what values do I want to pass on to my children? It should come as no surprise that having children has drawn the "baby boomers" back to the churches. Socialization of children involves values to live by, stories which provide identity, and communities of belonging. Few sociological candidates can rival religion and the churches in providing these functions. Neither sex, race, class, ethnicity nor geographical location represents as strong a sociological indicator of belonging and identity in the United States as religion. The churches remain our largest single voluntary organizations and the overwhelmingly greatest recipients of voluntary charitable giving.

America stands out, among industrial nations, for its religiosity. Gallup poll and National Opinion Research Center data reveal a dreary monotony of high American statistics for belief in God, the divinity of Christ, life after death, the efficacy of prayer. Compared to Western Europe, American regular attendance at church remains abnormally high. Indeed, the United States ranks with India and Ireland as among the most religious populations in the world!

The primary founding acts of the United States are connected with religious themes. For our Pilgrim fathers and mothers, American exile was a new exodus, a new covenant with the land, a new Eden. The discovery of America for British settlers was a simultaneous discovery of religious freedom. Indeed, they expected a new "revelation" from the newfound land. For the American revolutionaries, Washington represented a new Moses and America a new Israel, a light to the nations. During the Civil War, Lincoln became a martyred Jesus figure. Berkeley sociologist Robert Bellah, in his award-winning 1976 book *The Broken Covenant*, argues that throughout the history of American literature and politics three cultural streams predominate: (1) biblical religion; (2) the English Enlightenment; (3) civic republicanism. And, in America, Enlightenment thought and the civic republican tradition became entangled with church theology. The churches were major carriers of these other traditions such that to retrieve them is also to return, at points, to biblical religion in America. We simply cannot understand our literary classics (Hawthorne, Whitman, Melville, Faulkner), or our main philosophical resources (Emerson, William James, Josiah Royce, John Dewey, Whitehead), without resort to the implicit theological and religious backdrop which undergirds them. Nor could there be a genuine *resourcement* in American culture without a return to its religious roots—a point culture critics such as Christopher Lasch, Robert Bellah and Daniel Bell strongly underscore.

Indeed, only those aspects of the counter-culture of the

1960s which found some explicit religious institutionalization in new religious movements of the 1970s—what Emory University sociologist Steven Tipton in his imaginative study of new religious movements, *Getting Saved From the Sixties*, calls "survivor units" of the 1960s—took any abiding cultural hold. We know now that these new religious movements—Buddhist, Sufi, Hindu groups in America—had a limited market of seekers. While these "extraordinary" religions have become more ordinary, assimilated to an earlier American religious tradition of "alternative altars" of theosophy and spiritualism, this "turning east" movement had limited scope. In fact, it presaged a renewed interest in spirituality and mysticism in its essentially Western Jewish and Christian forms. American religion after turning east turned back to its own substantive cultural sources.

Recently, Theodore Caplow and his associates, in an important sociological study of American religion, *All Faithful People: Continuity and Change in Middletown's Religion*, dispel any easy notions of a vaunted secularization of American society. They argue, instead, for the persistence and consolidation of church religion in America. What has demonstrably broken down, however, is an earlier regnant secular myth of rational progress. As University of Chicago theologian Langdon Gilkey trenchantly puts it, "The disintegration of the secular myth—not that of the traditional Christian mythos—constitutes the present crisis of American society." The Catholic culture critic, Joe Holland, echoes Gilkey:

> The two foundational sources of our nation's cultural energy—the Protestant Reformation and the Scientific Enlightenment—are no longer adequate guides to the future.
>
> American Protestantism, despite its important ongoing contributions, is now dominated by two destructive tendencies—a secularizing liberalism uprooted from the public power of Jesus' Gospel and reactionary fundamentalism promoting national idolatry.

American science and technology, despite continuing
gifts to the human family, have to a great degree become
blind slaves to definitions of progress and freedom unac-
countable to spiritual values, human community or the
ecology of the earth.

But as the secular myth of scientific enlightenment and
liberal Protestantism have experienced disarray, new forces
(evangelical Protestantism, Catholicism) emerge in the cultural
center of American life.

THE DECLINE OF LIBERAL PROTESTANTISM

The decline of liberal Protestantism in America—represented by the United Church of Christ, Presbyterianism,
Methodism, the Episcopal Church—is especially dramatic.
Mainline Protestantism—the cultural mainstay in America
from 1880 until 1960—has lost much of its energy, nerve and
cultural creative abilities. Sociologist Paul Chalafant captures
the statistics. "In the period from 1965–1970 Methodists,
United Presbyterians, Episcopalians, Lutherans and the
United Church of Christ began to suffer declines in membership. In the next five years, 1970–1975, other mainline
churches followed suit." Among the large American denominations only Southern Baptists and Roman Catholics held their
numbers or increased in membership. The 1970–1980 losses
are especially staggering: United Presbyterian Church—19%;
Disciples—17%; Episcopalians—15%; United Church of
Christ—11%; United Methodist—9%.

The liberal Protestant decline is as much a matter of ethos
as numbers. As Will Herberg noted several decades ago, "Protestantism in America today presents an anomaly of a strong
majority group with a growing minority consciousness." The

reasons given for this liberal Protestant eclipse are multiple. Dean Kelley points to the lack of inner church discipline and appropriate community mechanisms in liberal churches as he argues that their presence in evangelical churches explains *Why Conservative Churches Are Growing*. Lutheran author, Richard J. Neuhaus in *The Naked Public Square*, for his part argues that the liberal churches have sold out to prevailing fashions and accommodated too much to a secularity which is, in itself, in considerable disarray. Sociologist Dean Hoge, in a careful statistical study of church growth and decline in the 1970s, focuses on an emphasis on evangelism, a distinctive lifestyle and morality, and insistence on orthodox belief systems as three important predictors of church growth. Churches which are successful in providing clear identity symbols and a vivid sense of belonging prosper. Liberal Protestant churches are especially weak in maintaining the children of church members. They lack decisive criteria for church membership or belief.

In the political elections of 1980 and 1984, for example, evangelical Protestant and Catholic prelates had voice and impact in defining the moral issues. Liberal Protestants—the most articulate religious voice for American cultural values for a century—were strangely silent. As sociologist Benton Johnson notes, "many of the symbolic resources of the liberal churches have been depleted and cannot be renewed." As that center could not hold, new rivals for established cultural religion emerged.

RESURGENT EVANGELICAL MORALISM

With the eclipse of the liberal Protestant churches, the evangelical and fundamentalist churches have taken on a new cultural aggressiveness. Since the 1960s they have become more politically active and culturally affirming, tackling a host of foreign policy issues (e.g., anticommunist militarism, support for Israel, opposition to returning the Panama Canal), economic policy issues (ideological backing for the market capitalist economy) and social concerns: abortion, the women's movement and the ERA, the work ethic, the ethos of public school textbooks.

Like Roman Catholics, evangelical Protestants are an upwardly mobile group in American society. They are no longer rednecks! As sociologist Wade Clark Roof notes, "Whereas in 1960 only 7% of members of evangelical and fundamentalist denominations had attended some college, by the mid-1970s the figure was 23%." The new cultural prominence of the evangelical moralist voice in the 1970s is best explained by two major cultural shifts: (1) The counter-culture of the 1960s highlighted a massive breakdown of an earlier moral consensus on a host of issues—sex, abortion, family values, the work ethic, personal honesty. These had gradually eroded over time but came to abrupt symbolic consciousness in the late 1960s. Evangelicals continue to embody the earlier American consensus. While in terms of other cultural values they were marginal, they embodied the earlier cultural *moral* mainstream. (2) Since the late 1970s, there has been a dramatic halt to American economic growth. The symbolic crusade of the moral majority serves to displace any head-on economic confrontations as the real wages and purchasing power of ordinary Americans decline. Finally, groups experiencing membership growth relative to other competing groups often become culturally aggressive.

The presence of the evangelical moralist voice in American culture and politics seems likely to persist. Evangelicals are well-placed, geographically, in the expanding Sunbelt. They do better than liberal Protestants in maintaining the allegiance of their children and winning back fallen-away evangelicals. A careful sociological study of evangelical growth rates by Reginald Bibby, "The Circulation of the Saints," shows that these two factors—rather than a high conversion rate of non-evangelicals—explain evangelical growth. Moreover, the near religious monopoly of television and radio space by evangelicals guarantees their continued public presence. But voting studies have shown that evangelical and fundamentalist voters are not a monolith. They had much less impact on the 1980 and 1984 elections than the popular media suggest. What evangelicals will do as they become more mainstream is anyone's guess. What seems less guesswork, however, is historian of religion Martin Marty's comment that this group represents the new cultural mainstream in American Protestantism, its new establishment. Historians might expect that consolidation into the mainstream and access to power might temper some of the extreme positions of fundamentalists.

Already, as University of Virginia sociologist Jeffery Hadden (a keen observer of TV evangelists—in particular, Pat Robertson) notes, evangelicals are beginning to downplay their pre-millennial beliefs about a "rapture" and the speedy second coming of Christ and the end of our world. Jerry Falwell supports an Eastern establishment Republican such as George Bush for the presidency. Others calculate the positions needed for electability. If power does not always necessarily corrupt, it forces compromise on ideologically pure positions. Many social critics—such as Harvard theologian Harvey Cox—do not think a more pragmatic and "worldly-wise" evangelicalism is a bad thing for a renewed American culture. While not, at present, pluralist enough to embrace a full spectrum of American culture, evangelicals force us all to question the secularist assumption of a culture without any religious substance. Yet, as we saw Joe Holland assert, some critics think evangelical fundamentalism is so tied to the regnant forms of American culture that it promotes a national idolatry. It lacks transcendent substance. Still, fundamentalism has moved far enough along the pluralist spectrum as to eschew an earlier racism and anti-Catholicism. It seems premature to predict the further forms it might take.

THE CATHOLIC MOMENT IN AMERICAN CULTURE

A number of thoughtful commentators on American culture and religion—Martin Marty, Robert Bellah, Richard Neuhaus—point to a new Catholic moment in American history. They argue that the Roman Catholic leadership has interchanged position with earlier mainline Protestants with respect to the articulation of a social vision for America's future. Generally, these commentators point to the recent pastoral letters of the American bishops on arms control and the American economy. But a recent Gallup survey of American Catholics points to a deeper layer of Catholic strength. The Gallup Survey highlights, first, the evidence earlier amassed by Andrew Greeley about Catholic social mobility. The Catholic immigrants' children and grandchildren have become the best-educated and economically well-placed Gentile white group in America. Catholics are strategically situated in the political, economic and organizational life of the nation.

Secondly, as Mary Hannah demonstrated in her careful study, *Catholics and Politics*, the immigrants' descendants exhibit a political set of views at variance with earlier stereotypes. They show up consistently as tolerant, political liberals supportive of economic justice and civil liberties. They are the American group, for instance, least likely to support increased defense spending. Politically and economically more liberal than majority America, but socially conservative on several family and cultural issues, Catholics may inject a new vitality—Gallup argues—into American politics in the 1990s.

Finally, although Post-Vatican II Catholicism has shown several indices of important institutional decline, Catholics' weekly church attendance, adherence to core doctrinal beliefs (such as the divinity of Christ, belief in life after death) and inner sense of disciplined identity remain higher than for liberal Protestantism.

Will this Catholic center in American culture hold into the 1990s? Much will depend on structural adaptations to address the precipitous declines in ordained ministry, its ability to hold women and the new Hispanic immigrants, and some decentralization in decision making from what sociologist Joseph Fichter calls a "monophasic" to a "multi-phasic" (i.e., with plural centers of decision-making) church. Will Rome and the American bishops permit institutional and cultural adaptation to American religious patterns of voluntarism, pragmatism, a congregational style of parochial government and evangelical devotional styles? These are the patterns which church historian David O'Brien sees as quintessentially American.

Then, too, the success of a new Catholic moment in American culture will depend on combining new programs of personal renewal, focused on an adult lay spirituality, with concentration in religious education on the religious imagination. Andrew Greeley has stressed the issue of religious imagination for the renewal of American Catholicism. Joe Holland speaks eloquently to the question of an adult lay spirituality.

In recent pastoral letters and statements in defense of life at every level, Holland argues, the Catholic bishops are challenging the present direction of American culture. A consistent ethic of life is a new voice being heard in our land. But to bear fruit, Holland says, this consistent ethic of life must meet two conditions: (1) The bishops' concern for life needs to be restated, not as moral conclusions ordering life from the outside, but rather as arising from within an authentic lay spirituality rooted especially in the ordinary experiences of family and work. (2) Such an authentic lay spirituality will be possible only if we grow beyond the modern reduction of spirituality to privatized psychological experience.

Holland notes that we American Catholics "are nearly 60,000,000, a quarter of the nation, rooted in an ancient tradition, maturing in our post-European immigrant phase, being renewed after Vatican II, contributing a new wave of artists and intellectuals, and providing leadership across America's institutions." He seeks for this population "an authentic and public lay spirituality rooted in family and work, in service of the evangelical healing and renewal of American culture."

What Holland and others who are calling for a new Catholic moment in American culture desire is a deep *resourcement* of the substance of our culture, to see that substance come alive through vital church engagement as "communities of memory" and hope—to use a phrase of Robert Bellah et al. in *Habits of the Heart*. They seek a renewal of religious presence to the culture—a presence of discernment both of its spiritual vitalities and deflections from truth. In short, they envision the kind of cultural vitality liberal Protestantism once provided the culture. Some doubt the substantial depth of evangelical Protestantism to provide this public church. Joe Holland sees the monolithic views of evangelical Protestantism as an idolatry. Harvey Cox, on the other hand, thinks the evangelicals might provide essential resources for a post-modern culture. Richard Neuhaus, who applauds the evangelicals' attack on secular humanism, feels they substitute private revelation for public reasoned discourse. Catholic public policy rhetoric, on its part, has become more Bible-based, without sacrificing the traditional natural law appeals to reasoned discourse and a pluralistic consensus beyond revelational or confessional argument. It represents a new American synthesis of the three strands of American culture: biblical religion, Enlightenment concern for human rights and freedom, and the tradition of civic republicanism. It is a candidate for renewing American religious culture.

But the challenge to Catholicism at this moment of American history will consist in its willingness to risk, its willingness to permit American culture to become much more the form of its acculturated religion—without losing, in the process, inner church discipline and Catholic identity or sacrificing a rich traditional and Catholic identity or sacramental and analogical imaginative forms. Catholicism must engage in a delicate balance of pluralism and a renewed sense of spiritual authority. We should not trust the nay-sayers. For the foreseeable future, it will remain impossible to understand, let alone renew, American culture without resort to its religious substance, its formative and deforming religious substratum. As the early Puritan divine put it, "God may still have some fresh design and purpose for religion on this continent."

PLUS CA CHANGE?

In a thoughtful overview of American religion in the 1980s, historian Martin Marty espied three major spiritual energy resources in recent American culture: a passionate hunger for personal experience, a resort to authority in the face of relativism and chaotic pluralism, and a pull toward those institutions and movements which provide personal identity and social location. Upon reflection, these three forces and movements strike me as perennials in American culture. Thus, the revivalists drew on these three against the sterile established New England churches; immigrant Catholicism relied on them to forge a vital American Catholic church; in its heyday liberal Protestantism created a synthetic amalgam of personalism, authority and community. Indeed, were these not aspects of American religion De Tocqueville described? Thus, as I have argued in this essay, the substance of American religious culture persists more than meets the eye while the forms change. Religion has not declined as an American cultural force, although its terrain has shifted. But with the eclipse of earlier centers of cultural creativity (liberal Protestantism and scientific enlightenment), it is still too soon to tell whether the new candidates as center of American religious substance (Catholicism, evangelical Protestantism) will take, let alone hold. Most likely, as Martin Marty contends, no one center will ever emerge again in American religious culture. Like world Catholicism, it will become "multi-phasic."

Bernard Cooke

Christian Marriage: Basic Sacrament

In the traditional short definition of Christian sacrament, the third element is a brief statement about the effectiveness of sacraments: "Sacraments are sacred signs, instituted by Christ, to give grace." Sacraments are meant to do something. What they do is essentially God's doing; in sacraments God gives grace. We will devote the remainder of this book to studying the way in which the various Christian sacraments give us grace, beginning with the sacrament of marriage. Before looking at the sacramentality of human friendship and of marriage in particular, it might help to talk briefly about the kind of transformation that should occur through sacraments.

In trying to explain what sacraments do, we have used various expressions: celebrants of sacraments "administer the sacraments" to people; people "receive sacraments" and "receive grace" through sacraments; sacraments are "channels of grace." The official statement of the Council of Trent, which has governed Catholic understandings for the past four centuries, is that "sacraments contain and confer grace."

The traditional understanding of grace and sacraments would include at least the following. The grace given was won for us by the death and resurrection of Jesus. Without depending upon misleading images such as a "reservoir" or a "bank account," it seems that there must be some way that the graces flowing from Jesus' saving action are "stored up" so that they can be distributed to people who participate in sacraments. The grace given in sacramental liturgy is, at least for baptized Christians, a needed resource if people are to behave in a way that will lead them to their ultimate destiny in the life to come.

Beneath all such formulations—which we are all familiar with in one form or another—there lurks a basic question: What is this "grace" we are speaking about? It is all well and good to say that we receive the grace we need when we come to sacramental liturgy, and that we receive it in proportion to our good will. But what do we have in mind when we use this word "grace"? We have already begun to see that "sacrament" should be understood in a much broader sense, one that extends far beyond the liturgical ceremony that is the focus of a particular sacramental area. Now, with grace also, a deeper examination leads us to the conclusion that grace touches everything in our lives; it pervades everything we are and do.

Some brief discussion of grace at this point may help us to understand better the effectiveness of the various individual sacraments as we study them. In trying to get a more accurate notion of grace, it might help to remember a distinction that was sometimes made in technical theological discussions, a distinction that unfortunately received little attention and so was scarcely ever mentioned in catechetical instructions about grace. This is the distinction between "uncreated grace" and "created grace."

"Uncreated grace" refers to God himself in his graciousness towards human beings; "created grace" refers to that special ("supernatural") assistance God gives to humans to heal and strengthen them and to raise them to a level of being compatible with their eternal destiny. For the most part, our previous theological and catechetical explanations stressed created grace as a special help that enabled persons to live morally good lives, an assistance to guide and support them when they faced temptations. There was also a frequent reference to "the state of grace," the condition of being in good relationship to God and therefore in position to move from this present earthly life to heaven, rather than to hell. But there was practically no mention of uncreated grace.

During the past few decades, there has been a renewed interest in and study of grace. We have learned to pay much more attention to uncreated grace, that is, to the reality of God who in the act of self-giving and precisely by this self-giving transforms and heals and nurtures our human existence. Along with this new emphasis on God's loving self-gift as *the* great grace, there has been more use of the notion of "transformation" to aid our understanding of created grace. Under the impact of God's self-giving, we humans are radically changed; this fundamental and enduring transformation of what we are as persons is created, sanctifying grace.

In various ways, sacraments—in their broader reality as well as in their liturgical elements—are key agencies for achieving this transformation. Though the effectiveness of the different sacraments is quite distinctive, each area of sacramentality touches and changes some of the significances attached to human life. As these significances are transformed, the meaning of what it is to be human is transformed; our human experience is therefore changed, and with it the very reality of our human existing.

This process of transformation is what we now turn our attention to, hoping to discover what sacraments are meant to accomplish in the lives of Christians.

SACRAMENT OF HUMAN FRIENDSHIP

Explanation of the individual sacraments traditionally starts with baptism. Apparently it is the first sacrament Christians are exposed to, and the one all the others rest upon; it is the one that introduces the person to Christianity, etc. However, as we attempt to place the sacraments in a more human context, there is at least the possibility that we should begin with another starting-point. Perhaps the most basic sacrament of God's saving presence to human life is the sacrament of human love and friendship. After all, even the young infant who is baptized after only a few days of life has already been subjected to the influence of parental love (or its lack), which in the case of Christian parents is really the influence of the sacrament of Christian marriage.

Sacraments are meant to be a special avenue of insight into the reality of God; they are meant to be words of revelation. And the sacramentality of human love and friendship touches the most basic level of this revelation. There is a real problem in our effort to know God. Very simply put, it seems all but impossible for humans to have any correct understanding of the divine as it really is. God is everything we are not. We are finite, God infinite; we are in time, God is eternal; we are created, God is creator. True, we apply to God the ideas we have drawn from our human experience; we even think of God as "person." But is this justified? Is this the way God is?

Some fascinating and important discussion of this problem is going on today among Christian philosophers, but let us confine our approach to those insights from the biblical traditions. As early as the writings of the first chapter of Genesis (which is part of the priestly tradition in Israel that found final form around 500 B.C.), we are given a rich lead. Speaking of the creation of humans by God, Genesis 1:19 says that humans were made "in the image and likeness of God." That is to say, somehow the reality of human persons gives us some genuine insight into the way God exists. But the passage continues— and it is an intrinsic part of the remark about "image and likeness"—"male and female God made them." This means that the imaging of God occurs precisely in the relationship between humans, above all in the interaction of men and women. To put it in our modern terms, some knowledge of the divine can be gained in experiencing the personal relationship of men and women (and one can legitimately broaden that to include all human personal relationships).

The text provides still more understanding, for it points out that from this relationship life is to spread over the earth; humans in their relation to one another (primarily in sexual reproduction, but not limited to that) are to nurture life. And humans are to govern the earth for God; they are to image and implement the divine sovereignty by this nurture of life that is rooted in their relationship to one another. As an instrument of divine providence, human history is meant by the creator to be effected through human community, through humans being persons for one another.

Though the first and immediate aspect of the relationship between Adam and Eve as life-giving is their sexual partnership, the text does not confine it to this. Rather, Genesis goes on to describe the way Adam's own human self-identity is linked with Eve's. As Adam is given the chance to view the other beings in God's creation, he is able to name them, but he is unable to name himself until he sees Eve. The very possibility of existing as a self is dependent upon communion with another.

Implicit in this deceptively simple biblical text is a profound statement about the way human life is to be conducted. If life is to extend to further life, either by creating new humans or by creating new levels of personal life in already-existing humans, it will happen on the basis of people's self-giving to one another. And, if women and men are truly to "rule" the world for God, they will do this by their love and friendship, and not by domination. To the extent that this occurs, the relationship of humans to one another will reveal the fact that God's creative activity, by which he gives life and guides its development (in creation and in history), is essentially one of divine self-gift. Humans have been created and are meant to exist as a word, a revelation, of God's self-giving rule; but they will function in this revealing way in proportion to their free living in open and loving communion with one another.

Whatever small hint we have regarding the way God exists, comes from our own experience of being humanly personal. Our tendency, of course, is to think of the divine in human terms, even carrying to God many of the characteristics of our humanity that obviously could not apply directly to God, for example, changing our minds as to what we intend to do. Excessive anthropomorphism has always been a problem in human religious thinking and imagination; we have always been tempted by idolatry. Even today, when our religious thinking has been purified by modern critical and scientific thought, we still fall into the trap of thinking that God exists in the way we think God does. This does not mean, however, that we must despair of ever knowing God. On the basis of biblical insights (like those in Genesis 1:19 and even more in New Testament texts grounded in Jesus' own religious experience) we can come to some true understanding of God by reflecting on our own experience of being personal.

For us to be personal—aware of ourselves and the world around us, aware that we are so aware, relating to one another as communicating subjects, loving one another, and sharing human experience—is always a limited reality. We are personal within definite constraints of time and place and happenings. Even if our experience as persons is a rich one, through friends and education and cultural opportunities, it is always incomplete. For every bit of knowledge there are immense areas of reality I know nothing about; I can go on learning indefinitely. Though I may have a wide circle of friends, there are millions of people I can never know; I can go on indefinitely establishing human relationships. There are unlimited interesting human experiences I will never share. In a sense I am an infinity, but an infinity of possibilities, infinite in my incompleteness. Yet, this very experience of limitation involves some awareness of the unlimited; our experience of finite personhood points toward infinite personhood and gives us some hint of what that might be.

GOD REVEALS SELF AS PERSONAL

What lets us know the divine is indeed personal in this mysterious unlimited fashion is the fact (which as Christians we believe) that this God has "spoken" to humans; God has revealed, not just some truths about ourselves and our world, but about God's own way of being personal in relation to us. God in the mystery of revelation to humans is revealed as someone. What this means can be grasped by us humans only through our own experience of being human together. In our love and concern for one another, in our friendships and in the human community that results, we can gain some insight into what "God being for us" really means. These human relationships are truly insights into God, but not just in the sense that they are an analogue by which we can gain some metaphorical understanding of the divine. Rather, humans and their relationships to one another are a "word" that is being constantly created by God. In this word God is made present to us, revealing divine selfhood through the sacramentality of our human experience of one another.

One of the most important results of this divine revelation and genuinely open relationships to one another is the ability to trust reality. This might seem a strange thing to say, for reality is a given. Yet, the history of modern times has been one of growing uncertainty and strong distrust of the importance and goodness and even the objective reality of the world that surrounds us, the world of things and especially the world of people. Great world wars, among other things, have made many humans cynical about human existence and have made many others unwilling to admit that things are as they are. There is abundant evidence that our civilization is increasingly fleeing towards phantasy, taking refuge in a world of dreams, so that it does not have to face the real world. It is critically important, perhaps necessary for our sanity, that we find some basis for trusting life and facing reality optimistically and with mature realism.

Most radically, a culture's ability to deal creatively with reality depends on its view of "the ultimate," of God. We must be able to trust this ultimate not only as infinitely powerful but also as infinitely caring, as compassionate and concerned. The only ground, ultimately, for our being able to accept such an incredible thing—and when we stop to reflect, it is incredible—is our experience of loving concern and compassion in our human relationships. If we experience the love and care that others have for us, beginning with an infant's experience of parental love, and experience our own loving concern for others, this can give us some analogue for thinking how the ultimate might personally relate to us. Jesus himself drew from this comparison. "If you who are parents give bread and not a stone to your children when they ask for food, how much more your Father in heaven. . . . "

Experiencing love in our human relationships makes it possible for us to accept the reality of our lives with a positive, even grateful attitude. And this in turn makes it possible for us to see our lives as a gift from a lovingly providential God. If we have friends, life has some basic meaning; we are important to them and they to us. What happens to us and them makes a difference; someone cares. If love exists among people, there is genuine, deep-seated joy, because joy shared by people is the final dimension of love. If this is our experience of being human, then our existence can be seen as a good thing and accepted maturely and responsibly.

All of this means that our experience of being truly personal with and for one another is sacramental; it is a revelation of our humanity at the same time that it is a revelation of God. This experience of human love can make the mystery of divine love for humans credible. On the contrary, if a person does not experience love in his or her life, only with great difficulty can the revelation of divine love be accepted as possible. Learning to trust human love and to trust ourselves to it is the ground for human faith and trust in God.

To say that human love is sacramental, especially if one uses that term strictly (as we are doing), implies that it is a mystery of personal presence. Obviously, in genuine love there is a presence of the beloved in one's consciousness; the deeper and more intimate the love, the more abiding and prominent is the thought of the beloved. To see this as truly sacramental of divine presence means that human love does more than make it possible for us to trust that God loves us. The human friendships we enjoy embody God's love for us; in and through these friendships God is revealing to us the divine self-giving in love. God is working salvifically in all situations of genuine love, for it is our consciousness of being loved both humanly and divinely that most leads us to that full personhood that is our destiny. Such salvation occurs in our lives to the extent that we consciously participate in it, in proportion to our awareness of what is really happening and our free willingness to be part of it.

It is instructive to note that when Jesus, immediately after being baptized by John, was given a special insight into his relationship to God as his Abba, the word used in the gospel to describe his experience of his Father's attitude towards him is the Greek *agapetos*, "my beloved one." This was the awareness

of God that Jesus had, an awareness of being unconditionally
loved, an awareness that became the key to human salvation.
And John's Gospel describes Jesus at the last supper as ex-
tending this to his disciples. "I will not now call you servants,
but friends."

MARRIAGE, PARADIGM OF FRIENDSHIP

Among the various kinds of human friendship and personal love, the one that has always been recognized as a paradigm of human relationship and love, and at the same time a
ground of human community, is the relation between husband
and wife. There is considerable evidence that humans have
never been able to explain or live this relationship satisfactor-
ily, basic and universal though it is. In our own day, there is
constant and agitated discussion of the way men and women
are meant to deal with one another, and there is widespread
talk of a radical shift taking place in the institution of marriage.
As never before, the assumptions about respective roles in marriage are being challenged. Marriage is seen much more as a
free community of persons rather than as an institution of human society regulated for the general benefit of society; equality of persons rather than respect for patriarchal authority is
being stressed. And with considerable anguish in many instances, people are seeking the genuine meaning of the relation
between women and men, and more broadly the relationship
of persons to one another in any form of friendship.

Questioning the woman-man, and especially the husband-wife, relationship is not, of course, a new phenomenon.
As far back as we can trace, literature witnesses to the attempt
to shed light on this question. What complicates the issue is the
merging of two human realities, sexuality and personal relatedness, in marriage, a merging so profound that people often

are unable to distinguish them. We know, however, that in many ancient cultures there was little of what we today consider love between spouses; marriage was a social arrangement for the purpose of continuing the family through procreation. In not a few instances, there was so pronounced a cleavage between love and sexuality that the wife was considered the property of her husband and she was abandoned if she proved unable to bear him children. If men sought human companionship, they sought it outside the home. Apparently the marriages in which something like a true friendship existed between wife and husband were relatively rare.

SACRAMENTALITY OF MARRIAGE IN ISRAEL

In ancient Israel an interesting development began at least eight centuries before Christianity. Surrounded as they were by cultures and religions that worshipped the power of human sexuality, the Israelites assiduously avoided attributing anything like sexuality to their God, Yahweh. At the same time, these neighboring erotic religions were a constant temptation to the Israelites; the great prophets of Israel lashed out repeatedly against participation by Israel's women and men in the ritual prostitution of the Canaanite shrines. In this context it is startling to find the prophet Hosea using the example of a husband's love for his wife as an image of Yahweh's love for his people Israel.

Apparently, Hosea was one of those sensitive humans for whom marriage was more than a family arrangement; he seems to have had a deep affection for his wife, Gomer. The love was not reciprocated; his wife abandoned him for a life of promiscuity with a number of lovers; perhaps she became actively involved in some situation of shrine prostitution. At this point, Hosea was obliged by law to divorce her, which he seems to have done. But then "the word of the Lord came to Hosea," bidding him to seek out and take back his errant wife. And all this as a prophetic gesture that would reveal Yahweh's forgiveness of an adulterous Israel that had gone lusting after false gods.

Once introduced by Hosea, the imagery of husband-wife becomes the basic way in which the prophets depict the relationship between Yahweh and the people Israel. Tragically, the image often has to be used in a negative way. Israel is the unfaithful spouse who abandons Yahweh to run off with "false lovers," the divinities of the surrounding fertility religions. Yet, despite this infidelity on Israel's part, Yahweh is a merciful God who remains faithful to his chosen partner. "Faithful" becomes a key attribute of this God of Israel. Yahweh is a faithful divinity who keeps his promises to Israel. And the husband-wife relation becomes in the prophetic writings an alternative to the king-subject relation that the rulers of Israel and Judah (for their own purposes) preferred as a way of describing the covenant between Yahweh and Israel.

Our particular interest, however, is not the manner in which the use of the husband-wife imagery altered Israel's understanding of the covenant between people and God. Rather, it is the manner in which, conversely, the use of this imagery began to alter the understanding of the relation between a married couple. If the comparison husband-wife/Yahweh-Israel is made, the significance of the first couplet passes into understanding the significance of the second couplet, but the significance of the second passes also into understanding the first.

The understanding the people had of their god, Yahweh, and of his relationship to them, the depth and fidelity of his love, the saving power of this relationship, slowly became part of their understanding of what the marriage relationship should be. Thus, a "Yahweh-significance" became part of the meaning of married relatedness. The sacramentality of the love between husband and wife—and indirectly the sacramentality of all human friendship—was being altered. It was, if we can coin a term, being "yahwehized." The meaning of God in his relationship to humans became part of the meaning of marriage, and marriage became capable of explicitly signifying and revealing this God. This meant that human marriage carried much richer significance than before; it meant that the personal aspect of this relationship was to be regarded as paramount; it meant that the woman was neither to be possessed as property nor treated as a thing; it meant that marital fidelity was expected of both man and woman. Thus the "institution of the sacrament of marriage" begins already in the Old Testament.

MARRIAGE AS A CHRISTIAN SACRAMENT

With Christianity another dimension of meaning is infused into this relation between wife and husband, the Christ-meaning that comes with Jesus' death and resurrection. Several New Testament passages could be used to indicate this new, deeper meaning, but the key passage probably is the one in Ephesians that traditionally forms part of the marriage liturgy.

> Be subject to one another out of reverence for Christ. Wives, be subject to your husbands as to the Lord; for the man is the head of the woman, just as Christ also is the head of the Church. Christ is indeed the savior of the body; but just as the Church is subject to Christ, so must wives be subject to their husbands. Husbands, love your wives, as Christ also loved the Church and gave himself up for it, to consecrate it . . . In the same way men are bound to love their wives, as they love their own bodies. In loving his wife, a man loves himself. For no one hates his own body: on the contrary, he provides and cares for it; and that is how Christ treats the Church, because it is his body, of

which we are living parts. Thus it is that (in the words of scripture, "a man shall leave his father and mother and shall be joined to his wife, and the two shall become one flesh" (5:21–32).

In dealing with this text it is important to bear in mind what the author of the epistle is doing. As so often in the pauline letters, the purpose is neither to challenge nor to vindicate the prevailing structures of human society as they then existed. Just as in other cases the pauline letters do not argue for or against an institution like slavery, the passage in Ephesians takes for granted the commonly accepted patriarchal arrangements of family authority without defending or attacking them; in a patriarchal culture all authority is vested in the husband-father. However, Ephesians insists that in a Christian family this authority structure must be understood and lived in an entirely new way. The relation between the risen Christ and the Christian community must be the exemplar for a loving relationship between the Christian couple.

This text contains a rich treasure of sacramental and christological insight that has scarcely been touched by theological reflection. Mutual giving of self to one another in love, not only in marital intercourse but also in the many other sharings that make up an enduring and maturing love relationship, is used in this passage as a way of understanding what Jesus has done in his death and resurrection. He has given himself to those he loves. His death was accepted in love as the means of passing into a new life that could be shared with those who accept him in faith. Jesus' death and consequent resurrection was the continuation of what was done at the supper when Jesus took the bread and said, "This is my body (myself) given for you." Ephesians 5 tells us that we are to understand this self-giving of Jesus in terms of the bodily self-giving in love of a husband and wife, and vice versa, we are to understand what this marital self-gift is meant to be in terms of Jesus' loving gift of self in death and resurrection.

One of the important things to bear in mind in studying this text is that Jesus' self-giving continues into the new life of resurrection. Actually, his self-giving is intrinsic to this new stage of his human existence. The very purpose and intrinsic finality of his risen life is to share this life with others. The risen Lord shares this resurrection life by sharing what is the source of this life, his own life-giving Spirit. For Jesus to exist as risen is to exist with full openness to and full possession of this Spirit. So, for him to share new life with his friends means giving them his own Spirit. What emerges from this Spirit-sharing is a new human life of togetherness, a life of unexpected fulfillment, but a life that could not have been reached except through Jesus freely accepting his death. So also, a Christian married couple is meant to move into a new and somewhat unexpected common existing, which cannot come to be unless each is willing to die to the more individualistic, less unrelated-to-another, way of life that they had before.

Christ's self-giving to the church is more than the model according to which a man and woman should understand and live out their love for each other. The love, concern, and self-giving that each has for the other is a "word" that expresses Christ's love for each of them. The fidelity of each to their love is a sign that makes concretely credible their Christian hope in Christ's fidelity. In loving and being loved, each person learns that honest self-appreciation which is the psychological grounding for believing the incredible gospel of God's love for human-kind. In their relationship to one another, and in proportion as that relationship in a given set of circumstances truly translates Christ's own self-giving, the couple are a sacrament to each other and a sacrament to those who know them.

In this sacramental relationship, a Christian man and woman are truly "grace" to one another; they express and make present that uncreated grace that is God's creative self-giving. Though there certainly is mystery in this loving divine presence, it is revealed in the new meanings discovered in the lived relationship between Christian wife and husband. The trust required by their unqualified intimacy with one another and the hope of genuine acceptance by the other, which accompanies this intimacy, help bring about a new level of personal maturity. But this trust and hope are grounded in the Christian faith insight that open-ended love can lead to new and richer life. Perhaps even more basically, a Christian couple can commit themselves to this relationship, believing that it will not ultimately be negated by death. Instead, Christian hope in risen life supports the almost instinctive feeling of lovers that "love is stronger than death."

Psychological studies have detailed the ways a truly mature married relationship, one that integrates personal and sexual love, fosters the human growth of the two people, and it is not our intent to repeat such reflections here. But these same studies point also to the indispensable role that continuing and deepening communication with each other plays in the evolution of such a relationship. In a Christian marriage the communication is meant to embrace the sharing of faith and hope in that salvation that comes through Jesus. The Christian family is meant to be the most basic instance of Christian community, people bonded together by their shared relationship to the risen Jesus.

All of us can think of marriages where this ideal has been to quite an extent realized, where husband and wife have over the years supported and enriched one another's belief and trust in the reality and importance of Christianity. Various challenges can come to Christian faith, if it is real faith and not just a superficial acceptance of a religious pattern. These challenges can change shape over the years, they can come with suffering or disappointments or disillusionment or boredom, they can come to focus with the need to face the inevitability of death. At such times of crisis, when faith can either deepen or weaken, the witness of a loved one's faith and hope is a powerful and sometimes indispensable preaching of the gospel.

Perhaps the most difficult thing to believe over the course of a lifetime is that one is important enough to be loved by God. Nothing makes this more credible than the discovery of being important to and loved by another human. The fidelity of one's lover, not just in the critically important area of sexual fidelity but also in the broader context of not betraying love by selfishness or exploitation or pettiness or dishonesty or disinterestedness or insensitivity, makes more credible the Christian trust in God's unfailing concern.

One could go on indefinitely describing how a Christian couple "give grace" to each other, because the contribution to each other's life of grace (their being human in relation to God) involves the whole of their life together. The sacrament of Christian marriage is much more than the marriage ceremony in the church; that ceremony is only one important element in the sacrament. Christian marriage is the woman and the man in their unfolding relationship to each other as Christians; they are sacrament for each other, sacrament to their children, and sacrament to all those who come to know them. The meaning of what they are for each other should become for them and others a key part of what it means to be a human being.

SUMMARY

If we restrict "sacrament" to certain liturgical rituals, it is logical to think of baptism as the initial sacrament. If, however, we realize the fundamental sacramentality of all human experience and the way Jesus transformed this sacramentality, there is good reason for seeing human friendship as the most basic sacrament of God's saving presence to human life. Human friendship reflects and makes credible the reality of God's love for humans; human friendship gives us some insight into the Christian revelation that God is a "self."

Within human friendship there is a paradigm role played by the love between a Christian wife and husband. Building on the transformation of marriage's meaning that began with the Israelitic prophets, Christianity sees the love relationship of a Christian couple as sacramentalizing the relationship between Christ and the church, between God and humankind. God's saving action consists essentially in the divine self-giving. This is expressed by and present in the couple's self-gift to each other; they are sacrament to each other, to their children, and to their fellow Christians.

Avery Dulles

Vatican II Reform: The Basic Principles

On January 25, 1985, Pope John Paul II unexpectedly called an extraordinary session of the synod of bishops to meet from November 25 to December 8, 1985. This meeting, commemorating the twentieth anniversary of the conclusion of Vatican II, will give the bishops from the various national and regional conferences an opportunity to exchange and deepen the experience of applying the council to the life of the church. To allay any fears that he might be distancing himself from Vatican II, the pope declared that it "remains the fundamental event in the life of the contemporary church," and that for himself personally it has been "the constant reference point of every pastoral action."

In the past two decades Vatican II has become, for many Catholics, a center of controversy. A few voices from the extreme right and the extreme left frankly reject the council. Reactionaries of the traditionalist variety censure it for having yielded to Protestant and Modernist tendencies. Radicals of the far left, conversely, complain that the council, while making some progress, failed to do away with the church's absolutistic claims and its antiquated class structures. The vast majority of Catholics, expressing satisfaction with the results of the council, are still divided because they interpret the council in contrary ways. The conservatives, insisting on continuity with the past, give primary emphasis to the council's reaffirmation of settled Catholic doctrines, including papal primacy and infallibility. The progressives, however, hold that the true meaning of the council is to be found rather in its innovations. For them Vatican II made a decisive break with the juridicism, clericalism, and triumphalism of recent centuries and laid the foundations for a more liberal and healthier Catholicism.

Like most other councils, Vatican II issued a number of compromise statements. It intentionally spoke ambiguously on certain points, leaving to the future the achievement of greater clarity. Many commentators, accenting these problematical features, give the impression that the council left nothing but doubt and confusion in its wake. It may therefore be time to acknowledge that, while leaving many open questions, the council did present a solid core of unequivocal teaching on matters of great importance.

Vatican II addressed an extraordinary variety of issues, ranging from highly technical questions about the theology of revelation to eminently practical questions about marriage and family life. But its central focus was undoubtedly the self-understanding of the church, and this is the theme that the present pope evidently envisages as the agenda for the coming synod. As a contribution to the common reflection that will precede the synod, I shall here attempt to set forth, as simply as I can, the basic vision of the church as understood by Vatican II. I shall concentrate on practical and pastoral matters that have a direct impact on the lives of rank-and-file Catholics. For the sake of clarity, I shall arrange my observations under the rubric of ten principles which I regard as unquestionably endorsed by the council. Whoever does not accept all ten of these principles, I would contend, cannot honestly claim to have accepted the results of Vatican II.

1. AGGIORNAMENTO

This Italian term, which may be translated by English words such as "updating," "modernization," or "adaptation," was popularized by John XXIII, who made the concept fundamental to his own program for the coming council. Accepting this program, the fathers at Vatican II abjured the hostility and suspicion toward the modern world that had characterized the Catholicism of the nineteenth and early twentieth centuries. Especially in the *Pastoral Constitution on the Church in the Modern World* (*Gaudium et Spes*), the council declared its great respect for the truth and goodness that had been brought into the world through modernization (*GS* 42). It stated that we are witnesses to the birth of a new humanism in which people are conscious of their responsibility to one another for the future of the world (*GS* 55). The faithful, said the council, must "live in very close union with the men of their time" (*GS* 62). Catholics must, moreover, "blend modern science and its theories and the understanding of the most recent discoveries with Christian morality and doctrine" (ibid.), so that the church may keep pace with the times and enter fully into the new age now being born. In so doing the church can enrich itself and better understand the treasures she has received from Christ. Far from clinging to ancient forms, the church as pilgrim must press forward toward the consummation of history, when God's kingdom will be revealed in its fullness. Neither John XXIII nor the council, of course, held the absurd dogma that the new is always better than the old. In fact they frequently pointed out that modern techniques can easily be abused so as to distract people from the lasting goods of the spirit. But that is no excuse for burying oneself in the past.

The principle of *aggiornamento*, like all the others we shall consider, is only a principle. To apply it requires prudence and discretion lest the gospel, in being accommodated to the spirit of the age, lose its challenging power. Still the principle itself is sound and important. The church, glorying in its magnificent heritage, should not allow itself to become a museum piece. It must not become a relic of the Middle Ages or any past period, but rather a vital part of the modern world as it presses forward into God's future. Confident that the Lord himself remains with his people down through the centuries, Christians can have the courage to live out the gospel and bear witness to it under the conditions of today's world.

2. THE REFORMABILITY OF THE CHURCH

In recent centuries it has been common to look upon the church as a divine institution without spot or wrinkle. While admitting the faults of individual believers, Catholics have insisted that the church itself is pure and holy. Vatican II, however, depicted the church in terms of the biblical image of the people of God. As we learn from Scripture, this people, though always sealed by its covenant relationship with God, was sometimes unfaithful. *The Constitution on the Church* (*Lumen Gentium*), therefore, was able to admit: "The Church, embracing sinners in her bosom, is at the same time holy and always in need of being purified, and incessantly pursues the path of penance and renewal" (*LG* 8). Furthermore, in the *Decree on Ecumenism* (*Unitatis redintegratio*), the council declared: "Christ summons the Church, as she goes her pilgrim way, to that continual reformation of which she always has need, insofar as she is an institution of human beings here on earth" (*UR* 6).

The idea that the church might be reformable caught many Catholics by surprise. In the late Middle Ages there had been several councils having as their express aim the reformation of the whole church "in the head and in the members," but after the Protestant Reformation the idea of reform came under suspicion in Catholic circles. Thanks to Vatican II, however, we are relieved of the burden of having to defend the whole record of the past. We can freely admit that not only individual Catholics, but the church itself in its official actions, has committed errors and sins, such as the burning of heretics, the persecutions of Jews, and the excesses of holy wars. We can admit that Catholics had a large share of responsibility in bringing on the divisions among Christians that so weaken the Christian witness in our time.

Like the principle of updating, this second principle must be applied with discretion. Not everything in the church is suspect and fallible. Its basic sacramental structures, its scriptures, and its dogmas are abidingly valid. The grace of Christ, which comes through these channels, is more powerful than human infidelity and sin. The church, therefore, does not have an equal affinity to holiness and to evil. Evil is against its true nature. For this reason Vatican II, while speaking of the church of sinners, avoided the expression "sinful Church." The difference is a subtle one, but has a certain importance.

With regard to past historical events, we should be on guard against a kind of spiritual masochism that would transfer all the blame from the other party to our own. Often it is best to follow the principle of John XXIII: "We do not wish to conduct a trial of the past. We shall not seek to establish who was right and who was wrong. Responsibility is divided." Still, to set the record straight, it is well to disavow certain errors. An example would be the present investigation to determine whether the papal commission erred by condemning the theories of Galileo in the seventeenth century.

3. RENEWED ATTENTION
TO THE WORD OF GOD

In the Middle Ages and even more since the Reformation, Catholicism tended to become the church of law and the sacraments rather than the church of the gospel and the word. Catholics too often neglected the spiritual riches contained in the Bible. Emphasizing the precepts of the church, they allowed the proclamation of the good news to fall into abeyance. They celebrated the Mass in Latin—a language not understood by most of the people—and usually without any homily. In Catholic theology the Bible was viewed as a remote source of doctrine, hardly used except to find proof-texts for later church doctrines.

Vatican II, especially in its *Constitution on Divine Revelation* (*Dei verbum*), recovered the primacy of Scripture as the word of God consigned to writing under the inspiration of the Holy Spirit (*DV* 9). The teaching office of the Church, according to the constitution, "is not above the word of God but serves it, listening to it devoutly, guarding it scrupulously, and explaining it faithfully . . . " (*DV* 10). "The study of the sacred page," according to the same constitution, "is, so to speak, the soul of sacred theology" (*DV* 24).

The same constitution strongly recommended the use of Scripture by all Catholics. "Easy access to sacred Scripture," it stated, "should be provided for all the Christian faithful" (*DV* 22). The Scriptures were here compared to the Eucharist, since each in its own way offers to the faithful the bread of life (*DV* 21). And in the same paragraph we find the following eloquent sentence: "For in the sacred books, the Father who is in heaven meets His children with great love and speaks with them; and the force and power of the word of God is so great that it remains the support and energy of the church, the strength of faith for her children, the food of the soul, the pure and perennial source of spiritual life."

Besides rehabilitating the Bible, the council sought to renew the ministry of preaching. It called on Catholic preachers to provide the nourishment of the Scriptures to the people of God (*DV* 23) and warned that, as Augustine had said, "those who do not listen to the word of God inwardly will be empty preachers of the word of God outwardly" (*DV* 25). Thus priests as well as lay people were exhorted to read the Scriptures prayerfully.

Since the council, directives such as those I have just quoted have produced excellent fruits. Catholics have learned more about the Bible; many of them attend study and prayer groups that concentrate on the Scriptures. But in this respect, as in others, further progress remains necessary. There is as yet no danger that Catholics, in their enthusiasm for the word, will turn away from ritual and sacrament or that, in their devotion to the gospel, they will neglect the law of Christ and the church. The more relaxed attitude toward church law at the present time, while regrettable in some respects, can be viewed as a gain insofar as it helps to overcome an almost pharisaical scrupulosity to which Catholics were subject in the years before Vatican II. Ideally, of course, contrasting elements such as law and gospel, word and sacrament, should not be played off against each other but should rather be mutually reinforcing. The effort to achieve the right balance should be high on the agenda of Catholics today.

4. COLLEGIALITY

It is almost a platitude to assert that the Catholic church, from the Middle Ages until Vatican II, was pyramidal in structure. Truth and holiness were conceived as emanating from the pope as commander-in-chief at the top, and the bishops were depicted as subordinate officers carrying out the orders of the pope. In our day many conservative Catholics lean toward this military analogy of the church.

Vatican II did not deny the primacy of the pope as it had been defined a century earlier by Vatican I, but it did put the papacy into a significantly new context. The college of bishops, together with the pope as its head, was seen as having the fullness of power in the church. The individual bishops were portrayed not as mere lieutenants of the pope but as pastors in their own right. They were in fact called "vicars of Christ" (*LG* 28)—an ancient title that had been given to bishops in the early church but which, since about the eighth century, had come to be reserved to the pope.

The principle of collegiality runs through the documents of Vatican II like a golden thread. Just as the pope is surrounded by a college of bishops, so each bishop serves as head of a presbyteral college, called presbytery, and governs his diocese in consultation with presbyters, religious, and laity. Thus the principle of collegiality, understood in a wide sense, may be viewed as pervading all levels of the church. Pastors, according to the *Constitution on the Church*, "know that they themselves were not meant by Christ to shoulder alone the entire saving mission of the church toward the world. On the contrary, they understand that it is their noble duty so to shepherd the faithful and recognize their services and charismatic gifts that all according to their proper roles may cooperate in this common undertaking with one heart" (*LG* 30).

Since the council, many new institutions have been erected to implement collegiality on various levels; for example, the worldwide synod of bishops, national and regional episcopal conferences, national and diocesan pastoral councils, parish councils, priests' senates, and the like. If in some cases too many questions have been subjected to prolonged discussion and debate, it has been necessary to go through this stage to arrive at the proper mean. Parliamentarianism or democracy, if carried too far, is likely to provoke a reaction in the opposite direction, toward a revival of the preconciliar form of authoritarianism, which seemed relatively efficient and rapid. Here the council still calls upon us to devise mechanisms of decision making that respect both the traditional principle of personal pastoral authority and the nature of the church as a Spirit-filled community. Neither an army nor a New England town meeting is a suitable paradigm.

5. RELIGIOUS FREEDOM

Up to the very time when the council opened, it was far from certain whether the Catholic church could subscribe to the principle of religious freedom which had by then prevailed in most Protestant bodies and won approval in the Assembly of the World Council of Churches at New Delhi in 1961. More specifically, it was being asked whether the church could fully respect the right and duty of each person to follow his or her conscience with regard to the acceptance or nonacceptance of religious belief. For centuries the churches, Protestant as well as Catholic, had striven to gain control of the apparatus of civil power so as to obtain a privileged status. In the 1950s, when John Courtney Murray began to defend the idea of a religiously neutral state, his orthodoxy was questioned by other American theologians and even by some Roman authorities. Over the protests of his opponents, however, he was invited to Vatican II (not indeed to the first session but from the second session on) and he, probably more than any other individual, was responsible for the *Declaration on Religious Freedom*. This *Declaration* clearly taught that there is no need for the state to profess the true religion or give it a legally privileged status. It approved of civil tolerance for all faiths and rejected, on theological grounds, any coercion in the sphere of belief.

For most Americans the principle of religious freedom offers no difficulties. We almost take i. for granted. Our danger is rather to fall into the opposite extreme, religious indifferentism. We have to remind ourselves that the *Declaration* itself asserted the unique status of the Catholic faith and the obligation of all believers to profess and defend that faith. Those who sincerely believe and love the truth received from Christ will strive, as did Christ and the apostles, to bear witness to it by their words and deeds, and to share their faith with others.

6. THE ACTIVE ROLE OF THE LAITY

In the Catholic church, at least in modern times, priests and religious have borne almost total responsibility for the mission of the church. The apostolic spirit of the clergy and religious orders has been admirable, but generally speaking, the laity have been rather passive. Seeking to remedy this situation, the movement known as Catholic Action, in the period between the two world wars, sought to involve elite members of the laity in the apostolate of the hierarchy. Not satisfied with this, some progressive theologians during the decade before Vatican II held that the laity, besides associating themselves with the apostolate of the hierarchy, should exercise an active apostolate in their own right as baptized believers. The council, endorsing this development, exhorted lay persons to advance the kingdom of God by engaging in temporal affairs and by discharging their familial and vocational obligations in a manner faithful to Christ.

Since the council, some have maintained that the clergy have as their proper sphere of operation the inner affairs of the church, whereas lay persons should regard secular matters as their area of competence. The council, however, does not authorize such a sharp division of labor. It provides for active participation of the laity in divine worship, in pastoral councils, and even in the sphere of theology. In this last area Vatican II calls upon the laity to speak freely and openly. "In order that such persons may fulfill their proper function," says the *Pastoral Constitution*, "let it be recognized that all the faithful, clerical and lay, possess a lawful freedom of inquiry and of thought, and the freedom to express their minds humbly and courageously about those matters in which they enjoy competence" (*GS* 62).

In the past two decades, we have seen in the church a great increase of lay ministries—not only the canonically erected ministries of reader and acolyte, but also ministries of teaching, music, social action, counseling, and even the distribution of the Eucharist. There has likewise been a great and welcome influx of laymen and laywomen into theology. These new developments, predictably, have called for adjustments that have in some cases been difficult. It is the task of the pope and the bishops to see that these new developments do not disrupt the community. In some cases this means proceeding slowly, but on the whole we must be thankful that so much has been accomplished in so short a time. In a period of diminishing vocations to the clerical and religious life, it is urgent that lay persons assume greater responsibility than ever for the faith and life of the church.

7. REGIONAL AND LOCAL VARIETY

From the late Middle Ages until Vatican II the characteristic emphasis of Catholicism had been on the universal church, commonly depicted as an almost monolithic society.

Vatican II, by contrast, emphasized the local churches, each of them under the direction of a bishop who is called, as already mentioned, a "vicar of Christ." Many of the council texts portray the universal church as a communion, or collegial union, of particular churches. "In and from such individual churches," says the *Constitution on the Church*, "there comes into being the one and only Catholic Church" (*LG* 23). The local bishop, on the ground of his ordination and appointment, is given authority to be a true pastor of his own community, making responsible decisions rather than simply carrying out Roman directives (*LG* 27).

Vatican II made provision also for regional groupings. Speaking of the differences between Eastern and Western Christianity, the council declares: "Far from being an obstacle to the church's unity, such diversity of customs and observances only adds to her comeliness, and contributes greatly to carrying out her mission" (*UR* 16). Vatican II accordingly recognizes a legitimate variety among regional churches, even in the formulation of doctrine. Elsewhere it states: "The variety of local churches with one common aspiration is particularly splendid evidence of the catholicity of the undivided church" (*LG* 23). "The accommodated preaching of the gospel," says the *Pastoral Constitution*, "ought to remain the law of all evangelization" (*GS* 44). Each nation, we are told, must develop the ability to express Christ's message in its own way, and must foster a living exchange between the church and the particular culture (ibid).

The differences between the Catholicism of different regions are much more evident today than twenty years ago, when the customs and liturgy of the Roman church, with its Latin language, were universally enforced. This diversification has not yet run its course. John Paul II, in a visit to Zaïre, spoke in favor of Africanization.

Americanization has been and is taking place in our own

Catholicism. Because of our distinctive cultural and political tradition, we have different views from most other nations on how the church ought to relate to politics and economics. We have different conceptions regarding human rights, growing out of our common-law tradition. Probably, too, we are more prepared than many other countries to see women rise to positions of leadership in the church, as they have in political and economic life.

While seeking a sound inculturation, we must avoid thinking that our own national traditions are above criticism, or that Americans are a superior people who have nothing to learn from other countries. Even where legitimate differences exist, we must take care that they do not disrupt our communion with the rest of the Catholic church. In this regard we should respect the authority of the Holy See, which has the responsibility before God both to "protect legitimate differences" and to make sure that "such differences do not hinder unity but rather contribute to it" (*LG* 13).

8. ECUMENISM

Since the Reformation, Catholics have commonly adopted hostile and defensive attitudes toward other Christian churches, and especially toward Protestantism. Such hostility may even be found in official documents of the Holy See, notably between Pius IX and Pius XI. In this regard John XXIII and Vatican II effected a quiet revolution. The council in its *Decree on Ecumenism* expressed reverence for the heritage of other Christian churches, called attention to their salvific importance for their own members, and acknowledged that they possess true elements of the church of Christ. As a result, anathema has yielded to dialogue. In the ecumenical dialogues since the council, great progress has been achieved in overcoming major differences that have divided the churches for centuries. While formal reunion between the Catholic church and other communions remains only a distant prospect, Christians of different confessional groups have achieved a far greater measure of mutual understanding, respect, and solidarity.

The proper implementation of ecumenism, as of the other principles we are here considering, requires realism and good judgment. On the one hand, we must overcome our habitual attitudes of hatred and suspicion and be open to appreciate all the sound values in other forms of Christianity, both Eastern and Western. On the other hand, we cannot surrender what is true and valid in our Catholic tradition or act as though all the ecumenical problems had already been solved. Instead of simply wishing away the remaining disagreements, we must work patiently over a long period to achieve, through prayer and dialogue, a consensus based on the truth.

9. DIALOGUE WITH OTHER RELIGIONS

The Second Vatican Council was not slow in perceiving that the changed attitude of Catholics toward other Christian churches called for a corresponding shift in their attitude toward other religions and their adherents. The council accordingly drew up a *Declaration on the Non-Christian Religions*, which contained a major section on Jewish-Christian relationships. Since the council, there have been important dialogues between Catholics and Jews, both in this country and abroad. Christians are finding that the riches of other religious traditions, such as Hinduism, Buddhism, and Islam, can help to revitalize their own faith and worship. Missionaries are finding new ways of helping non-Christians to relate better to God within the faiths of their ancestors.

The principle of interreligious dialogue, like the other

principles I have mentioned, challenges us to a mature and responsible reaction. Some commentators have introduced an antithesis between mission and dialogue, as if the importance of the one must undercut the necessity of the other. The council, however, kept mission and dialogue in balance. While recognizing elements of truth and goodness in all the great religions, and hence the desirability of respectful dialogue, the council insisted on the God-given uniqueness of the church of Christ and consequently on the "absolute necessity" of missionary activity so that Christ may be acknowledged among all peoples as universal Lord and Savior.

For most Americans the most obvious application of the *Declaration on the Non-Christian Religions* has to do with Judaism. In some parts of the country there is still among many Catholics a latent attitude of hostility, deeply rooted in ethnic and cultural factors. We need to make a special effort to rise above these negative attitudes, which are utterly contrary to the gospel precept of love. As I mentioned earlier, the church collectively has much to repent of in its historic dealings with the Jewish people. Let us not add to these crimes.

10. THE SOCIAL MISSION OF THE CHURCH

Since the Reformation the Catholic church has tended to regard its mission as an exclusively religious one, aimed at preparing individuals through faith, worship, and right behavior to attain eternal life. Gradually, with the social encyclicals of popes such as Leo XIII and Pius XI, the church began to assume responsibility to teach the principles of a just social order, but this order was viewed in terms of conformity to the natural law rather than as an implementation of the gospel.

With John XXIII and Vatican II, the emphasis shifted. The apostolate of peace and social justice came to be seen as a

requirement of the church's mission to carry on the work of
Christ, who had compassion on the poor and the oppressed.
This changed attitude was eloquently expressed in Vatican II's
"Message to Humanity," released nine days after the opening
of the council in 1962. It was more fully elaborated in the *Pastoral Constitution on the Church in the Modern World*, which described the church as endowed with "a function, a light, and
an energy which can serve to structure and consolidate the human community" (*GS* 42). Since the council this trend has
gained momentum. It was reflected in the encyclical of Paul
VI on the *Progress of Peoples* (1967) and even more clearly in the
synod document on *Justice in the World* (1971), which depicted
the struggle for justice and the transformation of society as constitutive dimensions of evangelization. Seeking to carry out the
council's mandate to discern the signs of the times in the light
of the gospel (*GS* 4), popes and episcopal conferences have
given increasingly concrete directives concerning matters of
public policy. The theme of the church's special solidarity with
the poor, already broached at Vatican II (*GS* 1), has given rise
in Latin America to the idea of a "preferential option" for the
poor.

   This tenth principle is no easier to implement than the
other nine. It would be irresponsible for the church to avoid
all comment on the moral and religious aspects of public policy
issues, for the world legitimately looks to religious leaders for
advice in reshaping society according to what Bishop James
Malone has called "a God-given value system." On the other
hand, ecclesiastical authorities must respect the freedom of individuals and groups within the church to reach conscientious
decisions about policies on which intelligent and committed
Catholics can disagree. The turbulent debates surrounding the
collective pastorals of the American bishops on peace and on
the economy make it evident that, while real progress is being

made, the right approach to sociopolitical issues is only gradually being found through a process of trial and error.

These ten principles are not intended to exhaust the achievements of Vatican II, even in the field of ecclesiology. But they do show, in my opinion, that the council, in spite of all hesitations and compromises, gave clear directives on a number of crucial issues. The extraordinary synod of 1985, commemorating the twentieth anniversary of the close of the council, may wish to reaffirm and clarify some of these basic, unequivocal teachings. It could in this way assist Catholics all over the world to address the problems of the coming decades with greater confidence and unanimity.

Tad Guzie

The Church as a
Eucharistic Community

It is a truism to say that we live between an "already" and a "not yet," and that the kingdom of God consists of both elements held in tension. This truth has to do not only with the church. It is the way the world lives, the way economics and politics and world affairs go; and a good case can be made for interpreting history according to this formula. Many people are preoccupied with what already is and how to preserve it. Others are more interested in what could be and how to bring it about.

This tension is evident in the life of worship that we lead as Catholic Christians. Right now, we are standing between two poles: the tradition that we inherited from recent centuries, and the renewed liturgy that came out of Vatican II. The old eucharistic tradition is rooted in medieval and Tridentine theology. For sake of a shorthand term, I will call this the *sacrificial* tradition. The renewal, which I will call the *ecclesial* tradition, is rooted in biblical and patristic sources which the liturgy of recent centuries had overlooked. The sacrificial tradition is an "already" which many Catholics are afraid to see lost. The ecclesial tradition is a "not yet" in the sense that we are still in the process of absorbing it.

It is interesting to look back at the *General Instruction of the*

Roman Missal, published in 1970, which promulgated the revised eucharistic liturgy. The brief introduction to this document, which takes only three pages of the *Roman Sacramentary*, tries to bridge the two traditions I just mentioned. It first describes the sacrificial nature of the Mass, the real presence of Christ proclaimed by the words of consecration and the central role of the ministerial priesthood. The sacrificial tradition having been affirmed, the instruction goes on to talk about the worshiping community, the celebration of the eucharist as the action of the whole church and the people of God brought together and strengthened in unity by sharing in the body and blood of Christ. In the literary genre of ecclesiastical documents, it is stated that all these ideas bear witness to the "unity and coherence" of the church's tradition, and that Vatican II has done little more than "complete and perfect" the liturgical norms of the Council of Trent.

If only it were that simple. The *General Instruction* was an official document promulgating a radical revision of the Mass to the entire Roman church. It could hardly take any other tack than it did. But the fact is that we are dealing here with two different theologies. This is made most evident by a basic ambiguity which the *General Instruction* makes no attempt to resolve. It is stated that the priest "offers sacrifice in the person of Christ;" and a paragraph later it is said that the people of God also give thanks in Christ "by offering his sacrifice." Contained in this ambiguity are two sets of images communicating two quite different views of the church.

The sacrificial tradition developed under the impetus of an ecclesiology which all but excluded the people of God from the essential action of the eucharist. The ordained priest became a stand-in for Christ, and thus was imaged as one who offers sacrifice "in the person of Christ." In this view of things, "the priest was imaged as a surrogate for the rest of the church.

He did not call *the church* to offer sacrifice; he did not call *the people* to the ministry of reconciliation; he did not invite *the assembly* to initiate, to heal, or to bless. All these he did on behalf of the church. The work of Christ that properly belongs to the whole church became solely the work of the ordained" (Peter Fink, "The Sacrament of Orders: Some Liturgical Reflections," *Worship*, 56 [November 1982] 486; italics added).

THE ECCLESIAL TRADITION

On the other hand, in what I have called the "ecclesial" tradition, there is no place for a surrogate action on the part of the priest. It is the liturgical assembly itself—the people of God, not the priest—which represents and images Christ. And so "whatever the priest is called upon to do, he can only do *with* the people of the church. His act of forgiveness must be at the same time a summons to the church to be with him in that forgiveness; his act of offering, at the same time a summons to the church to offer itself. The ordained priest must be seen as standing in the midst of the assembly, and his ministry ordered to those whose own 'Amen' is needed to complement and complete what he does" (Fink, p. 487).

When the *General Instruction* sets about laying down the norms for celebrating the eucharist, it clearly favors the ecclesial tradition over the sacrificial tradition. The assembly of the people is primary, not the ministry of the priest. Each celebration must "take into account the nature and circumstances of each assembly," and the various liturgical forms contained in the rite are to be "selected and arranged," taking into account the "individual and local circumstances" of each assembly (Chapter 1).

This is quite a radical *principle of adaptation* which urges that final decisions about the elements to be contained in a particular liturgy can only be made locally. It is probably the least observed of all the norms in the *Sacramentary*. Liturgical planners are constantly told that many legitimate adaptations are not permitted. That the celebration belongs to the *assembly*, not to the bishop or even the local priest, is an abstract principle that is quickly overridden in the concrete in a great many communities. This points to the tension of images and traditions which I mentioned above. The sacrificial tradition, with its emphasis on the centrality of the ordained minister, is an "already" which is hard to overcome. The ecclesial tradition, which gives primacy to the assembly, is a "not yet" in the sense that it is has not fully matured; it has not become a total part of our communal consciousness, and, therefore, is not fully implemented.

At this point it should be clear that when we speak of the "church as a eucharistic community," there is a choice to be made. We have two theological traditions, two ways of imaging both church and eucharist. Ever since the Middle Ages, and owing to the particular history of the theology of sacrifice, there has been a certain disharmony between the two traditions. This has not always been the case. In the patristic era, the two traditions were developing alongside each other, as complementary understandings of the eucharist; and they did not yet convey different images of the church.

Augustine of Hippo shows us both traditions standing in harmony. (I intend to use Augustine as a witness for the kind of things said about the eucharist during the high patristic era. I have great difficulty with Augustine's ideas on some other subjects, but his thoughts on the eucharist are representative of the church fathers. I might have used the baptismal catechesis of Ambrose, Chrysostom, or Theodore of Mopsuestia to make the same points that I will make here.)

AUGUSTINE

Augustine develops the "ecclesial" tradition in one of his Easter sermons, which expands on Paul's image of the *body of Christ:* The bread and wine which you see on the alter, sanctified through the word of God, are the body and blood of Christ. If you receive worthily, "you are what you have received." You are to "become bread, that is, the body of Christ" for one another because "in the bread you learn how much you ought to seek for unity with one another." The bread was made from many grains ground together, mixed with water, baked with fire. You were ground and refined by your practice of Lent, baptized with water, anointed with the fire of the Holy Spirit. This "being what you have received" is what Paul meant when he said that as the bread is one, so we though many are one body (Sermon 227).

The "body of Christ" is therefore both the church and the eucharist. Augustine cannot speak of the eucharistic body without speaking in almost the same breath of the body which is the church. The one does not make sense without the other; the one necessarily images the other. Both church and eucharist are the *corpus mysticum.* Or more precisely, "mystical body" is the patristic term for referring to the church precisely as a eucharistic community (see Henri de Lubac, *Corpus Mysticum* [Paris: Aubier, 1949]).

"Sacrifice" is simply another image which expresses the same reality. In the same sermon, Augustine speaks of the eucharist as a sacrifice, which is another "sign of what we are," because Christ "wished us to be his sacrifice." He develops this image further in his *City of God* (10.6), in some classic texts which the sacrificial tradition would later distort. The sacrifice of Christians, says Augustine, is precisely that we, though many, are one body in Christ. This consciousness of being church, this awareness of being the body of Christ in this world, *this being church* is "the sacrifice which the church continues to celebrate in the sacrament of the altar, in which it is clear to the church that she herself is offered in the very offering she makes to God."

The link between the altar and the cross, between the eucharistic celebration and the work of Christ, is the ecclesial body living for God. The image of "sacrifice" therefore communicates exactly the same thing as the image of "body of Christ." The anchor-point for both images is the church, the people of God, the assembly.

This harmonization of what I have called the sacrificial and ecclesial traditions broke down during the Middle Ages. First of all, the meaning of "body of Christ" changed. During the patristic era, this term referred at once to three realities: the personal body of Jesus, the church, and the eucharist. With the increasing clericalization of the eucharist, the faithful no longer imaged themselves as an essential part of the eucharistic body. And so the middle term—the ecclesial meaning of "body"—was lost. Theology now had to find some other way to link the bread and wine with the historical or heavenly body of Jesus. The solution was found in extremely physical notions of the real presence.

The theology of the "real presence" of Christ in the eucharist has its own curious and sometimes complex history, which we do not need to pursue here (see my book *Jesus and the Eucharist* [Paulist, 1974], chapter 4). I will simply note that, beginning around the ninth century, theological reflection became fixated on the elements of bread and wine because the *ecclesial* meaning of the body of Christ—the church, the people of God as eucharistic community—had been lost. I suspect that the theory of "transubstantiation" would not have come about otherwise. It is crucial for catechists and teachers to note that the theology of real presence handed down by Trent and the Baltimore Catechism *prescinds entirely* from that "body" which is the church. That is, the traditional theology of the real presence is explained exclusively in terms of a change in the elements of bread and wine. The theory of transubstantiation, as it is usually presented, unfolds without any reference to the eucharistic *community*.

"IN THE PERSON OF CHRIST"

A similar fate befell the understanding of eucharist as "sacrifice." In Augustine's hands, "sacrifice" refers to a triad of realities analogous to the body of Christ: namely, the sacrifice of the cross, the church as the living sacrifice of Christ, and the sacrifice of the altar. The middle term—the people of God, the assembly—was lost from the image of sacrifice. Theology had to find a way to link the sacrifice of the altar with the sacrifice of Jesus, again without the essential middle term. This was done by creating a notion of the ordained priest as one who offers sacrifice "in the person of Christ."

Note that in traditional sacrificial theology, the priest does not act in the person of the *community* but in the person of Christ. In this theology only Christ and the cross are needed; the assembly is absent. In other words, the community of the church is not an integral part of sacrificial theology as it was handed down to modern times.

Here we find the ultimate justification for the practice of multiplied private Masses: The priest, acting more in the person of Christ than as a representative of the church, renews the sacrifice of Calvary as often as canon law will permit. The only brakes put on this practice—brakes which preserved the last vestiges of an ecclesial understanding of the eucharist—came from the canonical regulation that a priest must have a server. Members of religious communities of priests will remember how this regulation was observed in practice, before concelebration came along. Priests served one another's Masses if there were no seminarians around. Often enough this was an opportunity for one priest to read his breviary while his brother priest was saying his private Mass.

Augustine's words were now twisted in another direction. In the passage from *City of God* mentioned above, Augustine adds that "Christ Jesus is both the priest who offers and the oblation that is offered. And it was his will that as a sacrament of this reality there should be the daily sacrifice of the church which, being the body of him, her head, learns to offer itself through him" (10.6). By "daily sacrifice" Augustine meant the church, the assembly, living its life unto God. But with the church eliminated from the triad of cross-church-altar, the sacrificial tradition came to read the "daily sacrifice" as the Mass, offered by the priest who is a stand-in for Christ.

I have tried to demonstrate how the two eucharistic traditions which we have been living with were originally harmonious. Owing to medieval developments, the harmony was broken, leaving us today with two traditions in tension. But let us note first things first. Of the two traditions, is there one which is more essential to the church's self-understanding? Yes. The sacrificial tradition broke free of its ecclesial roots and created around itself a cleric-centered image of the church and of the eucharist itself. The lesson of history is that the notion of the eucharist as a "sacrifice" cannot stand alone.

But the converse is not true. What I have called the ecclesial tradition, which is anchored in the basic notion that it is the *people* who celebrate the eucharist, does not require the notion of eucharist as "sacrifice" in order to be complete. The idea of eucharist as sacrifice is secondary and supplementary to the much more basic notion of the eucharist as the *church's* remembrance of Jesus. The image of sacrifice is optional, not essential.

This point is implicit in the ecumenical dialogues of recent times (e.g. Roman Catholic dialogues with Lutherans and with Anglicans). Churches which were once at loggerheads with one another have come to substantial agreement on the meaning of the eucharist. What I have described as the "ecclesial" tradition is common to all the major Christian churches. The "sacrificial" tradition was abandoned by most of the Reformation churches because of the abuses to which it had led. This no longer needs to be divisive, because all parties in these dialogues have agreed that there are different traditions, different ways of "imaging" the eucharist. The challenge for Catholics is to realize that the absence of sacrificial language and imagery from another church's eucharistic liturgy does not imply any fundamental difference in belief.

How are we to relate all of this to the biblical tradition? By biblical tradition I mean not only the written books, but above all the lived experience which the books record. Over the centuries, the texts of the New Testament which deal with the eucharist have been worked over time and time again, in defense or in refutation of doctrinal positions that were taken much later. Thanks to biblical studies and historical consciousness in general, we have learned that first-century texts do not give ready answers to twelfth, or sixteenth, or twentieth-century questions. In relation to the eucharist, first-century Christians simply did not *experience* the eucharist the way we do. For most of them, the breaking of the bread and the sharing of the cup was part of a larger meal, a dining experience. This practice of communal meals seemed to decline by the end of the first century, and the ritual of the bread and cup came to stand on its own. But it was still a good while before there was a *regulated* ritual, much less an institutionalized system of ministers who were ordained precisely to preside at the eucharist.

How do our two traditions, the ecclesial and the sacrificial, fit into the scenario of the very early church? They do and they don't. They do, in the sense that a variety of *images* of the

Lord's supper as a remembrance of the sacrificial act of Jesus are in the air. They don't, in the sense that there is no articulate theology which resembles *either* the ecclesial view *or* the sacrificial view of the eucharist discussed above. Images take time to develop. Images have to be savored, enacted in ritual, and reflected upon. The earliest Christians broke bread together in a simple way and with simple words. However profound their faith, they did not describe this experience and could not have done so with the kind of sophisticated imagery—"ecclesial" or "sacrificial"—which Augustine used in the fifth century.

BENEATH THE TRADITION

All of this suggests that there must be a theology of the eucharist *beneath* the received tradition, whether sacrificial or ecclesial. There is such a theology, but we have not given any attention to it. Sacramental theology has attended to the generic whole, the community, the assembly, the people of God. Even when theology got fixated on priests and clerics, these persons were imaged as stand-ins for the community. What sacramental theology has not done is to discuss the reality of any community *smaller than* the large assembly, the parish assembly, the Sunday assembly, which has been our norm for understanding the meaning of the eucharist.

This is the point at which I want to push you to think beyond the received tradition, sacrificial or ecclesial. The essence of the matter is that the Christian eucharist has its roots in table fellowship, not in the kind of assembly we know on Sundays. Unless we recognize this fact, we are liable to miss the most basic meanings of the eucharistic meal.

Let me begin out of our Catholic tradition. The *Constitution on the Liturgy* of Vatican II did an excellent job of broadening the question of the "real presence" of Christ, which

Catholics had tended to reduce to the elements of bread and wine. This document (#7) speaks of many ways in which Christ is present: in the celebration of the eucharist (in the liturgical action, not just the objects of bread and wine), in all the sacraments, in the proclamation of the scriptures, and above all in the assembly itself which is gathered to pray and sing and worship. The fundamental point in this paragraph, which overrides centuries of dispute between Protestants and Catholics on the "real presence" question, is that it is *we the faithful* who are the presence of Christ in the world, before the bread and wine are brought to the table. The foundation for all of this is the saying in Matthew's gospel: "Where two or three are gathered in my name, I am in their midst" (18:20).

This saying of Jesus applies to our own families, not just to an assembly in a church. The primary condition for the presence of Christ is to be "gathered in my name." Certainly there is a particular dignity in a large Christian assembly like the Sunday assembly. But this in no way diminishes the particular dignity of a *family* gathered in the name of Jesus. The presence of Christ is just as "real" in a small group, like a family, as it is in a church assembly.

To illustrate my point that something smaller than the Sunday assembly gives us a norm for understanding the basic meaning of the eucharist, let me call on the gospel of Luke. Table fellowship seems to have been a key part of Jesus' own ministry. In Luke's gospel, meals are the setting for much of Jesus' teaching. When the Twelve returned from their first mission of preaching and healing, Jesus taught them that another essential part of their ministry was to break bread with people (Lk 9). Seeing the crowds, Jesus told the Twelve, "Give them something to eat." This command was no different from that other mandate they would hear later on: "Do this in memory of me."

When Levi, the tax collector and excommunicate, became

a follower of Jesus, he hosted a dinner. The legalists complained that Jesus was eating and drinking with known sinners. The meal was a healing and reconciling event in which Jesus broke through the divisions that the professional religious people of his time wanted to maintain (Lk 5). Later on, at a sabbath meal, Jesus expanded on the same point. He insisted that the Christian table should reach out to others, to the rejects of society, and not remain confined to a comfortable in-group (Lk 14).

A meal hosted by Jesus and his disciples was the setting for the great mercy parables, including the story of the prodigal son, whose return and forgiveness were celebrated by a feast (Lk 15). And Zacchaeus, from his branch in the sycamore tree, accepted Jesus' offer of table fellowship. There he returned to honesty and determined to share his wealth with the needy (Lk 19).

So when Luke comes to the story of the Last Supper, he has already laid out the implications of the words "Do this in memory of me." To share a meal together means forgiveness. It means reconciliation, unity, harmony restored, love celebrated, commitment to caring for others and sharing one's blessings. These are the themes of table fellowship. Not that Luke created these themes. Rather, his stories show how Jesus knew the profound meaning of sharing a meal together, and he drew on *the meaning of sharing a meal* to state the heart of his message.

Isn't this the starting point for eucharistic theology? Preaching and teaching and theologizing about the eucharist invariably begin and end with the "macro" picture, the Sunday church assembly. Here the theological tradition universally follows one writer, Ignatius of Antioch, the father of the "normative" eucharist, the first writer to insist that the eucharist be celebrated in the presence and under the presidency of the leader of the assembly, the *episkopos*. Ignatius was concerned with unity and harmony, and his teaching on the eucharist was one of his ways of expressing it. But however legitimate the concerns of Ignatius might have been, we are not finished until we have focused on the "micro" picture as well.

TABLE FELLOWSHIP

My point here is very simple, very biblical (Lukan at least), and something that catechists have often intuited: How can we really grasp the import of a Christian assembly gathered to celebrate the eucharist on the Lord's Day unless we have a sense of the *holiness of a meal shared in Jesus' name in our own homes?*

This won't be every meal, nor does it have to be, because not every meal is a gathering in the name of Jesus. Many of our meals are casual feeding times, and sometimes we feed in front of the TV set. The problem is that we have become so used to eating and running that we have lost touch with meals as truly holy events.

My readers know, I am sure, that in Jesus' time (and for religious Jews today) every meal is a sacred meal. The Passover meal, though lavish in its symbolism, is basically a *family* meal with special foods and blessings. Whatever connection the followers of Jesus made between the Last Supper and the Passover meal, a far more basic factor at work in their minds was the symbolism of any family meal. The Passover is celebrated only once a year, and yet we know that the first Christians met regularly in their homes for the breaking of the bread (Acts 2:42). This they never could have done unless the eucharist were based, not primarily on the symbolism of the Passover, but on the symbolism inherent in *everyday table fellowship.*

To share a meal in peace and harmony is a great grace, one of God's most precious gifts to us. We are a sacred and precious people, and that sacredness is not first celebrated in a large assembly. We need to recognize the gift that a meal carries, accept it with awareness, and so enjoy at least some of our meals in an atmosphere of thanksgiving and reverence.

To make this concrete, let me sketch a little ritual of table fellowship. Begin with your Sunday dinner, or some other meal of the week which is important for your household. Or begin with meals at special times: holidays, birthdays, anniversaries. Select a cup which you will set aside as your "blessing cup." As you use it, it will become a sign of your solidarity and your care for one another.

You might begin the meal with a short reading from scripture—a passage which speaks of the season or the occasion, or one which simply puts into words the hopes you share together. Those around the table might then offer petitions, express their joys or worries, or pray in silence for their needs.

Then fill the blessing cup with wine, or whatever beverage everyone enjoys. Let the filling of the cup itself be a ceremonious act, which might be given to different members of the household at different times. The leader (a role which might also be rotated) then recites a prayer of blessing: "Blessed are you, Father, for all the gifts you have given to us. Blessed are you in Jesus, your son and our brother, who was poured out for us." The cup is then passed around the table.

After the cup has been shared, the leader takes a piece of bread, breaks it and passes it on a plate around the table, reciting another blessing: "Blessed are you, Father, for giving us bread to eat. Blessed are you in Jesus, your son and our brother, who was broken for us. We recognize him and we give you thanks, here in the breaking of the bread." After the bread is eaten, all might join hands around the table and recite the Lord's Prayer or sing a song. The meal then continues as usual.

This simple ritual is not written in stone. Through experience, a family or household will come to know what words and prayers and gestures are most fitting and comfortable around the table. The best table prayer finally comes from concrete experience, and above all from the conviction that what we do at table is a blessed event.

Let me put into an historical context what I am proposing here. Traditional theology, following the lead of Ignatius of Antioch, simply does not discuss the eucharist or the presence of Christ except in terms of the assembly. If a priest is talking, he might say that the honest-to-goodness really real presence of Christ happens when he pronounces the words of consecration. I am trying to get behind all of this, to something more basic that theology has left unsaid. The Christian eucharist originated within Jewish table fellowship. Afterwards, in the patristic era, a whole theology of the eucharistic assembly evolved, essentially the "ecclesial" theology I have described. Then, during the Middle Ages, "sacrificial" theology took over with all of its emphasis on the altar, the objects of bread and wine, and the priest who consecrates them.

| TABLE FELLOWSHIP | ⟶ | THEOLOGY OF THE ASSEMBLY | ⟶ | THEOLOGY OF BREAD AND WINE |

The liturgical theology of the past decades has been leading us back to basics: from adoration of the Host and the sacrificial theology of the Middle Ages, back to a rediscovery of the holiness of the Christian assembly and its ecclesial action of breaking bread together. This is the evolution or, perhaps better, the revolution expressed in the Liturgy Constitution of Vatican II and implemented in the *General Instruction of the Roman Missal* of 1970. We now have a further step to take, I would urge, and that is to recover a sense of the sacredness of table fellowship, in our own families and households.

| TABLE FELLOWSHIP | ⟵ | THEOLOGY OF THE ASSEMBLY | ⟵ | THEOLOGY OF BREAD AND WINE |

In this schema, the dotted line represents the road we still have to travel if we are to link our received eucharistic theology with a concept which is still more basic.

How do we relate the concept of table fellowship to the received tradition of the church, whether "sacrificial" or "ecclesial"? Let me refer once more to Peter Fink's excellent article on the meaning of holy orders. The ordained ministry came about, he suggests, because of a certain "largeness" which our worship in a eucharistic assembly reflects. "Gospel and eucharistic prayer announce the largeness of Christ and the largeness of the church which remains only partially achieved in history. This largeness calls the church assembled into becoming. It is both a theological principle and an observable fact that without this dimension of largeness and its power to summon beyond what already is, a given assembly will close in on itself. Without the dimension of largeness the very impulse for growth is taken away. It is because of this largeness of both gospel and eucharistic prayer that the ministers who proclaim them have come to be appointed by the college of bishops, and not simply through the local ministry of the local church" (Fink, p. 491).

This is one of the best statements I have read about the basic reason why, in a nutshell, ordination came about. What I have been suggesting in the last few pages is a complement or corollary, not a contradiction. If the Christian community gathered in a Sunday assembly possesses a "largeness" which necessarily calls for an ordained ministry, our theologizing must also take account of the smaller units which make up this largeness—the unit of the family, the household, the small community, the "house church." These smaller units participate in the total ministry of the assembly in the sense of preceding it existentially: "Where two or three are gathered in my name, I am in their midst." The smaller unit therefore anticipates the assembly, hopes for it and calls for it.

But not all households are able to find an assembly in

which they can celebrate their faith in a way that is authentic for them. This is often a very painful situation. Many committed Catholics hope and cry out for an assembly, but they are not able to find one that rises above the lowest common denominator. They have no wish to avoid a larger community, but they are unable to find a community that is committed to prayer, reflection, and change of heart. When these elements are not part of an assembly's life, its liturgy is a contradiction. An increasing number of Catholics today feel that their own lived experience is violated when they try to celebrate with such an assembly. So they are left with nothing but their own household or some other small community in which they can pray, reflect, and celebrate the paschal mystery. The ray of hope in this situation is that we *can* celebrate as Jesus taught us to celebrate. The existence of an institutional church and an official ministry does not negate the authentic eucharistic ministry that belongs to every Christian household.

Our problem is that theological reflection has been devoted to the *macro-church*—the "largeness" which Fink accurately describes. But this is not where the eucharist began. It is the *micro-church*, the household church, which is the context for the thoughts of someone like Luke on the meaning of the Breaking of the Bread. There has been little or no theological reflection on the micro-church. The result is that our eucharistic theology, whether sacrificial or ecclesial, lacks roots in a Christian truth, a Christian reality which is more basic than what our theological tradition has handed down to us.

We have images for the assembly, and we have recovered many images that we had lost. We are in a good position, a better position than we have been for over a millennium, to speak of the church as a eucharistic community. But that is the macro-church. We have not developed eucharistic images for the micro-church. In some important respects, our eucharistic theology lacks roots in the teaching and historical ministry of

Jesus, because it does not take account of the context of table fellowship in which he broke bread, shared the cup, and celebrated with sinners. I hope this article will stimulate reflection in the direction of some basic truths which our inherited theology has overlooked. The "not yet" is a bigger world than we may have thought.

Monika K. Hellwig

Christian Initiation: Gate to Salvation

Christian reflection on contemporary experience has required us to consider again in great depth many aspects of Christian faith and practice which we took for granted. Not very long ago, the term "gate to salvation" would have suggested to Catholic readers either death or the Church as the ante-chamber to what lies beyond death. Among Catholics, at least, salvation was not envisaged in worldly or historical terms. It was otherworldly, beyond history and beyond death. Because it was outside history, it was understood also to be outside experience.

What this meant for our implicit understanding of the sacraments was that their meaning and effects were largely a matter of hearsay evidence. There was little sense that one's experience and life-style and worldly expectations would be radically changed by one's initiation into the Christian community. Baptism was seen as the entrance into the Church and therefore into a realm of grace. But the grace was by no means apparent. What was apparent to most initiates was rather a burden of moral and ritual obligations. This burden was experienced. The grace was believed to exist with a degree of conviction that depended heavily on the intensity of catechesis and of devotional reinforcement of the belief, but the connection between grace and experience was tenuous and remote for many Catholics.

The traditional Catholic tolerance of this discrepancy has been breaking down. Catholics are less credulous now about a profound and significant change in themselves which cannot be substantiated by experience. This reluctance has been both good and bad for Christian life in the Catholic community. It has been bad in that many have considered what they actually saw in themselves and other Christians, and have concluded that being Christian made no difference, and have therefore withdrawn from the Church and its observances. Yet it has also been good because it has led to a more honest and a more penetrating reflection on what we mean by the sacraments in general and by the sacraments of initiation in particular.

This more persistent questioning of the meaning of the sacraments and of the changes we expect to be brought about by them has grown out of a renewed understanding of grace and of the process of redemption. The groundbreaking work of Henri de Lubac (*Le surnaturel,* 1946; *Le mystère du surnaturel,* 1965) and of Karl Rahner ("Concerning the Relationship between Nature and Grace," 1961) shifted the whole inquiry ineluctably into the realm of what is experienced. This seems to be the most significant change which has prompted re-examination of our sacramental practice and understanding. It seems that Catholic orthodoxy has always been suspicious of the claims which put grace within the realm of experience, mainly because those claims tended to come from enthusiastic sects and groups which associated the idea of grace rather directly with emotional exaltation.

EXPERIENCE: A NEW VIEW

The new emphasis on experience is of a different kind. It is concerned not with a state of emotional stimulation but with the experience of a transformation in faith and hope and most of all in practical and effective charity which brings about a reintegration of life and goals for the individual and for the society in which the individuals concerned deal with one another. This emphasis on the palpable effects of grace in the community received much support, of course, from renewed New Testament studies and more particularly from careful readings of the Pauline letters in which the term, *charis*, clearly designates an observable quality in the lives of communities and their members.

There has been, however, another great shift in contemporary theological understanding which has caused a rethinking of our understanding of the sacraments. This is the shift caused by persistent, shrill socio-critical questions about Christian claims concerning the redemption. Coming from intellectual champions of the poor and the dispossessed of the world, these questions have challenged our perception of the relationship between the salvation offered in Christ through the ministry and continued presence of the Church, and the desperate and all too apparent practical needs of salvation experienced by the wretched of the earth. In the minds and imaginations of serious and committed Christians these questions will not go away. And because the whole process of redemption is more and more coming to be seen in the light of these socio-critical questions, therefore the meaning of the Church and of its sacramental ministry is coming under scrutiny of the same questions.

In their application to the sacraments of initiation, these two shifts of theological focus have come most opportunely as the rites of initiation were being revised. Liturgical and patristic scholarship had suggested closer attention to the historical development of the rites and a reconsideration based primarily upon the rite for adult initiation and the function which that rite ought to play.

Ever since the baptism of infants became almost the exclusive form in practice, the theory or theology of the sacraments of initiation was burdened by this. Because medieval reflection eventually turned Augustine's response to the Pelagians upside down, we came to relate initiation to death rather than life. That is to say that our concern became rather predominantly that of ensuring that people be baptized before death to ensure that they were qualified to enter heaven. The prompt baptism of the newborn was far more important than the gathering and instruction of the community that was to welcome that infant into its midst to experience a life of grace.

To understand the rites of initiation better, we traced their early history through the patristic era because that was the story of their formation. What we found were not only clues to the meaning of the symbolism which turned out to be far deeper and richer than had been apparent in more recent centuries. We also found out a great deal about what was expected of the community and of the candidates for initiation. Their initiation into the community was not a formality. Nor yet was it a rite that was expected to be effective without a radical turning about of the whole lifestyle and outlook, the expectations and patterns of association of the candidates. Moreover, whatever demands were made upon them were made without hesitation or embarrassment because they were assumed to correspond closely to the established way of life and pattern of the community of the faithful.

It is on the basis of what we learned from the early centuries that the adult catechumenate and the order of initiation of adults into the Church have been restructured in our own times. What is contained in the instructions and in the ceremonies themselves is momentous in implications and visionary in inspiration. But it is difficult and indeed embarrassing for us to make the demands implied because we can in no way assume that they correspond to the way in which most of the community included in our Sunday morning congregations actually lives. Perhaps it is especially for this reason that it is more important and more urgent that we achieve a certain depth and clarity of understanding for ourselves and for those being baptized and confirmed and also for the communities that must welcome them into their midst.

CREATION OUT OF FOCUS

Such an understanding of the meaning of initiation sacraments includes creation, sin and redemption, as well as the role of the Church community in the redemption and the function of sacramental activity in the life of the community. Therefore it begins with the vision of created reality as it really is—dependent on its relationship to the creator for existence, purpose and harmony, yearning and groaning for it knows not what until the true relationship to the creator is re-established and reintegrates within itself all the other relationships. Baptism and all the sacramental life of the Christian community is grounded in a magnificent vision of what creation is intended to be—a vision that sanctifies material and spiritual existence and establishes a natural harmony among persons.

Yet it is clear that Christian baptism does not invite the neophyte to a contemplative acceptance of what is in the world without further discernment or discrimination. It has been suggested (by Alexander Ganoczy, *Becoming Christian*, Paulist, 1976) that baptism is the sacrament of history, precisely because it does indeed invite one into critical distinction between what simply is and what ought to be. Baptism, and indeed the whole Christian initiation, only make sense in the context of a vivid consciousness of original sin. But that consciousness of sin is itself properly an historical and social consciousness as has been so clearly demonstrated in the work of Piet Schoonenberg (available in English in *Man and Sin*, Notre Dame Press, 1965).

The truth of our human existence is that we live in personal and historical ambivalence—a good creation which has lost its focus and its harmony, and has therefore lost sight of its purpose. The story of Adam is the story of each of us and all of us. Adam is a representative figure in a more intrinsic and less arbitrary sense than our post-Tridentine catechisms may have led us to believe. Adam seen against the background of the lost Eden is an inclusive tableau of the human situation in history. Initiation into the Christian community is meaningful in the context of a journey, in the context of bitter homesickness, of an anguished sense of loss and of alienation.

Baptism is essentially the great sacrament of repentance, of the turning about of one's life, the change of direction in one's journey. This becomes clearer with a deeper appreciation of what sin is. We are not concerned in the first place with particular actions which transgress rules and commandments, but rather with disorientation of personal and social existence. To be created is to be called into existence in response to God—a response of gratitude, dependence acknowledged and appreciated, contentment and joy in creaturehood and in co-creaturehood with others, focussed in discernment of the divine will and purpose. To sin is essentially to repudiate that relationship and set out on one's own to create a world, and other people and perhaps even a God, to one's own image and likeness and one's own purpose, setting oneself and one's own independent goals and projects at the center of this world to hold it together. Our common experience, of course, is that such a world and such a project do not hold together, but we maintain them by the external pressure of competition with the worlds and projects of other people which are in competition with our own.

SALVATION—A TURNING

Sin is essentially disorientation, alienation from God, from others and from one's true, peaceful self. Salvation then is by a turning, a re-orientation to God, to community with others, to peace with oneself—a re-orientation of the individual and a re-orientation of society in its community concerns and relationships and also in its structures large and small. And this is why baptism is the sacrament of the great turning; it is the return to community with others in the context of a turning of one's life to God and to God's purpose in the world and in history, and that is a return to one's true self, to the truth of one's self as creature before the creator and among other creatures. Baptism assumes not only the candidate's appreciation of what is at stake and the candidate's readiness to be brought to this turning. It also assumes a community to which the candidate can return—a community that is in some sense already that of the final reconciliation. The turning is in the last resort a community as well as a personal matter.

The redemption which Christians have experienced in Jesus Christ is a restoration of the focus and integration and therefore of the joy and the purpose of human existence. What was restored in the person of Jesus himself is shared with all who can be drawn into relationship with him. Because sin is essentially the state of disorientation and alienation, therefore salvation is essentially a matter of re-orientation and of reconciliation. It is re-orientation to God and that brings all else into perspective. It is reconciliation with God and that is worked out in some very specific and concrete reconciliations within creation. The very existence of Jesus in the world, in history, gives a new center to human existence—a center around which others, individually and in their social groupings and structures, can come together to become whole, to become authentically themselves as created by God, and therefore to find fulfillment and peace.

However, this re-integration of all human life in Jesus is made possible by the mediation of those who extend the presence of Jesus to one another across great stretches of space and time and cultural variations. It is a community of followers of Jesus, themselves transformed in his Spirit alive in them, that is able to forge the links through space and time and culture that channel the grace of Christ to others to transform their lives in turn. That quality of life, that open relationship with God and with God's good creation, which we call grace because it is wholly gift, does not drop into human hearts directly from heaven and is not "produced" by the performance of a ritual. Like all human relationships, and qualities and values, grace is communicated through the encounter with graced and gracious persons. And this grace is salvation in process.

Baptism and confirmation and first eucharistic communion, therefore, making up the process of Christian initiation, are sacramental and effective in this truly divine and truly human way. Sacraments give body to spiritual reality, specificity to what is otherwise diffused, visibility and palpability to what is otherwise elusive. The ritual gives expression and concreteness to the transition from a life of chaos and frustration to a life of reconciliation, purpose and communion. The ritual cannot substitute for this transition; it is intended to facilitate it and thereby mediate or confer grace.

This means, of course, that the welcome into the realm of Christ's grace is in fact more or less ineffective where, in the case of an adult candidate, there is no intention to allow one's life to be transformed—a condition which in our own times must be very rare because there is no other very evident advantage in being received into the Church. But it also means that the effect is somewhat hampered wherever the local community of Christians is not much interested in welcoming the newcomer to a transformed sort of life or wherever the local community of Christians is simply not a community or is not discernibly living a transformed sort of life. This has led many parishes to establish a carefully planned catechumenate for adult converts to the Church, in which the candidates can be guaranteed to meet deeply committed Christians of the local community who will draw them into circles of persons more seriously pursuing the Christian life. This is, of course, good, because it recognizes both the true sacramental nature of baptism and the exigencies of a sinful and confused history. Yet the scandal remains and nothing short of a conversion of the parish will remove it.

INFANT BAPTISM

What is a scandal in the case of adult initiation is worse in the case of infants, because the immediate circle that is to welcome them is not selected on the basis of Christian commitment but on the basis of blood relationship. This, of course, is why the Church has been so cautious about baptizing children unless there is some reasonable guarantee that they can be raised in the Christian faith and hope and community of charity. The American Catholic tradition has tried to deal with this problem by means of Catholic parochial schools, which at least provide an environment in which the Christian vision of reality is taken for granted and constantly explicitly presented. Ideally the schools draw young Christians into an adult community living a truly transformed Christian life. Because many of the schools have been conducted by religious or by apostolically minded lay persons who were sufficiently committed to work for lower salaries than could be had elsewhere, this has in fact happened more frequently than we might have expected.

Nevertheless, it seems that we have been guilty of a kind of superstition in relation to infant baptism, as though the mere performance of the ritual could bring the child into a realm of grace which would unfold more or less spontaneously. Now that we are brought to think of initiation with the adult candidate as the primary model from which the initiation of children is adapted, it becomes clear that, if we are not thinking superstitiously, we must think in terms of the infant baptism as an invitation or welcome into the community which is expressed in the ceremony of baptism but must be substantiated in the life of the community.

If the sacraments of initiation are really to be the gate to salvation, as they are indeed intended to be, there has to be present a community of salvation and there has to be a real catechumenate to introduce candidates to that community and its life-style in depth and in all facets of human existence. In the case of children there cannot be a catechumenate before baptism, therefore there must be one after. We have, of course, since shortly after the Council of Trent, made a habit of catechizing children, but we have assumed that their Christian commitment was made for them at baptism and that they need but have explained to them what they believe and how they are to behave in accordance with what they believe. In a less pluralistic society this seemed to work well enough in most cases, though it may have resulted in some very shallow and minimalist perceptions of what was involved in Christian faith and Christian life. In our own very pluralistic society it does not work. We can no longer pretend to tell people the commitment they made (or we made for them) and explain to them what they believe. We must invite them, respectful of their freedom, and we must invite them into something whose value they can test in their experience.

THE YOUNG ADULT

When we claim that the initiation into the Christian community is a gateway into salvation, young people come with certain felt needs for salvation, certain deprivations, fears and sufferings from which they know they need to be rescued, certain perceptions of what is wrong and unjust in the world which they know must be changed. They want to know whether the salvation the Church offers has anything to say to the real problems which they perceive. What is even more important, perhaps, is that they have a right to come with these questions and that their demands are in keeping with the true nature of the sacraments of initiation and the true nature of the Church.

The specific fears that haunt young people of our times and from which they want to be redeemed are important. There is the never wholly absent fear of nuclear holocaust which constitutes a pervasive threat to the future of the human race. There is the fear of being excluded in the fierce economic competition—a fear of joblessness, of incompetence, of failure, of being overwhelmed, of being unvalued and unwanted in the marketplace. There is also the fear of personal loneliness and isolation, of being left out, of being despised for nonconformity to the peer group expectations, of being ridiculed or made the butt of prejudice, of not being acceptable for what one is. There is also the fear of violence in our society, of the cold selfishness of others, of infidelity in marriages and families, and of the instability and vulnerability which spring from family infidelity. Moreover, there is often a realization among the young of the huge intractable problems of racial prejudice, oppression of poor and powerless masses, corruption in public life, warmongering for financial profit and so forth.

The young people whom we have baptized in infancy and whom we are inviting to full and adult membership in our

Christian communities want to know and have a right to know whether the salvation we claim to offer has any "cash value" in the world of these problems and fears that threaten and overwhelm them. If we are honest, we do not pressure them to complete their initiation in confirmation and solemn first eucharistic communion (for the solemn communion is not necessarily the first) unless and until they themselves are convinced that they have found the answer to their questions, a community that shares their search and can show grounds for hope in its present experience of fellowship and social concern. If we are honest, therefore, we do not sweep them through the preparation for and reception of confirmation in a peer group that generates a kind of herd pressure and gets them through with little conviction of their own. This would show little respect for the young people but it would also show little respect for the serious nature of the sacrament and for the serious nature of the community that continues to build itself out of the accretion of such newcomers.

Because of the nature of sin and the nature of salvation from sin, the Church is essentially, not accidentally, concerned with every one of these problems that concretely constitute the disorientation and alienation of the persons living in our time and culture. To bring into the Church should mean to bring into a community that lives in a reconciling manner, that is to say a community that constantly serves the needy, embraces the excluded, makes peace, is concerned to reshape the economy so that it serves the interests of all, respects the dignity of all, confronts every kind of suffering with courage and compassion and lives in mutual acceptance and support in a spirit of great hope and joy. This is what the newcomer should find. This is the apologetic, the demonstration of the reasonable grounds of credibility which can reasonably be expected.

In the context of such a community Christian initiation has its full meaning and efficacy as an entrance into salvation.

It is the ideal. Because we live in the confusion of a sinful history in which the wheat of redemption is much intertwined with the tares of original sin, we seldom find a community that really combines all these qualities in a significant number of its members, relationships and structures. Yet even if there is a serious striving after such attitudes and lifestyle in a small core group in a parish, there is a strong testimony to the ongoing process of redemption. Moreover, the whole manner of the redemption is grace, gift, surprise, breakthrough in impossible situations. To be joined to the Church always means more than becoming part of the local congregation of believers. It means becoming a member of the great tradition that reaches into our times from Jesus and his earliest followers. It means becoming heir to all that the great tradition has to offer, and a member of the universal community of the followers of Jesus spanning centuries, continents and disparate cultures.

ACTIONS OF CHRIST

Because initiation, while rooted in the present local community, also transcends the local community and its limitations and faults, we can heartily endorse within the perceptions and understandings of our own time the principle of St. Augustine concerning the efficacy of the sacraments. It is not the minister of the sacrament who gives it its value and efficacy for entrance into salvation. It is not even the local community of the present. It is Christ, in the whole mystery of redemption as it is worked out and lived in the Church universal throughout history, who gives the sacraments their efficacy. Therefore, our history bristles with saints who arose in times of corruption and indifference, kindled by the gospel that was being lived so inadequately around them, and in turn rekindling others. Yet the doctrine of the efficacy of the sacraments as actions of Christ must be balanced by an honest and realistic acknowledgement of how it is that Christ acts in sacraments, not by magic rituals but by constant transforming relationships with and among persons expressing themselves in lifestyle and in structures of society.

Perhaps, however, the most urgent question of all in our times concerning the meaning and efficacy of the sacraments of initiation has to do with exclusivity of claims. The question concerns the lack of discernible difference between Christians and others, or specifically between Catholics and others. As between Catholics and other Christians, of course, it could not be anything but cause to rejoice that we should discern deep faith and hope and pervasive effective charity among the followers of Jesus who are grouped in other church configurations than our own. On this also, Augustine's wisdom has become a permanent part of our heritage; the baptized are baptized into Christ no matter how schisms cut across the communities. Every valid baptism is an entry into the Christian sphere of salvation, into the history of salvation.

As between Christians and others, also, there seems to be no reason for anything but rejoicing whenever any community lives in peace and joy and harmony, whenever any community contributes to social justice and reconciliation in the world. There seems to be no good reason for any desire on our part to limit the grace of God to the channels explicitly offered by the Church.

Our concern, as Vatican II reminds us (*Lumen gentium*, #1), should be to be that kind of sacrament or sign of intimate union with God and of the unity of the whole human race, which makes the realization of union and unity more readily possible for everyone. Our concern is not with numbers, nor even with desperately holding onto those baptized into the Church as infants, as though they could not otherwise be saved. Rather, our concern is fidelity to our own calling and an invitation to others to join us in full freedom. Our calling (*Lumen gentium*, #9) as Church is to be a seed of unity and hope and salvation for the whole human race. Initiation into the Church is an entrance into the gift and task of salvation which we hope will be shared with the whole human community.

Elizabeth A. Johnson, C.S.J.

The Marian Tradition and the Reality of Women

I. INTRODUCTION

The Catholic marian tradition in its complex relationship to theory and practice regarding women in the church and in societies influenced by the church has come under increasing scrutiny in recent theological reflection. This issue concerning both Mary and women has arisen at a time when the post-Tridentine symbolization and synthesis of thought about Mary, called "Mariology," has for all practical purposes shattered under the impact of the Second Vatican Council's decisions regarding the place and emphases of marian teaching.[1] Accordingly, thought about Mary is now being reassembled in the light of biblical, patristic, and liturgical renewals, ecumenical discussions, and developments taking place in systematic theology, most pertinently in the areas of the theology of God, christology, pneumatology, theology of grace, ecclesiology, and eschatology. A theology of Mary for the present and future church is slowly taking shape in line with advances made in these other areas of post-conciliar development. But concomitant with these theological shifts, there is a sea change occurring in our society in the self-perception and self-definition of women, and consequently in the understanding of women's nature, capabilities, role, status, and relationship to men and male-created structures. These changes on the anthropological, psychological, economic, and social-political levels are affecting the way the marian tradition is being perceived and evaluated, at least by those who are aware of this portentous turning of the tide. It is from this point of view that the marian tradition is reflected upon here. It goes without saying that men are as affected by this issue as are women, for the two sexes as a whole make up the human race, and redefinition of the nature and role of one draws into its purview by implication the reenvisionment of the shape of the other.[2]

An example will serve to indicate the depth of the change in perception which accompanies the new awareness of women's reality. To the question "What is Mariology?," the noted Mariologist Juniper Carol answered in the 1950's:

> By its very definition, Mariology is the study of Mary. More precisely, it is that part of the science of theology which treats of the Mother of God in her singular mission, prerogatives and cult.[3]

His book's development of each of these stated aspects makes clear that Mary's singular mission includes its preparation through Old Testament prophecies, its fulfillment in divine maternity, and its consequences in her universal mediation and universal queenship. Her prerogatives include the Immaculate Conception, perpetual virginity, and Assumption; the legitimacy of her cult is an obvious corollary. To the same question, "What is Mariology?," Rosemary Radford Reuther responded twenty years later that Mariology has been a creation by male human beings which

> sanctifies the image of the female as the principle of passive receptivity to the transcendent activity of male gods and their agents, the clergy. . . . (It) is the exaltation of the

principle of submission and receptivity, purified of any relation to sexual femaleness. . . . Mariology exalts the virginal, obedient, spiritual feminine and fears all real women
in the flesh.[4]

Her development of this theme argues that Mariology comes
into being and grows as an exercise of male projection of idealized femininity. As such it is dissociated from the reality of
women and functions as a tool of repression, an instrument of
male power over women. Only if reflection on Mary is freed
from its androcentric presuppositions can Mary emerge as a
true sign of redemption, a sign of God's liberating favor toward
those who are broken and have nothing.

The change in perspective is startling. Rosemary Radford
Ruether is, of course, a feminist theologian and her writing as
a whole embodies the feminist perspective. A brief word about
that theological stance is in order before exploring its critique
of the traditional marian symbol.

II. THE FEMINIST PERSPECTIVE

The feminist theological perspective is an orientation to
theology as a whole which has as its critical principle the promotion of the full humanity of women, up to now marginalized
in theory as well as fact.[5] According to this critical principle,
whatever promotes the full humanity of women is judged to
reflect a true and right relation to the divine; whatever distorts
or diminishes the full humanity of women is appraised as non-
redemptive and non-reflective of the Holy. The uniqueness of
feminist theology is not the critical principle of full humanity,
for this operated as a principle in classical Christian theology.
What is new is that rather than allow men alone to consider
themselves as norms of authentic humanity, women claim this

principle also for themselves: women name themselves as subjects of authentic and full humanity.

The working out of feminist theology utilizes a complex
of sources: the human experience of women as a primary
source, and dialogue with usable tradition from Scripture,
classical Christian theology, alternative though suppressed
Christian movements, ancient non-Christian religions, and
critical post-Christian philosophies. In this effort several theological themes come to the fore as particularly valuable. These
include the priestly writer's vision of creation in which both
male and female are created in the divine image; the prophetic
insistence on the holiness of justice for the poor and oppressed;
the teaching of Jesus of Nazareth about the approaching reign
of God as well as Jesus' characteristic behavior which, in the
power of that reign, was inclusive of the marginalized even to
the point (dramatic in a patriarchal society) of choosing women
as disciples; early Christian praxis which baptized women and
men alike, breaking out in song which proclaimed that in the
light of the new creation there is "neither Jew nor Greek, slave
nor free, male nor female, for all are one in Christ Jesus" (Gal
3:38); and the eschatological vision of redeemed humanity before God, a humanity redeemed in *all* its dimensions.

These and other elements of usable tradition are faced
with the now conscious experience of the dehumanizing subordination of women, in theory and practice, throughout the
Christian tradition.[6] This situation, judged to be sinful injustice, prevents the fullness of creation/redemption from being
victoriously fulfilled in individual persons and in the human
community. Those who theologize from a feminist perspective
seek first of all to unmask the massive distortion of those aspects of the Christian tradition which have systematically sub-
ordinated women on the basis of their gender; to name such
discrimination as the sin of sexism blocking the reign of God,
which it is; to critique the supposed divine sanctions which are

adduced in support of it; and ultimately to move the church toward change, away from patterns of domination/subordination toward the ideal of freedom and the possibility of self-actualization for all persons. This involves equivalence in the valuation of women and men as persons, genuine mutuality in their relationships, and the correlative reshaping of institutional structures. From the feminist perspective it is not enough just to interpret the tradition in the light of today's questions. Rather, it is necessary to engage in radical critique of the tradition insofar as it has abetted a situation of oppression. The critical interpretation which then results intends to serve the full emancipation of women as persons in their own right and, not incidentally, the emancipation of men, also freed from being cast into preset, gender-determined roles.

Thought from the feminist perspective, then, is both critical and hopeful. It is critical, protesting in the power of the Spirit the radical distortion of the Christian tradition regarding women. It is also hopeful, drawn by the power of the same Spirit to believe in the eschatological promise, that what exists in the present is not all there is, that God's deepest hope for humanity is the liberation of all people and indeed of the whole universe. The Christian feminist perspective fundamentally demands conversion, and leads to a transformation of values in every dimension.

When this perspective is brought to bear on the Christian tradition about Mary, a distinctly different judgment is made about the blessing that Mariology, with its glorification of a single woman, has been for women as a whole. Prevailing wisdom would have it that "the dignity of woman was raised in her,"[7] that is, the dignity of Our Lady in being the Mother of God is for Christians the measure of women's dignity which is modeled on hers. While there is some truth to this insight, it is not without ambiguity and in effect states only half the story, omitting consideration of the ways in which the marian tradition has functioned to block the self-realization of women as persons. A sampling of judgments by women religious writers makes this clear:

Patricia Noone: It is a question whether Mary is really there for women or is not rather a Trojan horse raised to ambush women's aspirations for personhood, human dignity, and coresponsibility for the church and society.[8]

Kari Børresen: The figure of Mary is a patriarchal construct: virgin, wife, mother, and adjunct to the male. She embodies the essential connection between femininity and subordination forged by the patriarchal mind-set. To make her the model for free women is absurd, until that connection is broken.[9]

Mary Daly: Women are enslaved symbolically in the cult of the Virgin Mary, who is glorified only insofar as she accepts the subordinate role assigned to her.[10]

Elisabeth Schüssler Fiorenza: Mary has almost never functioned as a symbol of women's equality and capacity to lead; adherence to her can deter women from becoming whole persons.[11]

Mary Gordon: It is necessary to reject the traditional image of Mary in order to hold onto any hope for one's own intellectual achievement, independence, and sexual fulfillment.[12]

Marina Warner: Mariology is a weapon in the armory of male chauvinism and an effective instrument of female subjugation. Clothed in theology legitimation, it is the instrument of a dynamic argument from the Catholic Church about the male-dominated structure of society and of the church, presented as a God-given order.[13]

The list could go on and on. Notice that the charge is not that of irrelevance, heard from other quarters about the marian tradition. It is rather that of complicity in the oppression of women. Mariology has legitimated women's subordination, has presided over the evil rather than challenging it.

Ten years ago, in his apostolic exhortation *Marialis Cultus*, Pope Paul VI took note of what he termed this "alienation" of women from the marian tradition, suggesting that traditional, culturally conditioned images of Mary were at the root of the problem. His solution was to replace timid, submissive images of Mary with the picture of one who gave active and responsible consent, one who proclaimed God's vindication of the humble and oppressed.[14] Similarly, the bishops of the United States in their pastoral letter *Behold Your Mother: Woman of Faith* proposed that Mary be envisioned as intelligent, apostolic, inquiring, creative, courageous, a woman of faith, indeed, the "model of all real feminine freedom."[15] While these are worthy suggestions which have the possibility of making a contribution, they have not led women to flock back in large numbers to the honoring of Mary. Women have developed what Patricia Noone describes as the "painful habit" of laying church documents and rhetoric about Mary side by side with the actual condition of women in the church, a habit which gives rise to clear perception of contradictions.[16] Thus, the critique from the feminist perspective has grown stronger rather than weaker. It is simply not enough to replace one set of virtues with another more suited to our present value system and to propose this new Mary as worthy of emulation. The basic structures which give rise simultaneously to the glorification of Mary and the subordination of women, the root attitudes which generate this pattern, need to be exposed and corrected. There is too much deep prejudice involved in the marian tradition for the simple strategy of a redescription of Mary's virtues to resolve.

And thus the two questions which focus this consideration of the subject: first, in what ways has the marian tradition
functioned to the detriment of women, aiding and abetting a
system which has kept women in an inferior position because
of their gender? Second, in what ways might this tradition be
critically reinterpreted in such a way that it would serve the
goal of liberation and true mutuality between women and
men? Three distinct but interrelated considerations are proposed under each question.

III. DETRIMENTAL ASPECTS

*Critique I: The marian tradition has been intrinsically asso-
ciated with the denigration of the nature of women
as a group.*

An overview of the history of early Christian thought
about Mary and about the nature of women gives evidence of
this paradox: that the exaltation of the one woman, Mary, grew
in direct proportion to disparaging theory and vituperative
rhetoric regarding the rest of womankind. The growing honor
paid to Mary in theology and cult redounded to her benefit to
the exclusion of other women, and this because of one fundamental assumption: that Mary was not a type (*typos*), exempli-
fying the capacity of redeemed humanity including women,
but the great exception. Her glorious precedence prevented
any analogy between herself and other women, all of whom fell
short by comparison.

This is particularly evident in the Mary-Eve symbolism
introduced by Justin in the second century and developed by
Irenaeus and others with great embellishment. Just as the
woman Eve was the disobedient one responsible for the fall of
humankind and all of its attendant misery, so the woman

Mary, the new Eve, was the one who through her obedience brought forth the conqueror of death, the Savior. "Death through Eve, life through Mary" became the axiom, with the accent on the contrast between the two. Occasionally in the poetry and hymns of the East the opposition is mitigated and the two women are placed in positive relationship. A hymn of Ephrem envisions Mary rejoicing in the redemption that has come to the first mother, who can now experience peace because her daughter has paid her debt; a Syrian poem pictures Mary as a child comforting Eve, stretching out her hand to the downcast ancestress and raising her up. But more usually a sharp opposition is built between the two. Mary is the obedient and faithful woman, Eve the temptress and sinner. Since no other woman is as obedient or pure or holy as Mary, no other woman can resemble her. Rather, all other women have more in common with Eve and share her sinful character. Typical of this pattern of thought, Tertullian addresses women and alleges,

> Do you not realize that you are each an Eve? The curse of God on this sex of yours lives on even in our times. Guilty, you must bear its hardships. You are the devil's gateway; you desecrated the fatal tree; you first betrayed the law of God; you softened up with your cajoling words the one against whom the devil could not prevail by force. All too easily you destroyed the image of God, Adam. You are the one who deserved death, and it was the Son of God who had to die.[17]

Woman is the cause of the fall, the accomplice of Satan, the destroyer of humankind. Indeed, the fury unleashed against Eve and other women is almost flattering, so exaggerated is the picture of woman's fatal and all-powerful charms and man's incapacity to resist.[18]

Chrysostom, Jerome, Augustine, and others operated within the same fundamental dynamic, projecting responsibility for the sinful condition of humankind onto Eve and all other women who are in solidarity with her, instead of perceiving clearly the solidarity of the whole human race, both men and women, in sin and grace. Mary *alone of all her sex* is exempt from this condition, being the door through which the Savior arrived. Her uniqueness sets her apart from all other women. Thus, not necessarily but by a certain logic, denigration of women became the shadow side of the glorification of Mary in the early centuries of the church.

Adding to the complexity of this development was the fact that the prevalent intellectual tradition of these early Christian centuries gave credence to the kind of dualism which posited undying tension between the spirit and the flesh, prizing spiritual detachment from the world as of the highest value. In the battle which the aspiring male waged between the spirit and the flesh, women were placed on the side of the flesh due to their obvious appeal to sexual males as well as their connection with pregnancy and childbirth. Correlatively, in the light of the growing ascetic ideal of virginity also related at this time to an anti-flesh bias, the evils of sex were particularly identified with the female. The resulting powerful aversion of Christian male thinkers to female sexuality gave added impetus to the honoring of Mary for her uniqueness in having conceived virginally, that is, for the non-use of her sexuality vis-à-vis a man, and to the corresponding belittling of women who exercised their sexuality.[19]

Throughout most of the history of the Christian tradition this early pattern is repeated. Mary is the great exception rather than the type. The influential writings of Thomas Aquinas provide an interesting illustration of the logical gaps embraced under the rule of that assumption. To counterpose his texts which describe women as defective and misbegotten males, inferior not just because of the state of sin into which human beings have fallen but originally and by nature, with his texts on Mary which describe her as exalted above all creatures, even above the angels, is to expose a real inconsistency in his thought which he at least never resolved.[20]

Those who approach this issue from a contemporary psychological point of view have noted that the marian tradition, having been created primarily by male minds and hearts, bears an overload of male projection. Men have divided women's reality into good and evil elements, projecting the good onto Mary in an idealized fashion and the evil onto the rest of women who are then to be kept subject due to their low estate. The ideal of the good feminine which is projected onto Mary reflects the desire for a woman who is untroubling to the celibate male psyche, with a-sexuality and passive obedience being the most notable elements which characterize her image. The "Madonna-whore syndrome," of which this issue is a classic example, enables men to love and respect their ideal of woman in Mary but to ignore or dominate concrete real women with impunity and with immunity even from the searchings of their own conscience.

To claim, as official rhetoric does, that the dignity of woman is raised in Mary is at best a half truth. In its root dynamic, the marian tradition has persisted in idealizing the one to the detriment of the many. Instead of seeing Mary as a type, a symbol of the capacity of women, it has exalted Mary as the great exception in comparison to whom all other women are denigrated. Further evidence for this judgment is provided by sociological observation. In those countries where the cult of Mary still flourishes strongly, women have not emerged in a significant way toward involvement in public and political life. The same is true of those churches which have the strongest official attachment to Mary: they are the least likely to be open to full participation of women in ecclesial public life and ministries.

Critique II: The marian tradition has dichotomized the being and roles of women and men in the community of disciples following Christ.

As with the first criticism, the subject of this second also results from a fundamental and false assumption, namely, that the relationship between Jesus Christ and Mary in theological interpretation should serve as the model for the relationship between concrete historical men and women in the sociological and interpersonal spheres. On the basis of such an assumption, despite heroic efforts to the contrary, it is inevitable that women are relegated to a hopelessly inferior position. God takes initiative and Mary responds. Her son is the Messiah of God, and she is caught up in the mystery of salvation centered in him. This is, of course, theologically sound. But then, God is envisioned as male: *he* took the initiative and *she* responded. Jesus' undoubted maleness is brought to the fore and interpreted in naive fashion: he is Messiah and *she* is oriented to *him*. The pattern is translated into normative social mores which shape relationships and structures on the premise that men are active, women passive; men take initiative, women respond; men are slated for the public sphere, women for the private, men exercise power, women are supportive of them.

Within this pattern the question of how men and women are related to each other is usually answered by the concept of complementarity. According to this concept each of the sexes is identified with a distinct role supposedly supplementary to one another, but roles which in actuality give the lion's share of influence to the male and reserve for women the stance of passive receptivity to and support of the primary male role. For example, the argument has been mounted that since Christ "operated" while Mary, totally dependent upon him, "cooperated," in her cooperation is revealed the intention of the divine plan concerning the whole of femininity (rather than the whole of humanity). From this divinely revealed pattern, a conclusion is drawn regarding the proper roles of women and men in the church, namely, that man preaches the word and woman receives it; her role is her listening silence by which she renders service to the man who speaks.[21] Beyond the debatability of the role definitions, the point to note is that the argument is being mounted from the marian symbol in relation to Christ, applied sociologically in direct fashion. It is a form of argumentation frequently heard. Another more recent example: man is the icon of Christ, woman the icon of the church which images Mary. As Christ is the head of the church which in turn is loved by him while he remains head (Eph 5), so the fatherhood exercised by the priest is not abrogated but complemented by the spiritual motherhood of women in the church. Likewise, the husband as head of the domestic church is complemented by the mothering role of the wife. The conclusion is drawn that "as Mary fulfills her complementary role we can see how the beautiful complementarity of man and woman, Christ and the Church, enriches the human race and the new people of God."[22]

Suffice it to say that from a feminist perspective, complementarity conceived of in this way is far from beautiful. It is a mask for an ideology which places woman in a stereotyped role on account of her gender, a role where she is praised for living at less than full capacity. (We might also note that it does the same for men with the difference that the preordained role of the male is that of the superior.) The marian tradition has been used to legitimate this conception of the relationship between the sexes, for Mary the woman is exalted precisely for accepting the secondary role assigned to her in view of the priority of

Christ the man. A true theological affirmation has become a destructive and oppressive symbol by being applied in naive analogical fashion to personal and sociological relationships. As Simone de Beauvoir critiqued the effect of the Christmas crib scene:

> For the first time in human history the mother kneels before her son; she freely accepts her inferiority. This is the supreme masculine victory, consummated in the cult of the Virgin—it is the rehabilitation of woman through the accomplishment of her defeat.[23]

The marian tradition has provided justification for a dichotomization of the being and roles of the sexes, casting woman in an auxiliary, receptive mold complementary to the dominative male.

Critique III: The marian tradition has truncated the ideal of feminine fulfillment and wholeness.

This effect of the tradition has resulted from several coalescing assumptions: that Mary is the model for the behavior of women; that the particularities of her life should therefore be directly imitated by women; and that these particularities are accessible to our knowledge through a literal reading of the scriptures. Although even with regard to Jesus the concept of "following" is replacing that of "imitation," since the historically-conditioned character of his life makes a literal imitation impossible in later ages, the tenacity of the imitative idea persists with regard to Mary. As Cahal Daly expressed it with unintended irony:

> Some of the resentments occasionally expressed by women about motherhood and child-bearing would hardly

be expected to come from people who had reflected seriously upon the privilege and grace of Christian motherhood as this is revealed preeminently in Mary. Some of the more strident formulae of some exponents of "women's liberation" are very far removed from the understanding of women's vocation which is given to us in the example of the Mother of Jesus Christ.[24]

Precisely! It is particularly the aspects of the image of Mary which portray her as handmaid, virgin, and mother which have defined the shape of the feminine ideal for centuries of believing women, curtailing the exploration of the full range of possibilities of human wholeness.

Handmaid. Luke's narrative of the Annunciation (1:26–38) presents a powerful image of a human *fiat* to the invitation of the transcendent mystery operating within history. But Mary's *fiat*, far from being seen as the radical autonomous decision of a young woman to risk her life on a messianic venture, and more fundamentally as a free human act of faith in God, has (especially in the Counter-Reformation centuries) been interpreted as an act of submissiveness to the will of God, who is imaged furthermore as male. In preaching and spiritual writing, Mary has stood forth as a model of dependence upon this male God's initiative, a model of humility understood as a lack of possession of a personal ego, a model of obedience understood as acquiescence: "I'll do whatever you say." The overwhelming passivity connected with the marian image has rendered Mary "a psychological model of a perpetual minor,"[25] hidden and enclosed, timid and sweet, taking direction from others with no inner purpose of her own. Since she is held up as the feminine ideal, women learn that they find their true vocation in being submissive, self-sacrificing, silent, deferential.

Even when women as members of the laity are actively engaged in church ministries, the image of Mary still haunts them with the passive ideal. One theologian in the 1950's described the virtues which the blessed Virgin models for the apostolate of the laity, including in his list

> her silence, her subordination to the legally prescribed religious life of her people, her self-effacement in the public life of her Son, . . . her unpretentious membership of the community at Pentecost, when she is in herself the central point yet in no way detracts from the official rights of Peter and the Twelve. . . .

It was Karl Rahner who wrote that,[26] demonstrating the powerful pervasiveness of the passive ideal, accepted without examination by him at a time when he was critically revising other foundational concepts (although to his credit he has since written about Mary and the image of woman admitting that an ambiguity now exists on the question).[27] The marian tradition with its emphasis on Mary the handmaid has legitimated the image of woman as a vessel of passive receptivity, a receptivity moreover to the primary activity of males, be they divine or human, God, fathers, husbands, or priests. Note how the problem is compounded by the thoroughly masculine character of the deity.

Virgin. As already noted, emphasis on Mary's virginity grew in an environment which was innately suspicious of the body and of the exercise of sexuality. Mary has been idealized as the Virgin *par excellence* from whom any trace of human sexuality has been exorcised, while the value of feminine sexuality has been correlatively undermined. The usual perception is well phrased by Cahal Daly, who asserted that "Mary's virginity is the highest peak of the history of the female sex."[28] The highest peak of the history of female sexuality is its non-use. In an age when women are discovering their own sexuality and becoming comfortable with the gift which it indeed is, such an ideal embodied in Mary is emphatically rejected. The ideal is furthermore critiqued for having divided the women in the Roman Catholic Church, because it carries the implication that women who live a life of virginity are closer to the ideal than those who actively exercise their sexuality. It is a regrettable deficiency that nowhere in the Christian tradition is there a highly honored symbol of the exercise of female sexuality—nor of male sexuality, for that matter. The need for a Christian theology of sexuality and a theology of marriage to counteract the influences of our ever more secular culture is not filled by the tradition of Mary's a-sexuality. Rather, the image of her virginity has functioned to impede the integration of women's sexuality into the goal of wholeness.

Mother. Historically Mary was indeed the mother of Jesus and, no doubt, can be assumed to have had influence on the kind of man he became. However, concentration on Mary's motherhood in the tradition has served to reinforce the perception that motherhood is the *raison d'etre* of a woman's life, the one divinely approved accomplishment, rather than the gospel proclamation that Mary's blessedness consists in hearing the Word of God and keeping it. It has thereby legitimated domesticity as the primary vocation for women.

In the history of the marian tradition, emphasis on Mary's motherhood gave rise rather early to the practice of intercession (the *Sub tuum praesidium* can be dated to the late third or early fourth century). Implicitly prerequisite for the practice as it developed was the projection of the patriarchal model of the human family into the heavenly sphere. One of the key roles of the mother in the patriarchal family is intercession or merciful influence with the male head. Such a role is now attributed to Mary, a move which also created the possibility for the later medieval aberrations which envisioned Mary as the zone of mercy over against Christ or God the Father, angry and just judges needing to be placated.[29] More to the point here, the mother's role vis-à-vis the children is presumed to be total dedication and service. In a linguistic study of 216 marian hymns done at the Institute Catholique in Paris, one researcher discovered that the word "mother" was used 85% of the time, usually linked with the imperative mode of the verb.[30] The supplicant requests, pleads, gives orders for the fulfillment of needs to which Mary the Mother is supposed to respond. What image of woman is assumed here? One always at the beck and call of her children? Perpetually available? Is she ever thought of as an independent individual, someone with a right to a room of her own, in Virginia Woolf's memorable phrase? The thought is never entertained. The connotation is rather that the natural order of things for a woman is motherhood, expressed in total devotion to the needs of the children. The other side of that relationship, as Laurentin has pointed out, is that too frequently the devotees are kept in a state of perpetual childhood, narcissistically looking to the mother for the satisfaction of needs, a state which is the antithesis of adult responsibility for the world.[31]

To sum up: being responsive to the inspiration of the Spirit, being virginal, and caring for the needs of one's children are not bad things—in fact they are quite excellent values in themselves. But when in the tradition about Mary they are set within an androcentric framework, so that the ideal of woman becomes the passively obedient handmaiden, the a-sexual virgin, and the domestically all-absorbed mother, then the tradition implicitly and explicitly supports the truncation of woman's fulfillment and is vigorously contested in the interest of greater wholeness.

IV. REINTERPRETATIONS

Is there any hope? Is there any possibility of retrieval of the marian tradition such that it would serve rather than hinder the cause of liberation/salvation for the whole of the human race? A number of feminist theologians are negative on this point, judging the interconnectedness of the cult of Mary and the oppression of women so intricate that the effort to save something from it is scarcely worthwhile. On the other hand, it can be argued that it is important to set Mary free from the image that has been made of her and from projections attached to her by male theologians and priestly hierarchy. Out of a deep sense of solidarity or sisterhood some feminist theologians do not want simply to let go of Mary.[32]

In addition, as critical analysis of the marian tradition brings to light the mechanisms used to make Mary an impossible model detrimental to women, in no way critical of men, and legitimating of the gap which persists between (female) sexuality and the mediation of holiness, the effort toward resymbolization can aid in the creation of new patterns of thought and relationship within those communities where that tradition is strong. Again, the marian tradition did keep alive the memory of a woman closely associated with the saving action of God on our behalf, a memory which some theologians in the churches of the Reformation have recently been seeking to rediscover for their own tradition.[33] An area coming under increasing scrutiny is that of God in the image of a female as well as a male person; reinterpretation can bring to light the many ways in which the marian symbol has usurped functions of the divine, thus clearing the way for renaming God with female imagery such as Mother.[34]

Finally, for all of its debilities, the marian tradition has borne to the present one of the few female-focused symbols which has persisted in the Christian community. Since we are inheritors of the long marian tradition, it is arguably a vitally important task to probe this tradition from the scriptures onward, seeking a resymbolization of Mary which could serve the liberating intent of the gospel. There is as yet no coherent renewed theology of Mary as a whole, but I would like to identify three new directions which hold some promise, each one roughly counterpoint to the above critiques.

Proposal I

This approach is imaginatively historical in tone, identifying Mary as a real person in human history, a woman who has more in common with the rest of women than she has separating prerogatives. Biblical criticism has led to the realization of how very little is known of the historical Mary, most of the Scripture scenes in which she figures being theological interpretations of the gospel message in narrative form rather than historically accurate reportage.[35] This leaves the woman of Nazareth in historical shadows, but paradoxically makes her more accessible as a human person in her own right, the Mary behind the symbolism, so to speak. She did not live a glorified life but can be identified within the context of the Judaism of the first century as a woman of the people, poor, faithful, expectant; a woman with her own life history, her own very real struggles, and her own journey of faith, about which we know very little. The very paucity of the historical record regarding her is a point of identification with all women, whose history has been largely hidden and unremarked.

The new imagery developing from this approach, while not necessarily historically based, is pervaded with a realism which puts Mary within imaginable reach; for example, she is now addressed in feminist litanies as unwed mother, refugee woman with child, widow, traveling woman, mother of a son executed as a common criminal, a woman of pain, passion, and purpose. Some suggest that in solidarity with Mary as a woman of our history believers now invoke her as our "sister" in faith who reveals to women their own real resources.[36] This line of approach is revaluing the marian symbol not because of Mary's glorious difference from all the rest but because as a real woman with much to contend with she gave herself to her life and to her God, in her own time and place and way. We are associated with her by the bond of human history and still more in the communion of saints. She is one of the cloud of witnesses (Heb 11–12) whose story encourages our own faith. As the fourth Eucharistic prayer of the renewed Catholic liturgy so well expresses it, we praise God in her company—in the company of Mary and all the saints.

Proposal II

A second promising approach, more theological in its orientation, sees Mary as a type of the church and, more specifically within that broad concept, as a disciple who hears the Word of God and keeps it (Lk 11:27–28). She is thereby a type of the community of believing disciples which is the church. The early Christian understanding that Mary is a type of the Church was reincorporated into current discussion mainly as a result of Vatican II's statement on Mary and has been the source of fruitful reflection ever since. It holds Mary forth as the symbol of the community of redeemed humanity, gifted with the healing grace of God, responding wholeheartedly, and called to the mission of spreading the gospel in the world. The advance made here over much of the tradition is that as type, Mary represents not just believing women but the *whole* church saved from the enchainment of sin. In her precisely as woman is symbolized the fact that all those needy and oppressed by sin have received the self-communicating grace of the transcendent mystery which we call God, source of both

maleness and femaleness; all are therefore called in the Spirit
to the mission of working for the coming of the reign of God;
all are therefore capable of presencing Christ in the world and
have a responsibility to do so.[37] As type of the church which
receives the grace of Jesus Christ and which is the sacrament
of Christ in the world, the symbol of Mary calls into question
by implication the Mary/Christ-based dichotomization of the
nature and roles of women and men in the redeemed community.

One specific interpretation of the exemplarity of Mary for
the Church designates her as a disciple, in fact as a first and
preeminent disciple in the community of disciples which is the
church. Biblically based, this approach understands that Mary
is not to be imitated in terms of the socio-cultural conditions
of her historical life, which are scarcely able to be reproduced
today, but

> for the way in which in her own particular life she fully
> and responsibly accepted God's will; because she heard the
> Word of God and acted on it; and because charity and a
> spirit of service were the driving force of her action. She
> is worthy of imitation because she was the first and most
> perfect of Christ's disciples.[38]

As both biblical scholars and theologians have been show-
ing, there is a great deal of promise here.[39] But a caution needs
to be sounded in the light of our history. Hearing the Word of
God and keeping it, which are the primary characteristics of
Mary as a disciple, cannot be interpreted as a mandate to passive obedience on the part of women. It must be made explicit
that the Word of God which one hears may well be a call to
critical prophecy, and that the Word of God which one keeps
may well impel the hearer toward conflict with the powers
which oppress people not only outside the church but also

within it. Furthermore, discipleship may well involve the mandate for action in the public sphere, and here again the symbol of Mary cannot be naively applied.

Historically there is no evidence that the mother of Jesus was ever actively engaged in ministry, that she ever preached or taught or evangelized or healed or administered or led a community. Many feminist theologians have discovered in other women of the New Testament, particularly in Mary of Magdala, much more potent models of female discipleship. It is at least historically ascertainable that this Mary followed Jesus during his public ministry, witnessed his death and burial, and was a commissioned witness of his resurrection, which commission she carried out.[40] The lack of Mary of Nazareth's public involvement has led some to make the distinction between Mary as the model of the believing disciple and Peter as the model of the apostolic disciple, a distinction which again turns the marian symbol into a potential tool of patriarchal power. The symbol of Mary as a disciple needs to be interpreted in such a way that she is seen to embody the personal spirit of discipleship while no strict analogy is made between her own personal history and the lives of women today, called to be disciples in a world she never dreamed of.

Proposal III

A third promising approach is concerning itself with specific aspects of the image of Mary, both discovering a new symbolic aspect of Mary as the proclaimer of liberation and reinterpreting the meaning of the traditional qualities of virginity and motherhood.

In a genuinely new movement of interpretation, the Mary of the Magnificat (Lk 1:46–55) is coming into focus. Proclaiming words of praise and prophecy, she is a symbol of tremendous power as the singer of the song of justice in the new age of redemption. Liberation theologies of all types have claimed Mary under this aspect, recognizing that her proclamation of the greatness of God who puts down the mighty and exalts the humble, fills the hungry with good things but sends the rich away empty, fits well with the understanding of the importance of engagement for justice and peace. Feminist theologians find particular meaning in this symbol. It is noted that the Lukan community found such a proclamation a fitting expression for Mary, with its focus on the social and political rather than on the maternal and private.

With the Magnificat Mary appears as an active agent in salvation rather than the passive handmaiden, an image also countered by the idea of Mary as disciple. She is highly exalted because through her God is working a radically new reality into history, a transformation of the given order of things in which the victims will be justified. It is a revolution in which she finds great joy. And Mary does not just proclaim this. In her own person she herself embodies the humble and the hungry, the oppressed who are being liberated by God's action. Luke's sensitivity to women as members of the poor and despised classes adds this dimension to the image of Mary singing of justice: she herself represents the subjugated who will be lifted up and filled with good things in the messianic revolution. With this insight it becomes particularly appropriate to see in Mary a type of the church. She is the personification of those who, having nothing, are gifted by the action of God and charged to continue the liberating action of God in the world. It is precisely in her femaleness that she is this sign of the new redeemed humanity, the powerless who are empowered in the reign of God. Pray the Magnificat from a feminist perspective, and whole new meanings are declared.

In the Mediterranean world in which the image of Mary grew up, the cults of the great goddesses frequently portrayed them—Venus, Ishtar, Isis, Astarte—as virgins despite their lovers. Virginity symbolized their autonomy, their ability to refuse men or accept them because as female deities they were powerful, independent, self-directed. They were honored as virgins because they retained freedom of choice, not being identified by their relationships with men. Virginity then did not necessarily connote bodily integrity or sexual abstinence, but rather the notion of female independence. A virgin was "one-in-herself," autonomous. It is noted today that in the scriptures Mary is never portrayed as subject to Joseph or under control of any man, but in a unique way as free from parental and connubial control. Whatever the actual historicity of the infancy narratives, the image of Mary as a virgin has significance as the image of a woman from whose personal center power wells up, a woman who symbolizes the independence of the identity of woman.

Mary's motherhood is also being revalued. It is a genuine gift to be so creative, to be so fruitful as to be able to bring a new person into the world. The feminist vision rejects making the role of motherhood the exclusive or even necessarily primal role of a woman's life in a sort of biological determinism. But the actual free bearing of children is a thing to be prized, and Mary's freely chosen motherhood is seen as another aspect of her creative womanly being which creates solidarity with other women.

The combination of both of these attributions, virgin and mother, far from being seen as an impossible ideal for other women to emulate, may be understood to embody at least one aspect of a holistic goal for contemporary women. With the joining of the two, the emphasis is placed neither on bodily generativity alone nor on the value of the purely independent woman, but affirmation is given to the woman who combines both, home and career, if you will, or interrelationship and autonomy: mother and virgin.[41]

V. CONCLUSION

The marian tradition has consistently been integrated into the patriarchal framework of Christianity, and has served to legitimate it. Under the guise of a theologically correct understanding of the "feminine," the tradition about Mary has frequently functioned to undermine the real female self and to obstruct both the liberation of women and genuine mutuality between women and men in the church. Women as well as men have had complicity in this. Symbols can be said to participate in the reality which they signify, and thus they are born—and die—according to their ability to bear the power of a reality to people in different situations.[42] Recognition of the complicity of the traditional marian symbol in the assignment of inferiority to women throughout Christian history has resulted at the present time in its fracture or death among those who have entered into the feminist perspective. That symbol is unable to bear the power of a liberating vision of redemption in the lives of women and men.

Is then a resymbolization possible, so that the image of Mary can empower rather than impede the journey of women and indeed of the whole church toward greater wholeness? I dare to think and hope that it is possible, but caution strongly against letting that hope too quickly lead to a state of complacency. One can indeed imagine a renewed tradition about Mary which would include a non-stereotypical understanding of the nature of woman, one which recognizes the values of autonomy, integrity of conscience, courage, correct use of power, the goodness of female sexuality, self-assertion, and the relations of motherhood and sisterhood. One can also imagine such a renewed tradition playing a role as an integral part of a wider renewal which would result in a church that prized mutuality and reciprocity between women and men rather than one which rests content with the patriarchal pattern of domination and subordination. But this imagined renewed marian tradition is not yet reality. The experience of women in the churches is still that of systemic subordination.

If it be true that the image of Mary is tied to the image of woman in any given age,[43] then both images have a history. That history has entered a new phase as far as women are concerned. It seems a sure judgment to say that the future of the marian tradition is closely tied with the future history of women in the church, and that it will be regenerated or remain collapsed of its own weight depending in large measure on what happens in that history. A renewed marian tradition will be credible only in a church which recognizes and embodies in theory and practice the full dimensions of the dignity of women. It will be viable only in a church which as institution and community of persons learns to love and accept its women who have persisted in fidelity throughout the centuries of explicit and implicit subordination. Theological reflection reaches its limit at this point, and waits upon experience and orthopraxis within the church as the matrix from which a renewed, revitalized marian tradition can grow. Ultimately, what is at stake in this question is not only the redirection of the tradition about Mary, but the search for our common humanity: the essence of woman, of man, and of redeemed humanity, the church itself.

NOTES

[1]*Lumen Gentium*, ch. 8, in *The Documents of Vatican II*, ed. Walter Abbott (New York: America Press, 1966). See commentaries by Otto Semmelroth, *Commentary on the Documents of Vatican II*, ed. H. Vorgrimler (New York: Herder and Herder, 1967), 1:285–96; and René Laurentin, *Pastoral Reform in Church Government*, Concilium 8 (New York: Paulist, 1965), pp. 155–72.

[2]See the papers of the World Council of Churches' Conference in Sheffield, England, 1981, entitled *The Community of Women and Men in the Church*, ed. Constance Parvey (Philadelphia: Fortress, 1983).

[3]Juniper Carol, *Fundamentals of Mariology* (New York: Benziger, 1956), p. 1.

[4]Rosemary Radford Ruether, "Christology and Feminism: Can a Male Savior Help Women?," *Occasional Papers* (United Methodist Board of Higher Education and Ministry) 1/13 (1976), 5–6; and "Mariology as Symbolic Ecclesiology: Repression or Liberation?" in her *Sexism and God-Talk* (Boston: Beacon Press, 1983), pp. 139–58.

[5]For what follows, see Ruether, *Sexism and God-Talk*; this work's first chapter treats of methodology, sources, and norms (pp. 12–46). For other descriptions of the tasks and goals of feminist theology, see Elisabeth Schüssler Fiorenza, "Feminist Theology as a Critical Theory of Liberation," *Theological Studies* 36 (1975), 605–26; and Anne Carr, "Is a Christian Feminist Theology Possible?," *Theological Studies* 43 (1982), 279–97. A fine description of what is meant by "women's experience" is given by Judith Plaskow, *Sex, Sin, and Grace: Women's Experience and the Theologies of Reinhold Niebuhr and Paul Tillich* (Washington, DC: University Press of America, 1980), pp. 9–50.

[6]For example of distortion in theory, see Kari Elisabeth Børresen, *Subordination and Equivalence: The Nature and Role of Woman in Augustine and Thomas Aquinas* (Washington, DC: University Press of America, 1981); for analysis of practice, see Mary Daly, *The Church and the Second Sex* (New York: Harper & Row, 1975).

[7]Jozef Tomko, *L'Osservatore Romano* (English) 43 (October 26, 1981), 6.

[8]Patricia Noone, *Mary for Today* (Chicago: Thomas More, 1977), p. 12.

[9]Kari Børresen, "Mary in Catholic Theology," in *Mary in the Churches*, Concilium 168, ed. H. Küng and J. Moltmann (New York: Seabury, 1983), pp. 54–55.

[10]Daly, p. 61.

[11]Fiorenza, pp. 620–24.

[12]Mary Gordon, "Coming to Terms with Mary, *Commonweal* 109 (January 15, 1982), 11.

[13]Marina Warner, *Alone of All Her Sex* (New York: Knopf, 1976), pp. 49, 338.

[14]*Marialis Cultus*, E. T. *Devotion to the Blessed Virgin Mary, The Pope Speaks* 19 (1974–1975), #34–37, pp. 73–75.

[15]*Catholic Mind* 72 (1974), #142, p. 60.

[16]Noone, p. 12.

[17]*De cultu feminarum*, libri duo I, 1, (PL I, 1418b–19a).

[18]Warner, p. 58.

[19]See Rosemary Radford Ruether, "Misogynism and Virginal Feminism in the Fathers of the Church," in Ruether, ed., *Religion and Sexism: Images of Women in the Jewish and Christian Traditions* (New York: Simon and Schuster, 1974), pp. 150–83.

[20]*Summa Theologiae*, I, q. 92; passim; q. 96, art. 3, corp.; q. 99, art. 2; ST III, q. 27, passim; q. 30, passim; q. 37, art. 4, corp.; ST Suppl., q. 52, passim; q. 81, passim. See William Cole, "Thomas on Mary and Women: A Study in Contrasts," *University of Dayton Review* 12 (1975–76), 25–64.

[21]Jean Galot, *L'église et la femme* (Gemblour: J. Duculot, 1965), p. 57.

[22]Giles Dimock, "Mary, Model for the Church Today," *Aids in Ministry* (1982), 8.

[23]Simone de Beauvoir, *The Second Sex* (New York: Knopf, 1953), p. 171.

[24]Cahal Daly, "Mary and the Vocation of Women: I," *The Furrow* 25 (1974), 648.

[25]René Laurentin, "Mary and Womanhood in the Renewal of Christian Anthropology," *Marian Library Studies* 1 (1969), 78. While positing equality of nature between men and women, Laurentin nevertheless argues for a "functional hierarchy" between them (p. 89).

[26]Karl Rahner, "Mary and the Apostolate" in his *The Christian Commitment* (New York: Sheed and Ward, 1963 [1954]), p. 123.

[27]Karl Rahner, "Maria und das christliche Bild der Frau," *Stimmen der Zeit* 193 (1975), 795–800.

[28]Cahal Daly, "Mary and the Vocation of Women: II," *The Furrow*.

[29]See Hilda Graef, *Mary: A History of Doctrine and Devotion* (New York: Sheed and Ward, 1963), 1: esp. chaps 4–6.

[30]Bernadetter Gasslein, "Images de Marie, image de la femme," *Supplement* 127 (1978), 583–92.

[31]René Laurentin, *The Question of Mary* (New York: Holt, Rinehart and Winston, 1965), pp. 72ff.

[32]See Catharina Halkes, "Mary and Women" in Küng and Moltmann, eds., *Mary in the Churches*, pp. 66–67; Carol Frances Jagen, ed., *Mary According to Women* (Kansas City, MO: Leaven Press, 1985); Anne Carr, *Transforming Grace: Christian Tradition and Women's Experience* (San Francisco: Harper & Row, 1988), pp. 189–94.

[33]See, e.g., Ross MacKenzie, "Mariology as an Ecumenical Problem," *Marian Studies* 26 (1975), 204–20; and Lukas Visher, "Mary—Symbol of the Church and Symbol of Humankind," *Mid-Stream* 17 (1978), 1–12.

[34]See Ruether, *Sexism and God-Talk*, pp. 47–71; Joan Chamberlain Engelsman, *The Feminine Dimension of the Divine* (Philadelphia: Westminster, 1979); Elaine Pagels, "What Became of God the Mother?" in Carol Christ and Judith Plaskow, eds., *Womanspirit Rising* (San Francisco: Harper & Row, 1979), pp. 107–19; Geoffrey Ashe, *The Virgin* (London: Routledge and Kegan Paul, 1976).

[35]See Raymond Brown et al., eds. *Mary in the New Testament: A Collaborative Assessment by Protestant and Roman Catholic Scholars* (Philadelphia: Fortress, and New York: Paulist, 1978).

[36]Noone, p. 167. Noone's whole book does an effective job of resymbolization along the lines of this first proposal. See also Glenys Huws and Clare Guzzo Robert, "A New Image of Mary: Protestant, Catholic and Feminist Perspectives," *America* 141 (1979), 403–06.

[37]Rosemary Radford Ruether, *Mary—The Feminine Face of the Church* (Philadelphia: Westminster, 1977), pp. 76–88.

[38]Paul VI, *Marialis Cultus* #35, p. 74.

[39]See Raymond Brown, "The Meaning of Modern New Testament Studies for Ecumenical Understanding of Mary" in his *Biblical Reflections on Crises Facing the Church* (New York: Paulist, 1975),

pp. 84–108; Patrick Bearsley, "Mary the Perfect Disciple: A Paradigm for Mariology," *Theological Studies* 41 (1980), 461–504.

[40]See Elisabeth Moltmann-Wendel, "Motherhood or Friendship" in Küng and Moltmann, eds., *Mary in the Churches*, pp. 17–22; Ruether, *Sexism and God-Talk*, pp. 8–11; Schüssler Fiorenza, pp. 624–26. See also Elisabeth Schüssler Fiorenza's study of the discipleship of other women (not including Mary of Nazareth), *In Memory of Her: A Feminist Theological Reconstruction of Christian Origins* (New York: Crossroad, 1983).

[41]This is still a partial ideal for it omits reference to adult relationships which are constitutive for wholeness. For discussion, see Beatrice Bruteau, "The Image of the Virgin Mother" in J. Plaskow and J. Romero, eds., *Women and Religion* (Missoula, MT: Scholars Press, 1974), pp. 93–104.

[42]Paul Tillich, *Theology of Culture* (New York: Oxford University Press, 1964), pp. 54–58.

[43]Karl Rahner, "Maria und das christliche Bild der Frau," p. 800.

Philip S. Keane

Why Ethics and Imagination?

THE POSITIVE STATE OF MORAL THEOLOGY TODAY

Without doubt, many significant advances have been made in moral theology over the course of the past generation. To help set our context, we shall briefly consider these advances as they have occurred in three categories: Roman Catholic fundamental moral theology, Roman Catholic thinking on special questions in ethics, and ecumenical advances in ethics.

Catholic Advances in Fundamental Moral Theology

In Roman Catholicism, the Vatican II and post-Vatican II years have seen the development of a moral theology which is much more conversant with biblical themes than was the case in previous generations.[1] The use of biblical themes has resulted in a moral theology which is much more alive and vital than some former approaches were. Roman Catholic moral theology has also become a great deal more united with spiritual theology or asceticism. The old split between moral and spiritual theology separated many persons' moral decisions from prayerfulness and liturgical piety and sometimes led to an undue legalism. Today, the theme of discernment of spirits, once again prominent, helps many believers make their life

128

decisions in a highly prayerful and spiritual fashion.[2] A new sense of the true meaning of sin and of our need for ongoing and daily conversion has also enriched today's moral theology both in theory and in the practice of many believers. An awareness of the importance of the contemporary research into moral development has helped many Catholic authors and teachers work out more creative patterns for the education of our young people.[3]

Besides these advances in fundamental moral theology, the Vatican II and post-Vatican II era has seen the revitalization of some of our most important traditional moral themes such as natural law and the principle of the double effect.[4] A dialogue with contemporary philosophical systems such as transcendental Thomism, existential phenomenology, historical critical methodology, and hermeneutical methodology has been a key factor aiding development in areas such as natural law and double effect reasoning. The advances in natural law and double effect thinking have not been without controversy, and more refinement is still needed on these two issues. But nonetheless a great deal of progress has been made, especially in dealing with the excessive preoccupation with physical and biological realities which marked some (but not all) past natural law and double effect thinking.

Other advances in Roman Catholic fundamental moral theology could be added to those just cited, but the point is clear: notable advances have been made in recent moral theology. One of the clearest signs of the recent progress is that within the past five years several significant full-length treatises on fundamental moral theology have been published.[5] Up to these past few years, there had been very few major full-length fundamental moral treatises since Vatican II. The appearance of these full-length books suggests that enough significant gains have been made since Vatican II to make full-length efforts at consolidation worthwhile.

Catholic Advances on Particular Moral Issues

Forward moving steps in Catholic moral theology have not been limited to fundamental issues. To illustrate this point some comments can be made on sexual ethics, medical ethics, and social ethics. In sexual ethics, four important developments can be mentioned. First, there is a renewed sense of the goodness of human sexuality. Second, there is an understanding that sexuality is profoundly interrelated with the whole fabric of our humanity instead of being limited only to certain levels of our personality. The third development is a greatly increased pastoral sensitivity to persons dealing with difficult sexual dilemmas. Finally, and perhaps most notably, current approaches to sexual ethics include a much deeper understanding of women as truly co-equal sharers with men in a common humanity.[6] Of course there remain some controversies in Roman Catholicism on specific sexual questions, but these controversies, legitimate and honest though they be, should not obscure the great progress which has been made in Roman Catholic sexual ethics. A perusal of statements on homosexuality made by some American Catholic bishops over the course of the past decade ought to convince most anyone that moral theology has taken on a much different tone than it had a generation or two ago.[7]

In medical ethics, recent Roman Catholic thinking has continued the traditional leadership which Roman Catholicism has offered on issues such as death and dying and the right to life.[8] But new themes are beginning to appear in Roman Catholic writing and teaching about medical ethics. These new themes include the rights of patients, the question of how we should finance the costs of health care, and the establishment of adequate guidelines for medical research and experimentation.[9] Roman Catholic medical ethics has also become much more of a "hands on" reality than was the case in the past. A fair number of the Catholic religious communities involved in health care now employ full-time ethical consultants. Many individual Catholic hospitals now have human values committees and draw upon the services of nearby moral theologians or philosophical ethicists. Hopefully the result of all this is a deeper commitment to moral values on the part of Catholic health care systems. Hopefully, too, this kind of direct involvement has given moral theologians and ethicists a much more concrete sense of the many moral issues which exist in the health care field.

The renewal of Roman Catholic social ethics began with *Rerum Novarum* in 1891 and thus pre-dates the Vatican II period. Nonetheless, a deepening of the Roman Catholic approach to social questions has been a key aspect of the recent renewal of Roman Catholic moral theology.[10] Catholic social ethics today is more inductive, more biblical and perhaps more ready to address the really difficult questions. Pope John Paul II has given excellent leadership in the field of economic ethics, especially with his encyclical *Laborem Exercens*,[11] a document which, if read without automatic pre-conceptions in favor of a free market, could lead Catholics in the Western countries to a major reassessment of some aspects of their approaches to economic systems and social justice. The effort of the American Catholic bishops in issuing a pastoral letter on the nuclear arms question could prove to be one of the most remarkable events in the entire history of American Catholicism.[12] The style which the bishops employed in developing the pastoral (broad consultation, etc.) may become a paradigm for the Church's future handling of many complex ecclesial and social issues.

In reviewing these very notable advances in Roman Catholic moral theology, we should not lose sight of another different sort of advance—an advance in who does moral theology on a professional level. A generation ago, almost all Catholic moral theology was done by clerics, many of whom were canon lawyers who were only secondarily interested in and educated to do moral theology per se. Nowadays, there are religious women and men, married persons of both sexes, and single persons who are making significant contributions to the developments described in the last few paragraphs.[13] This diversity among the contributors to moral theology has greatly enriched the discipline of moral theology.

Protestant Moral Advances

I write as a Roman Catholic, and thus with a special awareness of the progress Roman Catholic moral theology has made in recent decades. It would be wrong, however, not to acknowledge that equally important accomplishments have also been made in recent Protestant writing on Christian ethics. Because both Protestant ethics and Catholic moral theology share many of the same basic concerns, it should not be surprising that much of the progress in Protestant ethics has been of a similar nature to what we have already seen in Roman Catholicism. In these areas of similar accomplishment, both Protestant and Catholic scholars have contributed with genuine originality, so that it is not a case of Protestant ethics being derived from Catholic ethics or vice versa.

On fundamental moral issues, several Protestant developments similar to those in Roman Catholicism can be mentioned. Modern biblical scholarship has had a marked influence on Protestant ethics. The area of spirituality, especially the theme of discernment of spirits, has emerged as a major concern for some Protestant ethicians. Important full-length Protestant books on fundamental Christian ethics are appearing such as the major new work by James Gustafson.[14]

Recent Protestant ethics also offers parallels to Roman Catholic thought on specific moral issues. Medical ethics, for instance, has become a major area of research for some leading

Protestant scholars. This development is particularly remarkable since Protestant medical ethics was almost unheard of before the mid-1950's.[15] Protestantism has also accomplished much in recent decades in the area of social justice. As with Catholicism, a renewed Protestant social ethics began around the turn of the century. But specific progress has taken place in recent years, with the nuclear arms issue again being a key example.[16]

Although these examples are similar to what has been happening in Roman Catholicism, there are also developments in Protestant ethics which are more unique. From the great hostility to natural law which existed in the Barthian era and earlier, certain Protestant scholars have begun a much more serious and intensive dialogue with the natural law tradition, so that, in the opinion of some contemporary observers, Protestantism and Catholicism can be said to be moving from two very different starting points towards a common middle ground on the natural law.[17] To get to this common ground Catholics have moved from static and sometimes overly physical approaches to natural law, while Protestants have moved from a tendency to rely on Scripture and to disregard philosophy and science as sources of moral knowledge.

Protestant authors have also contributed most notably to the development of a contemporary ethics of virtue.[18] This Protestant concern for virtue (which is beginning to be echoed by some Catholic authors) is ironic since in the past virtue was always such a key concept in Roman Catholic moral thought. As Catholic writers in the Vatican II period dealt with virtue ethics much less than before, some Protestant authors significantly revived the theme of virtue. Some older Protestant scholars saw the life of faith and justification as rather extrinsic to our human nature and human actions. The newer Protestant concern for virtue sees human interiority and the life of faith as important sources for moral life and action.

THREE PERSISTING PROBLEMS IN MORAL THEOLOGY

Based on the considerations mentioned so far, it seems that today's moral theology can be given a good deal of positive praise. At the same time however, any vital discipline always stands in need of further renewal, with moral theology being no exception. To set a context on imagination and moral theology, I would like to describe three problems which I see as present in today's moral theology, three problems which have caused me increasing concern over the fifteen years during which I have taught moral theology. These problems in no way gainsay the progress outlined earlier, but they are very real.

What Do Moral Principles Mean?

To explain the first problem, we must begin with one of the greatest strengths of Roman Catholic moral theology, i.e., its insistence on clear and definite principles for moral behavior. Roman Catholicism should be deeply proud of its devotion to moral principles, and nothing will question our need to make decisions on the basis of clear and well-articulated moral principles. However, there is a serious problem in that, while many believers know what our moral principles are, rather few believers know what many of these moral principles really mean. Perhaps part of the problem is that some of our moral principles have been around for so long that many people have forgotten the once hard-earned lesson of what these principles really mean.[19]

This forgetfulness of the real meaning of moral principles has created two quite opposite responses. Some persons, often including conservatives and/or authority figures, realizing that many moral principles are no longer understood, insist on an inflexible and sometimes legalistic following of our principles. Such an approach leaves very little room for the openness in interpreting principles which marked the work of many traditional scholars such as Aquinas with his teaching on *epikeia*. In some respects, our present situation makes a legalistic approach to principles understandable, and I for one can sympathize with the goals of those who proceed in this fashion. If many people have forgotten what our principles mean, there is logic to insisting on inflexible descriptions of moral principles. People who do not understand the principles they practice are more likely to make mistakes in their practice of the principles. The conservative position helps avoid such mistakes. There is, of course, an unacceptable paternalism in the conservative approach to defining moral principles, a paternalism which assumes that since persons do not now understand the meaning of many moral principles, they never will be able to understand them. But the cautious approach clearly has its own inner consistency and logic.

The second response to the fact that many moral principles are not well understood at a core level is the response taken by those who largely or completely abandon the use of moral principles in decision making. These persons find the routine and often shallow presentations of moral principles to be frustrating, and they see no course open to them other than to give up relying very much on moral principles. As with the first response, it is easy to see why persons with limited understandings of moral principles take this second response. However, the second response is ultimately unacceptable because of its antinomianism. It cuts itself off from the very real help which moral principles can offer. What is really needed is neither a legalistic nor an antinomian approach to principles. What is really needed is a deeper grasp of what our principles mean in the first place.

To give just one example of a moral principle with a forgotten meaning, consider one of our best known traditional principles, namely that genital sexual activity belongs in marriage and not elsewhere. It is a principle which seems to be observed as much today in its breaching as it is in actual practice. I doubt that we will have very much success in helping people in our society to practice this basic principle of sexual ethics unless we can find some ways to convey to people a whole new sense of what this principle really means. I also doubt that we will have much universal success in considering whether or not this principle might ever admit any objectively moral instances of genital sexual activity outside marriage unless we can come to a better grasp of what this principle means at its heart.

How Do We Apply Our Moral Principles?

A second problem which concerns me in today's Christian ethics or moral theology has to do with how we go about applying our moral principles to particular cases. The fact that we are so often unsure of the deepest meaning of our principles is one clear reason why applications can be difficult. But even when our principles are fairly well understood, applications can be difficult. So often we can face cases in which two or more of our central moral principles collide or at least appear to collide. So often, too, we get bombarded with new information which makes it hard for us to know which of our principles are relevant to a given situation and how we should apply the principles which are in fact relevant.

Two examples of this difficulty in applying moral principles come quickly to mind. In the current debate over nuclear arms, relatively few persons have doubts about the classic strength and validity of the just war theory. The principles of the just war theory developed by Augustine of Hippo still seem sound in themselves to many scholars. The traditional applications of the just war theory to ancient, medieval, and pre-nuclear modern wars were acceptable to many. But can a nuclear war ever be just? Or would a sound application of the just war theory in our changed, post-nuclear era call on us to reject all nuclear wars or even all wars in general as unjust? These are "application of known principles" questions and they are tough questions.[21]

The second example comes from medical ethics. One of the better accomplishments of traditional Roman Catholic morality was the set of principles pertinent to care for the dying.[22] We knew clearly that life was a value to be protected. But we also knew clearly that we did not always have to prolong life. We had a good distinction between ordinary means of preserving life (which we were obliged to use) and extraordinary means of preserving life (which we were not always obliged to use). Today however, in spite of all these clear principles, Catholic hospitals sometimes have a most difficult time in fostering good decisions in death and dying cases. There are so many new medical technologies that it is often unclear how we should go about rendering appropriate medical care. Doctors fear lawsuits and thus are very hesitant not to treat all patients vigorously, even when there are surely good reasons not to treat a given patient vigorously. People in general find it hard to talk about death (is this another instance of our not really grasping basic Christian values?), with the result that the patient, the doctor, the family, the pastoral minister, *et al.* can find it hard to begin a dialogue on what treatment is in the best interest of the patient. Even with our clear principles, the factors just mentioned can sometimes lead to less than satisfactory death and dying decisions. Where ethics committees exist in Catholic hospitals, they seem to struggle with this issue more than with any other single question.

In general two responses can be made to this difficulty in applying moral principles, two responses which basically parallel the earlier described responses to the problem of understanding principles well. One response is more cautious and opts for only carefully agreed upon applications of principles. At certain stages in our moral development, carefully worked out applications may well be all we can handle. But in the challenging crises of life, people will often have to move toward new and not so standard applications, applications which do not deny our principles but rather apply them in new ways to new cases. Many persons' moral development will not be able to proceed adequately if they cannot learn to move beyond the cautious applications to more creative ones.

The opposite response to the cautious standard-applications-only approach is the approach of those who will make esoteric and sometimes highly personalistic applications of principles, applications which are often mere rationalizations which undercut the essential meaning of principles. Such an approach is obviously not an acceptable application of principles, even if one can understand why it happens in an age in which many persons find it so difficult to apply principles.

In describing these two opposing approaches to the applying of moral principles, I am not trying to suggest that an acceptable and moderate middle ground is as of now completely unavailable. But we do find the middle ground difficult to hold today.[23]

Seeing the Social Side of Moral Issues

The third difficulty which strikes me concerning the state of moral theology today is that so many people have trouble in grasping the social dimensions of moral issues. In a general sense many believers have a hard time in making connections between their lives of prayerful openness to the Spirit and the social problems of the world around them. Such believers see prayer and spirituality as belonging in church while social problems are the world's business. Such believers find it hard to understand why Catholic bishops have spent so much time reflecting on nuclear arms. Once such a mindset is adopted, and social problems are detached from religious experience, it becomes quite difficult for social problems to be viewed as moral issues.

This difficulty can appear in various ways. Sometimes people can tend to think that only personal issues are true moral issues. Sometimes people will look at a moral issue which is both personal and social, but only be able to appreciate the personal moral aspects of the issue. Still other times, people will be aware of a given social issue, but without understanding that the issue is moral, as well as social, and therefore crucially important. In all these different cases there is a common root problem, namely the failure of people to see the social side of moral issues.

Several examples can serve to illustrate the difficulty many have in seeing the social side of moral issues. The first example will show the tendency to limit moral concern to personal issues alone. Very often when someone who was educated in traditional moral theology uses the phrase "moral problem," the phrase clearly refers to a sexual or a medical problem and to nothing else. When a program for a study week for priests states that a day will be devoted to moral problems, what is often meant is that the day will be devoted to sexual issues, or possibly to sexual and medical issues. This common and exclusively personal view of the term "moral problems" represents a serious failure to see the social side of human morality.

Two further examples show how people will look at issues which are both personal and social, but see only the personal side of such issues. In courses which deal with the problem of rape, many students tend to see rape as a sexual problem and nothing more. Such students cannot see that rape is profoundly connected to the way in which we organize society and to the many ways in which society systematically oppresses women. These students see rape only as the failure of certain isolated individuals to control their sexual instincts.[24] Similarly, in courses dealing with death and dying decisions, many students have a tendency to base death and dying decisions only on the suffering of the patient and/or on the anguish the situation is creating for the patient's family. Surely the needs of the patient and of his or her family are crucially important in death and dying cases. But the practice of medicine in death and dying cases is also very important for society as a whole and for the trust (or lack thereof) which all persons in society place in the medical profession. While direct mercy killing might appear to some to be reasonably justified based on the needs of the patient alone, the social dimensions of medicine raise a whole new series of questions about mercy killing, questions which cannot be ignored.[25]

A final example will show that people sometimes know about a social issue but fail to see that the issue is a moral issue. Perhaps the best current example of this type is unemployment. For years people have seen the growing statistics on unemployment and have known that it is a social problem. Especially today, when there are so many unemployed persons, there is much awareness that high unemployment is a social problem. However, the social problem of unemployment has not really struck most persons as a moral issue. Even when people know about unemployment, they fail to see that the lack of a job has a profound effect on the human dignity and worth of the unemployed persons and thus stands out as a major moral crisis. Government leaders are of course concerned about unemployment, but the comments of such leaders often seem to lack a grasp of the human dignity or moral side of the unemployment issue.

RATIONALITY AND IMAGINATION

A Common Source for the Three Problems?

Without doubt, other problems could be cited in today's moral theology. But the three problems described above all support my contention that, for all its recent gains, today's moral theology still has some significant limitations when it is used in teaching, preaching, and counseling. Ongoing work is essential on what moral principles mean, on how we apply them, and on how we see them as social.

To pursue this question a bit further, it might be asked whether these three problems have any common root or source. Obviously, each of the three problems has unique factors. But is there a common thread to the three problems? A survey of recent moral literature suggests one very important common thread, namely that each of the three problems is rooted in the tendency of moral theology to rely too heavily on forms of moral argument which are logical, discursive, and positivistic. We will not fully understand our moral principles on a discursive basis. Nor will we adequately apply our principles or see their social side if we proceed only with logical arguments. A substantial number of moral authors have recognized this common thread of over-reliance on discursive reasoning. These authors have begun to search for other means which can help us achieve moral wisdom.

One point must be clear from the outset: the turn to other elements of morality besides the discursive does not mean that logical clarity and discursive thinking are wrong or unnecessary in moral theology. Indeed, moral theology very much needs clear logical thinking as a means of explicating moral principles. The point therefore is not that we should abandon discursive moral thinking. The point is that we need more than discursive logic to successfully address the kinds of problems noted above. The major purpose of this book will not be to attack moral principles; the major purpose will be to get at the "more" which we all need, especially at the "more" which imagination can help offer us.

As an illustration of our need for more than the discursive in moral theology, let us consider one of the most interesting developments in moral theology in recent years: the effort to reinterpret the double effect principle.[26] Many scholars including myself have taken this issue up over the course of the past two decades. The contemporary investigation into the principle of double effect has had some very worthwhile results, although more discursively oriented research into the double effect is still needed to help clear up some of the questions which remain unanswered in the recent research. However, and most importantly in the present context, the key moral controversies which rage in the Church today will not be solved only on the basis of continued research into the principle of double effect. We also must turn in other, less logically oriented directions.

Efforts To Move Beyond the Discursive

The move in less discursively oriented directions has already been taken up by a number of moral theologians and philosophical ethicists. Authors such as Hauerwas and MacIntyre have stressed the importance of story (whether narrative, or drama, or journal) for moral theology. The same authors have also emphasized the role of character and virtue in the moral life.[27] Edward Shils and Daniel Callahan have emphasized the theme of tradition.[28] Paul Ramsey and a number of others have begun to explore the question of liturgy and ethics.[29] Bernard Häring and those who have been inspired by him have sought to tie Christian spirituality and ethics much more closely together. Häring has also introduced the notions of beauty and glory into moral theology, thereby opening up the whole question of moral theology and aesthetics.[30] Daniel Maguire has specifically raised the issue of imagination and moral thinking.[31] Maguire and Hauerwas have reflected upon the importance of the tragic and the comic as sources for Christian ethics.[32] For now we simply note the basic point: the move beyond an exclusively logical approach in moral thinking is clearly underway in an impressive group of ethical scholars.

Similar and helpful moves in less discursively oriented directions can also be found in philosophy, systematic theology, and Scripture.[33] In philosophy, the hermeneutic or interpretation theories of scholars such as Gadamer and Ricoeur point to notions such as a "surplus of meaning" to be found in literary and artistic classics.[34] In systematic theology, David Tracy has articulated a theology of the analogical imagination.[35] In Scripture, frustration with positivist approaches to studying the Bible is beginning to produce some important new schools of biblical interpretation such as rhetorical criticism and literary criticism (in the new sense which views the Bible as literature). All this suggests that the recent problems of moral theology and the efforts to address these problems are not an isolated case but part of a larger whole. In what follows we will need to give a good deal of attention to the larger whole.

So far, in describing a common source for the three problems, I have made use of the two terms logical and discursive, but I have not used the term rational. Critics who hold that moral theology is sometimes one-sidedly logical or discursive are also prone to say that moral theology can be excessively rational or rationalistic. If the word rational is understood as a term equivalent to logical or discursive, it can be appropriate to critique some moral theology as excessively rational or as rationalistic. It must be remembered, however, that, in a deeper sense, the word rational can and should be used to describe all of our human thought processes, not simply our logical processes. With this deeper sense in mind, it is not accurate to describe imagination as anti-rational or as critiquing rationality. Instead, I argue that imagination is indeed a rational process even though it involves a different kind of rationality from what we find in logical thought.

Why Imagination?

The last few paragraphs have suggested a common root problem in moral theology today and a variety of responses involving themes such as virtue, tradition, beauty, literature, and imagination. Surely these varied responses all belong in a common framework, and surely this book will need to look at all the elements in the common framework: the elements are part of a whole. Why then does this book plan to focus on the specific area of imagination and creativity? There are three main reasons. First, while there has been some writing on imagination and moral theology, this theme has not been treated as extensively as some of the related themes such as story, virtue, character, and vision. It is clearly a theme which deserves further investigation. Second, imagination as a moral theme appears to offer some specific benefits not available in the related themes. For instance, imagination might help us focus on how we grasp the Christian story in the first place and on how we relate our knowledge of the Christian story to the specific moral dilemmas we face. Similarly, imagination might help us to more accurately assess how we become virtuous and how we act concretely on the basis of our virtue. These questions have not yet been addressed in the contemporary literature as well as might be desired, with the result that the move beyond more logical categories in moral thinking may not yet have reached all of its potential in terms of practical or concrete impact.

Third, by taking up the theme of imagination we will also be able to attend to the theme of aesthetics and moral theology, a theme which offers much potential for our effort to work out a moral theology which moves beyond the discursive. Connected with this, it can be argued that music, art, literature, and beauty are always highly precious realities in themselves and that a sensitivity to them can contribute much to moral perception and judgment. Even many forms of athletic activity can be said to be beautiful and thus to have an important impact on human development and moral awareness. Some of our greatest theologians such as Karl Rahner have sensed all of this and written impressively on poetry and art.[36]

As our considerations unfold, the issue of aesthetics and moral theology will prove to be both fascinating and troubling. The fascination will come from an awareness of the potential benefits which the whole area of aesthetics might bring to moral thinking. The trouble will come from the fact that in our highly technical era, fewer and fewer of our young people get very many of the traditional opportunities for aesthetic experience. While not all of these concerns will be fully addressed in this book, the basic theme of imagination and moral theology may well help open up some of the aesthetic issues which are so important for human moral growth and development.

NOTES

[1]The best summary of the work of Vatican II on moral theology can be found in Josef Fuchs, *Human Values and Christian Morality* (Dublin: Gill and Macmillan, 1971), pp. 1–75. The major work which best expresses the spirit of Vatican II, especially its

biblical emphasis and its reunion of the moral life and the spiritual life, is Bernard Häring, *Free and Faithful in Christ* (cf. abbr. *F&F*).

[2]A summary of discernment literature through the mid 1970's can be found in Philip S. Keane, "Discernment of Spirits: A Theological Reflection," *American Ecclesiastical Review* 168 (1974), pp. 43–61. More contemporary thinking on discernment can be found in James M. Gustafson, *Ethics from a Theocentric Perspective* (cf. abbr. *ETP*), pp. 327–342. A helpful connection of discernment with story, character, vision, etc. can be found in James A. Donahue, "Religious Institutions as Moral Agents: Toward an Ethics of Organizational Character," *Issues in the Labor-Management Dialogue: Church Perspectives*, ed. by Adam J. Maida (St. Louis: The Catholic Health Association, 1982), pp. 139–159.

[3]Much will be said about moral development in Chapter 6. A simple basic text reflecting the Catholic interest in the theme is Ronald Duska and Mariellen Whelan, *Moral Development: A Guide to Piaget and Kohlberg* (New York: Paulist Press, 1975).

[4]Important examples of contemporary writing on the natural law include Franz Böckle, *Fundamental Moral Theology* (New York: Pueblo Publishing Co., 1980), pp. 180–247, and Charles E. Curran, *Themes in Fundamental Moral Theology* (Notre Dame, Ind.: University of Notre Dame Press, 1977), pp. 27–80. Most of the major recent writings on the double effect can be found in *RMT No. 1: Moral Norms and the Catholic Tradition* or in Richard A. McCormick and Paul Ramsey, eds., *Doing Evil To Achieve Good: Moral Choice in Conflict Situations* (Chicago: Loyola University Press, 1978).

[5]In addition to Häring's *F&F* and Böckle's *Fundamental Moral Theology*, other new full length works in this area include Timothy E. O'Connell, *Principles for a Catholic Morality* (New York: Seabury Press, 1978), and Daniel C. Maguire, *The Moral Choice* (cf. abbr. *TMC*).

[6]Many of these four developments can be found in the *SCDF's Declaration on Certain Questions Concerning Sexual Ethics*, Dec. 29, 1975. The English text was published by the *USCC* (Washington: 1976). Books which have reflected this kind of thinking, sometimes in a controversial fashion, include: Anthony Kosnik, *et al.*, *Human Sexuality:*

New Directions in American Catholic Thought (New York: Paulist Press, 1977); André Guindon, *The Sexual Language* (cf. abbr. *TSL*); and Philip S. Keane, *Sexual Morality: A Catholic Perspective* (New York: Paulist Press, 1977).

[7]Cf. Bishop Francis Mugavero, "Pastoral Letter: The Gift of Sexuality," *Origins* 5 (1976), pp. 581–586; Archbishop John R. Quinn, "A Pastoral Letter on Homosexuality," *Origins* 10 (1980), pp. 106–108. See also the report of the task force of the archdiocese of Baltimore on ministry to lesbian and gay Catholics, in *Origins* 11 (1982), pp. 549–553.

[8]For the recent official Catholic teaching on death and dying see *SCDF, Declaration on Euthanasia,* May 5, 1980 (in *Origins* 10 [1980], pp. 154–157). On abortion, see *SCDF, Declaration on Procured Abortion,* November 18, 1974 (in *Origins* 4 [1974], pp. 385–392). Much of the Catholic (and other) writing on abortion is summarized and critiqued in Richard A. McCormick, *How Brave a New World?* (Garden City, N.Y.: Doubleday, 1981), pp. 117–206.

[9]To anticipate a point to be made shortly in the text, much of this new work on medicine and ethics is being done in an ecumenical context, involving Catholic, Protestant, Jewish, and philosophical ethicists. Key sources for the issues mentioned are Warren T. Reich, ed., *Encyclopedia of Bioethics,* 4 vols. (New York: Macmillan and Free Press, 1978); Tom L. Beauchamp and LeRoy Walters, eds., *Contemporary Issues in Bioethics* (cf. abbr. *CIB*); and Thomas A. Shannon, ed., *Bioethics* (cf. abbr. *Bio*).

[10]Two important recent Catholic works on social ethics in America are Charles E. Curran, *American Catholic Social Ethics: Twentieth Century Approaches* (Notre Dame, Ind.: University of Notre Dame Press, 1982); and John A. Coleman, *An American Strategic Theology* (New York: Paulist Press, 1982).

[11]September 14, 1981. Eng. tr.: *On Human Work.* In *Origins* 11, pp. 225–244.

[12]*NCCB, The Challenge of Peace* (cf. abbr. *TCP*).

[13]Three of the more well-known non-clerics now writing moral theology are Margaret Farley, R.S.M., Daniel C. Maguire and William E. May.

[14]Cf. abbr. *ETP*.

[15]The first well-known Protestant medical ethics text was Joseph Fletcher, *Morals and Medicine* (Princeton: Princeton University Press, 1954).

[16]For a spectrum of Protestant (as well as some Catholic) reflection on the nuclear issue see *Christianity and Crisis* 41 (1982), pp. 370–398. This is a special issue titled *In Amsterdam Thinking About the Bomb*. It reports testimony from a World Council of Churches hearing on nuclear arms.

[17]The best source describing this movement to a common middle ground is James M. Gustafson, *Protestant and Roman Catholic Ethics* (cf. abbr. *PRC*).

[18]Most significant of the Protestant writers on the virtue theme is Stanley M. Hauerwas whose work will come up often in this book—e.g., his *Vision and Virtue* (cf. abbr. *VV*).

[19]For this notion of forgetting the real meaning of some of our basic truths, cf. Karl Rahner, "Forgotten Truths Concerning the Sacrament of Penance," *Theological Investigations* (cf. abbr. *TI*) 2, pp. 135–136.

[20]Omitted in this edition.

[21]In *TCP*, nos. 8–12, the bishops are very clear in making the distinction between principles and concrete applications.

[22]For a classic article which set forth the traditional Catholic position, see Gerald Kelly, "The Duty of Using Artificial Means of Preserving Life," *TS* 11 (1950), pp. 203–220.

[23]Profound questions about how theology works are at stake here. Some would hold that theological opinions which diverge from the magisterium ought only to be given private expression to the Vatican, preferably in Latin. Others seem to suggest that theologians are free to say anything about anything. Neither of these approaches is satisfactory.

[24]Of the much important work which has been done on rape, I believe the most significant text is Susan Brownmiller, *Against Our Will: Men, Women and Rape* (New York: Simon and Schuster, 1974).

[25]Cf. Paul Ramsey, "On (Only) Caring for the Dying," *The Pa-*

tient as Person: Explorations in Medical Ethics (New Haven: Yale University Press, 1970), esp. pp. 157–164.

[26]Cf. the sources cited in note 4 above. My own latest comments are in Philip S. Keane, "The Objective Moral Order: Reflections on Recent Research," *TS* 43 (1982), pp. 260–278.

[27]Hauerwas, "The Self as Story: A Reconsideration of the Relation of Religion and Morality from the Agent's Perspective," *VV*, pp. 68–89; *idem*, "Towards an Ethics of Character," *VV*, pp. 48–67; *idem*, "A Story-Formed Community: Reflections on *Watership Down*," *A Community of Character* (cf. abbr. *CC*), pp. 9–35; Alasdair MacIntyre, *After Virtue* (cf. abbr. *AV*), esp. pp. 190–209.

[28]Edward Shils, *Tradition* (Chicago: University of Chicago Press, 1981); Daniel Callahan, "Tradition and the Moral Life," *The Hastings Center Report* 12, no. 6 (1982), pp. 23–30.

[29]For Ramsey and other authors on this point, see the special issue titled *Focus on Liturgy and Ethics* in *JRE* 7 (1979), pp. 139–248.

[30]Häring, *F&F* 2, pp. 102–152.

[31]Daniel C. Maguire, *TMC*, pp. 189–217.

[32]Maguire, *TMC*, pp. 343–369. Stanley Hauerwas, *Truthfulness and Tragedy* (cf. abbr. *TT*), esp. pp. 57–70, 147–202.

[33]Specifics on these developments in philosophy, systematic theology, and Scripture will be found in Chapter 3.

[34]Cf. Paul Ricoeur, *Interpretation Theory: Discourse and the Surplus of Meaning* (Fort Worth: Texas Christian University Press, 1976).

[35]Tracy, *The Analogical Imagination* (cf. abbr. *AI*).

[36]Examples of Rahner's writings on this theme include "Priest and Poet," *TI* 3, pp. 294–317; and "Poetry and the Christian," *TI* 4, pp. 357–367.

The Eucharist and Social Justice

A discussion of the Eucharist and liturgy with respect to social justice and peace issues is probably more relevant in our own age than in past centuries of the church's life. Two converging currents seem to have become prominent and urgent in our own day.

First, we are all vividly aware of pressing social justice concerns: the millions of people living in dehumanizing and conflict situations, the rapidly expanding resource gap between the Third World peoples and other countries, worldwide problems of hunger, the scourge of wars that seem never to end, the proliferation of nuclear armaments, conflicts among nations, international terrorism, to mention but a few. Instant, worldwide communications have made these massive problems part of our everyday awareness.

At the same time the church has ever more frequently proclaimed the principles of social justice and has eloquently called us to be disciples of Christ truly concerned with the problems and needs of all our brothers and sisters. Pope John XXIII, the Second Vatican Council, Pope Paul VI, and Pope John Paul II, have issued encyclical letters, public statements, and personal pleas that the world family might be formed according to God's plan of harmony, peace and justice.[1] In all of the countries to which he has journeyed, Pope John Paul II has constantly called people to become authentic followers of Jesus Christ through lives committed to justice and peace. He visits the poor, the powerless, the sick and the sorrowing, to share his solidarity with them after the example of Christ.[2]

Second, the renewal of liturgy following the Second Vatican Council has provided a more vivid and tangible link between the Eucharist and the genuine problems that touch people's lives.

These converging currents produce a certain tension which I would like to explore in the first section of this article. I would then like to focus on the words of Jesus at the Last Supper, and to share some insights on how the consecratory prayer of the Eucharist is a radical call by Jesus to his disciples to continue his saving message and actions. And finally, I would suggest ways in which the Eucharist becomes for us today a genuine celebration of Christ's hope for the world.

THE EUCHARIST AND SOCIAL JUSTICE: A TENSION

Given the many justice and peace issues prevalent in today's world, and the church's call to us to become "doers of justice and makers of peace," we experience a genuine tension when the issues of justice and peace come to expression as the church defines its calling and reality in celebrating the Eucharist.

At one extreme, there are those who very readily identify issues of justice and peace with politics, and demand that we keep politics out of liturgy. For these people, the celebration of the sacred and the holy should be politically neutral, and the cares and concerns of people for peace and justice should not be noted in our liturgies. This group would prefer liturgical Scripture readings which are comforting and consoling, and which do not challenge the depth of our Christian living nor make local, direct application to us, our families, and our com-

munities. People in this group become angry when the plight
of Southeast Asian refugees is brought into a Sunday liturgy;
when the needs of striking steel workers or farm workers are
made part of our Eucharist; or when the devastating costs of
the nuclear arms race are spelled out in a homily or prayer of
the faithful.

At the other extreme are those who perceive the Eucharist
and liturgy to be a forum for the promotion of some special
cause or concern. Many of us have experienced situations in
which the celebration of the Eucharist became a minor action
in a broader context. In a sense, the liturgy can be "used" to
validate some particular action or strategy on behalf of a laud-
able justice or peace issue. Some have requested the celebration
of the Eucharist, for example, to give the impression of the
church's endorsement for some cause or strategy. Others have
employed the liturgy to help attract greater Catholic participation, again signaling to the uninformed that a Catholic liturgy validates the particular action or strategy for the Catholic
community.

It is interesting to note that in the early days of the church
St. Paul needed to deal directly with a developing problem
when the community at Corinth gathered to celebrate the Eucharist. In his First Letter to the Corinthians (11:17–34), Paul
criticizes those early Christians because when they gather for
the Lord's Supper, some begin eating and drinking without
waiting for the entire community to gather; others become
drunk; and still others eat their meal with little or no concern
for the poor and the hungry who are present. He urges them
to celebrate the Eucharist only when their celebration reflects
authentically the Lord's celebration in its fullness.

In my opinion, neither of the above extremes is correct.
Both fail to grasp the profound meaning given by Jesus to the
celebration of the first Eucharist. I would contend that the
proper understanding of that first Eucharist is essential to

grasping the depth and fullness of the eucharistic celebration throughout the ages. And once we understand the depth of Jesus' actions, we can far more readily perceive and realize the genuine implications for today's justice and peace concerns.

THE FIRST EUCHARIST: THE FULLNESS OF ITS MEANING

The eucharistic institution narratives in the New Testament[3] contain a common thrust, an emphasis which is captured in the church's official eucharistic prayer texts: "This is my body which will be given up for you. . . . This is the cup of my blood, the blood of the new and everlasting covenant. It will be shed for you and for all so that sins may be forgiven." Jesus' emphasis on his body being given up for us and his blood being shed or poured out for us reflects dramatically his mission and work from the Father. Once we begin to explore the reality and the profundity of this total self-giving, we begin to fathom the richness and the implications of our sharing in the eucharistic offering.

Let me share with you four examples of Jesus giving himself up for us and pouring himself out for us. While one could list several more instances to complete the total mission of Christ, these four will help illustrate the point and to serve as examples for our own Christian lives.

The Proclamation of the Father's Love and Mercy—
the Response of Rejection.

Very early in his public ministry, Jesus proclaims clearly that his mission can be best summarized by the fulfillment of Isaiah's prophecy in his own life and ministry: "The Spirit of the Lord is upon me; therefore, he has anointed me. He has sent me to bring good news to the poor, to proclaim liberty for captives, recovery of sight to the blind, and release to prisoners, to announce a year of favor from the Lord" (Lk 4:18–19). When John the Baptist's followers inquire of Jesus whether he is the Messiah, he responds by outlining his ministry in terms of proclaiming the good news of the Father's love and mercy (Lk 7:22). The parable of the Good Samaritan is another vivid example of this love lived out in practical and concrete terms (Lk 10:25–37). The mandate, then, "Go and do the same" (Lk 10:37), cannot be lost upon us as we prepare to celebrate and live the Eucharist. The poignant description of the final judgment of the world leaves no question about our role as brothers and sisters of Christ (Mt 25:31–46).

And yet, throughout his ministry Jesus suffers contradiction, opposition, and rejection as he attempts to proclaim this "good news" from his Father. In his own hometown Jesus must use his power to avoid being thrown over the cliff at the edge of town (Lk 4:28–30). His curing of the sick is often met with rejection (Lk 6:1–11; 20:9). After Jesus proclaims the promise of the Eucharist in John's Gospel, many disciples leave his company. He must turn to his closest friends to inquire, "Do you want to leave me too?" (Jn 6:60–71). When Jesus offers himself totally in the Eucharist, then, he does so in the clear proclamation of the Father's love and mercy, but with the frequent response of rejection.

The Cost of Discipleship.

Jesus never misleads or deceives us about what it will cost to become and to remain his disciples. If we want to be his followers, then the requirements for discipleship are clearly proclaimed. Those requirements demand the same giving of ourselves, the same pouring out of ourselves as contained in the eucharistic giving of Jesus. Early in his ministry Jesus explains that self-denial, bearing one's cross, and full identity with his example are the guidelines for genuine discipleship.[4] It even becomes necessary for Jesus to correct Peter harshly when he refuses to accept these guidelines (Mt 16:22–23). When we celebrate the Eucharist, it is in this same spirit and with the same intensity of discipleship to which Jesus calls us. It is only within the context of this faithful discipleship that we can celebrate the eucharistic mystery of Christ's total self-giving.

The Forgiveness of Sins.

The total giving of Jesus in the Eucharist is for the forgiveness of sins and the reconciliation of all creation according to God's plan. So many of Jesus' parables and personal encounters with people focus on the forgiveness of sins. Early in his ministry Jesus offers his greatest gift—the forgiveness of sins—to the paralytic lowered down through the roof (Mk 2:5). The overwhelming forgiveness of the Father is so beautifully described in the parable of the lost son (Lk 15:11–32). The apostles struggle with the generosity of God's forgiveness of sins and of one another's faults, and Jesus must raise their sights and vision almost beyond belief (Mt 18:21–35). In his final commissioning of the apostles, Jesus stresses that their work must be an authentic continuation of the great gift of the forgiveness of sins and reconciliation (Lk 24:45–53).

Our sharing in the Eucharist, then, must keep alive and authentic Jesus' mission of reconciliation, forgiveness, and the removal of sins. This particular quality of our eucharistic celebrations must be clearly recognized and made available to all who share in the Eucharist.

Doing the Will of the Father.

Jesus' giving over his body and pouring out his blood probably reaches its point of totality in his faithfulness in living out the will of his Father. It is striking how often and how forcefully Jesus refers to his sole mission as that of doing his Father's will. We see this when Jesus is speaking with the Samaritan woman at the well (Jn 4:34). We experience Jesus' struggle with the will of the Father in the Garden of Olives (Mt 26:39, 42; Mk 14:36). But in a most special way do we observe Jesus' concern for the Father's will within his discourse on the Eucharist as contained in the sixth chapter of John's Gospel. In speaking openly and directly about his being the bread of life, about giving us his very body and blood as our food and drink, Jesus places that eucharistic gift in the context of his total self-giving to his Father's will: " . . . because it is not to do my own will that I have come down from heaven, but to do the will of him who sent me. It is the will of him who sent me that I should lose nothing of what he has given me: rather, that I should raise it up on the last day. Indeed, this is the will of my Father, that everyone who looks upon the Son and believes in him shall have eternal life. Him I will raise up on the last day" (Jn 6:38–40).

Each authentic celebration of the Eucharist necessarily becomes a total immersion in the will and work of the Father, after Jesus' example. Our sharing in the Eucharist must reflect that same depth of affirming the Father's will and plan in our own lives. Any contrary attitude totally dilutes the measure of our giving over our bodies and pouring out our blood after Jesus' example.

CELEBRATION OF EUCHARIST: IMPLICATIONS FOR DOING JUSTICE AND MAKING PEACE

We have briefly reflected upon the theological mystery of the Eucharist as the zenith of Jesus' self-giving. We have seen how Jesus' own life was a powerful example of commitment to proclaiming the Father's love and mercy even in the face of fierce opposition and rejection, to sharing with us the demands of discipleship, to reconciling all things to the Father especially through the forgiveness of sins, and to doing the will of the Father so that all things might be made new again. As we think about these essential aspects of Jesus' giving over his body and pouring out his blood on our behalf, we begin to realize that the celebration of the Eucharist can be a most powerful grace to the Christian community and to the entire world community as we attempt to bring about Christ's vision for the world.

There are five implications which I feel flow from this understanding of the Eucharist and which should guide us in our justice and peace struggles in the world.

The Eucharist as Life-giving.

Justice and peace concerns which are brought to this deeper understanding of the eucharistic offering become life-giving in that full sense of Jesus' promise throughout the sixth chapter of John's Gospel. The first Eucharist, and all subsequent eucharistic celebrations, become life-giving precisely because Jesus continues to pour out the fullness of his life through the bread of life and the cup of salvation. Our own sharing in the Eucharist becomes most effective and grace-giving when we imitate the self-giving of Jesus in our own lives and bring that gift to the world through the Eucharist. If our pride and selfishness limit our own self-giving, then our celebration of the Eucharist cannot have a full measure of effectiveness in touching the world through our lives.

So many people in the world are in desperate need to have life, and to have that life abundantly after the promise of Christ. The sick, the suffering, and the dying; the hungry and the thirsty; those deprived of their freedom; those captured in the web of materialism and self-indulgence; those whose lives have no apparent purpose or value—all these desperately need life and need to find it fully in Christ Jesus. But we are the ones called by the Lord to carry on his work and ministry, and to be sharers of Christ's life. As we bring social justice and peace concerns to our eucharistic celebrations, we have the ability to transform those concerns into life-giving graces. Let us be attentive and enthusiastic with our own self-giving so that Jesus' life-giving gift might be shared with those most in need of it.

The Eucharist as Call to Repentance.

Since Jesus gave us the great gift of the Eucharist "for the forgiveness of sins" in his memory, and for the proclamation of his death for our salvation until the end of the world, our continuing celebration of the Eucharist must clearly call all of us to be reconciled to the Father and to one another. So much human misery and tragedy is caused by people unwilling to accept forgiveness in their own lives and to offer forgiveness to others. Jesus' constant message of the Father's mercy, the forgiveness of sins, and the reconciliation of all people is contained most especially in the celebration of the Eucharist.

As we bring social justice and peace concerns to the celebration of the Eucharist, we must do so within the context of repentance and forgiveness. We must not allow barriers to be built among us, irreconcilable differences to develop, or the hardness of our hearts to impede reconciliation. Our most authentic celebration of the Eucharist will flow from a gathering of communities fully committed to repentance, to the forgiveness of sins, and to reconciliation among all people. If we do not enter our eucharistic celebrations with this spirit, we can stifle the full effectiveness of Jesus' total forgiveness through his body and blood.

The Eucharist as Hope for All Humanity.

Jesus' giving of himself for us and for all people through each age of history becomes a sign of great hope for us. His leaving us this powerful supper in his memory is a pledge of both presence and grace until the end of time. Those who have no hope from any source are able to receive it through the Eucharist. The poor, the outcast, the suffering, all those whom Jesus touches in his ministry are found in each age and in each nation down through history. They must be given new life and the brightness of genuine hope through our offering of the Eucharist. Jesus continues to give up his body and to pour out his blood for those most in need of his saving touch.

Our sharing in the Eucharist must be with the same full awareness of all peoples about us, whether in our families, communities, or scattered throughout the world. Our self-giving is brought to the Lord's Supper and made effective in bringing hope to those who have none. Our ability to share Jesus' spark of hope is contingent upon our generosity in sharing ourselves without reservation after the Lord's example. A desperate world eagerly longs for hope in each of our lives. This desperate world craves for witnesses to the hope of Jesus Christ, not just for proclaimers of that hope. Our own lives take on the fullest measure of Christ's hope when we give of ourselves most generously. We must bring the concerns of those treated unjustly and those living in conflict to our celebrations of the Eucharist, but not simply in lifeless intercessory prayers. We are called by Christ to give of ourselves as he gave of himself, and it is in this self-giving that genuine hope blossoms.

The Eucharist as Understanding the Signs of the Times.

Jesus first called our attention to the signs of the times in his own ministry, and the Second Vatican Council reiterated this call so that we as disciples of Christ might become more authentic witnesses to the concerns of the world in this age.[5] When we gather for the Eucharist, we first listen to the word of God proclaimed for us. We attempt to grasp more fully the implications of Jesus' message and life in the gospels, and to make that message and example our own. As we reflect on this word, we do so in the context of our own times and with the reality of society's strengths and weaknesses ever before us. We envision Jesus' self-giving ministry and the remarkable ways in which he touched so many lives with a proper understanding of God's plan of peace and salvation for all peoples. We, too, must continue to proclaim the glory of God's kingdom and the value of possessing that treasure at all cost. We must proclaim the gospel values so that they are more readily understood by people of today in the context of their lived experience.

We must bring to the celebration of the Eucharist a broad awareness of the signs of our own times so that these may be immersed in the life-giving sacrifice of Christ mirrored in our own lives. Then the world will receive back through us the grace and saving actions of Jesus so that all things might be made new through him (Rev 21:5).

The Eucharist as Source of Christian Action in the World.

By bringing to the celebration of the Eucharist our own gift of self after the example of Jesus, we are able to absorb most fully the meaning and grace-expression of Jesus' own gift of self. Our Christian action on behalf of social justice and peace issues will then have substance and will be in harmony with the intentions of Christ in sharing the Eucharist with us.

I contend that all social justice action and work for the cause of peace must flow from this radical understanding of Jesus' self-giving and our total identification with him in that saving action. Anything less either reduces the sacrifice of Christ to mere symbolism, on the one hand, or promotes an artificial and superficial understanding of Jesus' entire life and ministry as expressed in the Eucharist, on the other.

The world desperately needs the saving actions and grace of Christ, and it most urgently needs the authentic involvement of his disciples in the real human misery all about us. But that saving action can only have its maximum benefit and effect when it flows from an authentic understanding of the Eucharist.

As a conclusion to this reflection upon the Eucharist and social justice and peace concerns, I would like to quote a section from Pope John Paul II's letter to all the bishops *On the Mystery and Worship of the Eucharist.*[6] His sentiments most appropriately bring together the reflections which I have sought to share with you: "The authentic sense of the Eucharist becomes of itself the school of active love for neighbor. We know that this is the true and full order of love that the Lord has taught us: 'By this love you have for one another, everyone will know that you are my disciples' (Jn 13:35). The Eucharist educates us to this love in a deeper way; it shows us, in fact, what value each person, our brother or sister, has in God's eyes, if Christ offers himself equally to each one, under the species of bread and wine. If our eucharistic worship is authentic, it must make us grow in awareness of the dignity of each person. The awareness of that dignity becomes the deepest motive of our relationship with our neighbor.

"We must also become particularly sensitive to all human suffering and misery, to all injustice and wrong, and seek the way to redress them effectively. Let us learn to discover with respect the truth about the inner self that becomes the dwelling place of God present in the Eucharist. Christ comes into the hearts of our brothers and sisters and visits their consciences. How the image of each and every one changes, when we become aware of this reality, when we make it the subject of our reflections! The sense of the Eucharistic Mystery leads us to a love for our neighbor, to a love for every human being."

NOTES

[1]An excellent reference resource is *The Gospel of Peace and Justice*, ed. Joseph Gremillion (Maryknoll, New York: Orbis Books 1976). It contains all the major social justice and peace teachings of the church from Pope John XXIII (1961) through Pope Paul VI (1975), together with a very helpful overview and prospectus.

[2]The following few examples will highlight this remarkable example of Pope John Paul II: Dominican Republic: Poor people of the "Los Minas" district, 26 January 1979; Mexico: Indians of the region of Oaxaca, 29 January 1979; Mexico: Workers of Monterrey, 31 January 1979; United States: People of Harlem, Spanish speaking immigrants, and Homily at Yankee Stadium, 2 October 1979; Brazil: Poor of Brazil at Favela Vidigal, 2 July 1980; Brazil: Poor of Alagados, Salvador da Bahia, 7 July 1980; Philippines: Poor of the Philippines, 18 February 1981.

[3]Cf. Matthew 26:26–28; Mark 14:22–24; Luke 22:19–20; and 1 Corinthians 11:23–25.

[4]Cf. Mark 8:34–38; Matthew 8:18–22; Luke 14:25–27.

[5]Pastoral Constitution *Gaudium et Spes* on the Church in the Modern World 4, in *The Documents of Vatican II*, ed. Walter M. Abbott (New York: Guild Press 1966) 201.

[6](Boston: St. Paul Editions) 10–11.

Richard McBrien

Catholicism: A Synthesis

To what extent, however, is the *ecclesial experience* of Jesus Christ *distinctively Catholic?* To what extent are the *moral vision and commitments distinctively Catholic?* To what extent are the *hopes* in the coming Kingdom of God *distinctively Catholic?*

If Catholicism is distinguishable within the Body of Christ from Protestantism, Anglicanism, and Eastern Orthodoxy, it must be on the basis of some belief(s) or characteristic(s) which Catholicism alone possesses. One belief that is obviously distinctive is Catholicism's commitment to the Petrine office, the papacy. At this point in the history of the Church, the Catholic Church alone affirms that the Petrine ministry is an integral institutional element in the Body of Christ, and that without the papal office the Church universal lacks something essential to its wholeness. It is the one issue which still finally divides the Catholic from all other Christian churches and traditions, notwithstanding various other differences regarding liturgy, spirituality, theology, polity, and doctrinal formulations. When all else is stripped away, the official Catholic position on the Petrine ministry and office is different from every other official and/or representative position of every other formal Christian Church. This is not to suggest that it must always be so, however, and therein lies the difficulty in linking Catholic distinctiveness with the papacy alone.

The Lutheran-Roman Catholic consultation in the United States, for example, has achieved a remarkable measure of consensus already on the question of papal primacy (see chapter 23), giving promise of even greater breakthroughs. It is conceivable, in other words, that Catholicism's affirmations about the Petrine ministry will, at some later date, no longer be Catholicism's affirmations alone. They may be shared by Lutherans, Anglicans, the Orthodox, Presbyterians, Methodists, and others. Will all of Christianity at that point be identified simply with Catholicism? Will Lutheranism, Calvinism, Anglicanism, and Orthodox Christianity fade from the scene once and for all? Will there, then, be one theology, one spirituality, one liturgy, one canon law, one vehicle of doctrinal formulation? If so, it would be the first time in the entire history of the Church, not excluding the New Testament period itself (see, for example, Raymond E. Brown's *The Community of the Beloved Disciple*, New York: Paulist Press, 1979).

A more fruitful, and more theologically and historically nuanced, approach to the question of Catholic distinctiveness would seem to lie in the direction of identifying and describing various *characteristics* of Catholicism, each of which (apart from the commitment to the papacy) Catholicism shares with one or another Christian church or tradition. But how can one distinguish Catholicism from other theological, doctrinal, spiritual, liturgical, and institutional expressions of Christianity on the basis of characteristics which Catholicism presumably *shares* with one or another Christian church? It is true: There is no one characteristic, apart from the Petrine doctrine, which sets the Catholic Church apart from *all other* churches. On the other hand, a case can be made that nowhere else except in the Catholic Church are *all* of Catholicism's characteristics present in the precise *configuration* in which they are found within Catholicism.

The point is crucial. An example may help to illustrate it. The flag of the United States of America has individual characteristics which it shares with the flags of other nations of the world. (1) It is *tri-colored*. But so, too, are the flags of Australia, Belgium, Botswana, Colombia, the United Kingdom, France, Ireland, Italy, the Federal Republic of Germany. (2) Its three colors are *red, white, and blue*. But so, too, are the flags of Burma, Cuba, Czechoslovakia, France, the Netherlands, Panama, the United Kingdom, New Zealand, Yugoslavia. (3) It has *stars* in its basic design. But so, too, do the flags of Australia, the People's Republic of China, Honduras, Venezuela.

Despite these common characteristics, no flag in the entire community of nations is identical with the flag of the United States, a reasonably close similarity to the flag of the African nation of Liberia notwithstanding. What is *distinctive* about the United States' flag is not any one of its several *characteristics* but the precise *configuration* of those characteristics. So, too, with the Catholic Church in relation to all of the other churches and traditions within the Body of Christ.

GENERAL CHARACTERISTICS OF CATHOLICISM

As its very name suggests, Catholicism is characterized by a *radical openness to all truth and to every value*. It is *comprehensive* and *all-embracing* toward the totality of Christian experience and tradition, in all the theological, doctrinal, spiritual, liturgical, canonical, institutional, and social richness and diversity of that experience and tradition. Catholicism is not a post-biblical phenomenon. It does not emerge from some historical moment and from particular historical (i.e., national, cultural, political) circumstances which are removed in time from Jesus' proclamation of the Kingdom, his gathering of disciples, and the formation of the Church in the period encompassed by the New Testament. Catholicism does not begin as a distinctive expression of Christian faith in the sixteenth century, nor are its basic lines already fixed by the fourteenth. It is not itself a sect or a schismatic entity, although sectarianism and schism are not unknown to it. Nor is it inextricably linked with the culture of a particular nation or region of the world. Catholicism is, in principle, as Asian as it is European, as Slavic as it is Latin, as Mexican or Nigerian as it is Irish or Polish.

There is no list of "Catholic Fathers" (or Catholic "Mothers," for that matter) which does not include the great theological and spiritual writers of the period *before* as well as after the division of East and West and the divisions within the West. Gregory of Nyssa is as much a Catholic Father as is Augustine or Thomas Aquinas.

Nor are there *schools of theology* which Catholicism excludes, variations in their inherent strengths and weaknesses notwithstanding. Catholicism continues to read Ignatius of Antioch and Clement of Alexandria, Athanasius and Cyril of Jerusalem, Gregory of Nazianzen and Augustine, Anselm of Canterbury and Bernard of Clairvaux, Abelard and Hugh of St. Victor, Thomas Aquinas and Bonaventure, Robert Bellarmine and Johann Adam Möhler, Karl Rahner and Charles Journet, not to mention John and Luke.

Nor are there *spiritualities* which Catholicism excludes, their variations again notwithstanding. Catholicism is open to *The Cloud of Unknowing* and the *Introduction to the Devout Life*, to the way of Francis of Assisi and of Bernard of Clairvaux, to Ignatius Loyola and John of the Cross, to Marmion and Merton.

Nor are there *doctrinal* streams and mighty rivers that Catholicism closes off. Catholics are guided by Nicea as by Vatican I, by Chalcedon as by Lateran IV, by Trent as by Vatican II. They read Gregory the Great as well as Paul VI, Clement of Rome as well as Leo XIII, Pius XII as well as John XXIII.

Catholicism is characterized, therefore, by a *both/and* rather than an *either/or* approach. It is not nature *or* grace, but graced nature; not reason *or* faith, but reason illumined by faith; not law *or* Gospel, but law inspired by the Gospel; not Scripture *or* tradition, but normative tradition within Scripture; not faith *or* works, but faith issuing in works and works as expressions of faith; not authority *or* freedom, but authority in the service of freedom; not the past *versus* the present, but the present in continuity with the past; not stability *or* change, but change in fidelity to stable principle, and principle fashioned and refined in response to change; not unity *or* diversity, but unity in diversity, and diversity which prevents uniformity, the antithesis of unity.

There have been many moments in the history of the Catholic Church when these delicate balances were disrupted, often through events beyond anyone's control and at other times through narrow-mindedness, blindness, stubbornness, and malice. But the Church is at once holy and sinful, not in the sense that sin exists *alongside* grace, but in the sense that even graced existence is ambiguous, fragile, and subject to disintegration. The record is always mixed. The Kingdom of God is neither coextensive with the Church nor totally divorced from the Church.

One person looks at a glass and sees that it is half empty; another looks at the same glass and declares it half full. One person looks at the story of the Church and sees only the Church's complicity in the feudal system, the Crusades, the pretentious claims of Innocent III and Boniface VIII, its blindness to the gathering storm clouds of the Reformation, its insensitivities to the East, its arid Scholasticism of the post-Reformation period, its handling of the Galileo affair, its declaration of war against modernity in the nineteenth century, its suppressions of theological freedom under Pope Pius X, its diplomatic hesitancies in the face of Nazism.

Another looks at the same Church and notes the extraordinary, and finally inexplicable, manner in which it drew unity out of seeming chaos in the Christological controversies of the fourth and fifth centuries. Still another marvels at how the Church can be the Church of both John and Paul, of Luke and Timothy, of the martyrs and apologists, of Gregory of Nyssa and Augustine of Hippo, of Gregory the Great and Anselm of Canterbury, of Francis of Assisi and Thomas Aquinas, of monasticism as a protest against political and social privilege and later as the carrier of Western civilization, of heroic reformers like Catherine of Siena, of contemporary saints like John XXIII or Dorothy Day.

But perhaps more than anything or anyone else, one must marvel at the Church of *Vatican II*: a *pluralistic* Church open to pluralism, a *modern* Church open to modernity, an *ecumenical* Church open to the whole wide world (the literal meaning of *ecumenical*), a *living* Church open to new life and to the change it brings and requires, a *catholic* Church open in principle to all truth and to every value.

For Lutheran Church historian Martin Marty, of the University of Chicago, "Catholicism is a family of apostolic churches, rich in regional, national, ethnic diversity; it is a faith that teaches me that because you have a *core* or center, you can make room for a variety of apparently competitive and interactive elements" ("Something Real and Lumpy," *U.S. Catholic*, vol. 44, May 1979, p. 24).

Like the flag of the United States of America, there are colors here that others share; there are patterns here that others display; there are symbols here that others use. But no other church or tradition within the Body of Christ puts them all together in quite this way. It is in their special configuration that the distinctiveness of Catholicism is disclosed and expressed. It is expressed in its systematic theology, in its body of doctrines, in its liturgical life, especially its Eucharist, in its variety of spiritualities, in its religious congregations and lay apostolates, in its social teachings and commitments to justice, peace, and human rights, in its exercise of collegiality, and in its Petrine ministry.

THE PHILOSOPHICAL FOCUS OF CATHOLICISM: CHRISTIAN REALISM

Catholicism is not bound to any one school of theology, although there is something distinctively Catholic in the way the pluralism of theologies is integrated, systematized, and applied within the Catholic tradition. If the Catholic Church is not linked exclusively to a particular theology, much less is it linked to a particular philosophy: existentialist, process, phenomenological, even Thomistic. And yet there is a distinctively Catholic way of integrating the pluralism of philosophies underlying its various theological and doctrinal orientations. For want of a better term, that distinctively Catholic philosophical focus is "Christian realism," as outlined, for example, by Bernard J.F. Lonergan (see his "The Origins of Christian Realism" in *A Second Collection*, William Ryan and Bernard Tyrrell, eds., Philadelphia: Westminster Press, 1974, pp. 239–261).

Lonergan reminds us that infants, in contrast to adults, do not speak. They live, therefore, in a world of immediacy: of sights and sounds, of tastes and smells, of touching and feeling, of pleasure and pain. But as infants learn to speak, they gradually move into a larger world, a world mediated by meaning. That world includes the past and the future as well as the present, the possible and the probable as well as the actual, rights and duties as well as the facts.

The criteria of reality in the infant's world of immediacy are given in immediate experience. They are simply the occurrence of seeing, hearing, tasting, smelling, touching, pleasure and pain. But the criteria of reality in the world mediated by meaning are far more complex. They include immediate experience but also go beyond it.

"For the world mediated by meaning is not just given," Lonergan insists. "Over and above what is given there is the universe that is intended by questions, that is organized by intelligence, that is described by language, that is enriched by tradition. It is an enormous world far beyond the comprehension of the nursery. But it is also an insecure world, for besides fact there is fiction, besides truth there is error, besides science there is myth, besides honesty there is deceit" (p. 241).

Now this insecurity and ambiguity does not really bother too many people. But it does trouble philosophers and those whose sciences, like theology, depend in some significant measure on correct philosophical presuppositions. Philosophical answers to the question of reality differ. First, there is *naive realism*, which insists that knowing is simply a matter of taking a good look; objectivity is a matter of seeing what is there to be seen; reality is whatever is given in immediate experience. The offspring of naive realism is *empiricism*. The empiricist takes naive realism seriously. The only reality that counts is the reality that one can determine by quantitative measurement. Empiricism, in turn, begets its philosophical opposite, *critical idealism* (Kant), in which the categories of understanding of themselves are empty and refer to objects only insofar as the categories are applied to the data of the senses. This is the world of *phenomena*. We cannot know things in themselves, the *noumena*.

"Insofar as Christianity is a reality, it is involved in the problems of realism," Lonergan suggests. First, Christianity itself is mediated by meaning. "It is mediated by meaning in its communicative function inasmuch as it is preached. It is mediated by meaning in its cognitive function inasmuch as it is believed. It is mediated by meaning in its constitutive function inasmuch as it is a way of life that is lived. It is mediated by meaning in its effective function inasmuch as its precepts are put into practice" (p. 244).

But there is ambiguity within the Christian's world, as there is in human life itself. For the Christian world is not *exclusively* a world mediated by meaning. There is also the immediacy of God's grace creating the new creature in Christ by the power of the Holy Spirit. The grace of God is not produced by the preacher, nor is it the result of believing the Gospel, nor does it come as a reward for good works. Grace is present to the individual person, as we have seen (chapter 5), from the very beginning of the person's existence. Grace enters into the definition of what it means to be human.

Thus, the real is not only what I can see and touch, as naive realism suggests. Nor is the real just an idea in the mind, as idealism insists. The real is what I judge to be real. The reality of the world mediated by meaning is known not by experience alone, nor by ideas alone, but by judgments and beliefs.

It is this commitment to *critical* realism that has moved the Catholic Church, first at Nicea (325) and again and again in its official teachings, to deliberate, to issue decrees, to condemn, to explain, to defend, to make distinctions, to use technical terms, to engage in the most acute rational reflection. Indeed, it is this commitment to critical realism that is at the foundation of the medieval effort toward systematization and of our own contemporary systematic enterprises as well.

What does all this mean? It means that the Catholic tradition philosophically rejects both naive realism and idealism as adequate bases for Catholicism's theological vision. One contemporary form of naive realism is *biblicism*. For the biblicist, the meaning of the Word of God is obvious. "Just take a look," the biblicist seems to say. "The requirements of Christian existence are clear. The answers are readily available in the pages of Sacred Scripture." *Moralism* is another contemporary form of naive realism. "Just consult your gut feelings, or use your common sense," the moralist insists. "Of course, violence is against the Gospel of Jesus Christ." Or: "Of course, violence can be justified to counteract oppressive violence." But moralism provides no arguments, no warrants, no reasons. It is assumed that the convictions are self-evidently true and their intrinsic power compelling.

Idealism, on the other hand, makes of Christianity a system of principles and ideas, but without clear or meaningful connection with the pastoral situation or the human condition at large. One need not worry about the effectiveness of preaching and teaching, for example, if one is convinced that the ideas to be preached and taught are plainly, even though not infallibly, true. One need not engage in time-consuming and ultimately diverting moral speculation about what it is one must do in such-and-such a conflict-situation when there is a clear statement of moral principle already "on the books." The contemporary forms of idealism are *dogmatism* and *legalism*. Dogmatism assumes that salvation is linked primarily to "right belief" and that the rightness of beliefs is clear and almost self-evident. Legalism assumes that salvation is linked primarily to "right practice," i.e., of obedience to Church laws. There is never any serious doubt about what the law demands, so specific and so detailed is it.

Critical realism, or what Lonergan calls Christian realism, insists that experience itself is not enough. One can "take a look," but one cannot be sure that what one sees corresponds entirely to what is real. "Appearances can be deceiving," the old saying has it. Christian realism also rejects the notion that clear and distinct ideas (doctrines, dogmas, canonical directives) are equivalent to the real itself. Ideas are never formulated except in relation to other ideas, to events, to one's associates, to the problems and resources at hand, to the historical circumstances, to social, economic, and political conditions, to one's own background, age, sex, nationality, occupation, income level, social status, and the like. Just as Christian realism rejects biblicism and moralism in favor of a critical and systematic approach to reality, so Christian realism rejects dogmatism and legalism in favor of a critical and systematic approach to reality, an approach that goes beyond what seems to be there and that takes historicity into account in the use and interpretation of ideas and principles.

This critical realism carries over into everything the Church does. Thus, the Church's moral vision and its approach to the demands of Christian existence are qualified always by its confidence in the power of grace and by its readiness to expect and understand the weaknesses and failures rooted in Original Sin. And so Catholicism is a moral universe of laws but also of dispensations, of rules but also of exceptions, of respect for authority but also for freedom of conscience, of high ideals but also of minimal requirements, of penalties but also of indulgences, of censures and excommunications but also of absolution and of reconciliation.

THE THEOLOGICAL FOCI OF CATHOLICISM: SACRAMENTALITY, MEDIATION, COMMUNION

No theological principle or focus is more characteristic of Catholicism or more central to its identity than the principle of *sacramentality*. The Catholic vision sees God in and through all things: other people, communities, movements, events, places, objects, the world at large, the whole cosmos. The visible, the tangible, the finite, the historical—all these are actual or potential carriers of the divine presence. Indeed, it is only in and through these material realities that we can even encounter the invisible God. The great sacrament of our encounter with God and of God's encounter with us is Jesus Christ. The Church, in turn, is the sacrament of our encounter with Christ and of

Christ's with us, and the sacraments, in turn, are the signs and instruments by which that ecclesial encounter with Christ is expressed, celebrated, and made effective for the glory of God and the salvation of men and women.

A corollary of the principle of sacramentality is the principle of *mediation*. A sacrament not only signifies; it also causes what it signifies. Thus, created realities not only contain, reflect, or embody the presence of God. They make that presence effective for those who avail themselves of these realities. Just as we noted in the previous section that the world is mediated by meaning, so the universe of grace is a mediated reality: mediated principally by Christ, and secondarily by the Church and by other signs and instruments of salvation outside and beyond the Church.

Catholicism rejects naive realism, which holds to the immediacy of the experience of God as the normal or exclusive kind of encounter with the divine presence. Catholicism also rejects idealism, which holds that the encounter with God occurs solely in the inwardness of conscience and the inner recesses of consciousness. Catholicism holds, on the contrary, that the encounter with God is a mediated experience but a *real* experience, rooted in the historical and affirmed as real by the critical and systematic judgment that God is truly present and active here or there, in this event or that, in this person or that, in this object or that.

Finally, Catholicism affirms the principle of *communion:* that our way to God and God's way to us is not only a mediated way but a communal way. And even when the divine-human encounter is most personal and individual, it is still communal in that the encounter is made possible by the mediation of the community. Thus, there is *not* simply an individual personal relationship with God or Jesus Christ that is established and sustained by meditative reflection on Sacred Scripture, for the Bible itself is the Church's book and is the testimony of the

Church's original faith. The mystic (even in the narrow sense of the word) relies on language, ideas, concepts, presuppositions when he or she enters into, or reflects upon, an intimate, contemplative relationship with God. We are radically social beings; our use of language is clear evidence of that. There is no relationship with God, however intense, profound, and unique, that dispenses entirely with the communal context of *every* human relationship with God.

And this is why, for Catholicism, the mystery of the Church has so significant a place in theology, doctrine, pastoral practice, moral vision and commitment, and devotion. Catholics have always emphasized the place of the Church as both the *sacrament* of Christ, *mediating* salvation through sacraments, ministries, and other institutional elements and forms, and as the *Communion of Saints*, the preview or foretaste, as it were, of the perfect communion to which the whole of humankind is destined in the final Kingdom of God.

And so it is with the *mystery of the Church* that we come at last to the point at which the distinctively Catholic understanding and practice of Christian faith most clearly emerges. For here we find the convergence of those principles which have always been so characteristic of Catholicism: sacramentality, mediation, and communion—principles grasped and interpreted according to the mode of critical realism rather than of naive realism or idealism.

These principles, at once philosophical and theological, have shaped, and continue to shape, Catholicism's Christology, ecclesiology, sacramentology, canon law, spirituality, Mariology, theological anthropology, moral theology, liturgy, social doctrine, and the whole realm of art and aesthetics. The last item is a particular case in point. In contrast, Protestantism, as a religion of the word, has had a "mixed" record when it comes to the arts. It has been "uneasy about objectification of the divine drama in images which might themselves draw the devotion of the supplicant from the invisible God beyond the gods. It has often and maybe even usually been uneasy about unrestricted bodily attention, and has rather consistently feared the ecstasy of the dance through most of the years of its history" (Martin Marty, *Protestantism*, p. 228; for a broader view of Catholicism's aesthetical impact, see Kenneth Clark's *Civilisation*, pp. 167–192).

Baptist theologian Langdon Gilkey saw many of the same characteristics when he probed the reality of Catholicism in search of its distinctive identity. First, he concluded, there is Catholicism's "sense of reality, importance, and 'weight' of tradition and history in the formation of this people and so of her religious truths, religious experience, and human wisdom."

Secondly, there is, "especially to a Protestant, a remarkable sense of humanity and grace in the communal life of Catholics. . . . Consequently the love of life, the appreciation of the body and the senses, of joy and celebration, the tolerance of the sinner, these natural, worldly and 'human' virtues are far more clearly and universally embodied in Catholics and in Catholic life than in Protestants and in Protestantism."

Thirdly, there is Catholicism's "continuing experience, unequalled in other forms of Western Christianity, of the presence of God and of grace mediated through symbols to the entire course of ordinary human life." For Gilkey, a symbol points to and communicates the reality of God which lies beyond it. A symbol can be viewed and appropriated "as *relative*, as a 'symbol' and not God, without sacrificing this relation to the *absoluteness* that makes it a vehicle of the sacred." The experience of the symbol can unite "sensual, aesthetic, and intellectual experience more readily than the experiences of proclamation or of an ecstatic spiritual presence." The Catholic principle of symbol or sacramentality, according to Gilkey, "may provide the best entrance into a new synthesis of the Christian tradition with the vitalities as well as the relativities of contemporary existence."

Finally, there has been "throughout Catholic history a drive toward rationality, the insistence that the divine mystery manifest in tradition and sacramental presence be insofar as possible penetrated, defended, and explicated by the most acute rational reflection" (*Catholicism Confronts Modernity: A Protestant View*, pp. 17–18, 20–22).

A CONCLUDING WORD

It is not a question of arguing that the Catholic Church and the Catholic tradition are necessarily superior to all of the other churches and traditions on this point or that, but that there is within Catholicism a configuration of values which enjoy a normative character in discerning the Christian tradition as a whole.

These values include Catholicism's sense of *sacramentality* (God is present everywhere, the invisible in the visible, within us and within the whole created order); its principle of *mediation* (the divine is available to us as a transforming, healing, renewing power through the ordinary things of life: persons, communities, events, places, institutions, natural objects, etc.); its sense of *communion*, or of peoplehood (we are radically social and so, too, is our relationship with God and God's with us); its drive toward *rationality* and its *critical realism* (reality is neither self-evident nor confined to the realm of ideas); its corresponding respect for *history*, for *tradition*, and for *continuity* (we are products of our past as well as shapers of our present and our future); its conviction that we can have as radical a notion of *sin* as we like so long as our understanding and appreciation of *grace* is even more radical; its high regard for *authority* and *order* as well as for *conscience* and *freedom*; indeed its *fundamental openness to all truth and to every value*—in a word, its *Catholicity*.

Philip J. Murnion

The Community
Called Parish

Catholic Americans, like the majority of their fellow citizens, are a believing people in spite of our secularity. We continue to profess faith in a personal God, in Jesus Christ, and in the work of the Holy Spirit. The American Catholic continues to believe in life after death, in heaven and hell, and in prayer as a way of being in communion with God. In this respect, American Catholics are much like the Irish of both the South and North of Ireland; they too have retained their faith. On the other hand, fellow Catholics in the rest of Europe have considerably less faith in those realities that are explicitly supernatural. Study after study, comparing the United States with Western Europe, finds that people in the United States, and Catholics in particular remain people for whom God is important and religion is significant.

We would, nonetheless, be foolish to deny the significant problems we face in *living* according to that faith. Profession of faith is not the same as living the faith; it takes spirituality to turn the profession of faith into a life of faith. And spirituality is our challenge.

LOSS OF SPIRITUALITY

While people in the United States retain faith in God, that faith tends to be marginal, and increasingly so, to the rest of their lives. The Gallup organization, in particular, has found in its surveys that only one in ten Americans is strongly spiritual, that is, only 10 percent score high on a combination of those questions that ask how important religion is in one's life and how much of an impact it has on one's family and work. But we need not depend on public opinion measures to know that there is a seriously growing gap between faith and life. As a matter of fact, various other studies and personal experience give evidence that there is a considerable loosening of the connections between the two.

Church and parish life once embraced many realms of people's lives. Furthermore, American Catholics traditionally found the meaning of life in relation to their family and neighborhood, rather than in the labor of their jobs. Today the church is less of a self-contained community; now a significant portion of American Catholics measure the success of their lives by their careers. The measure of spirituality is the extent to which it guides a person's understanding of the world and the extent to which it provides a basis for discipline in one's life. Thus, Christian spirituality is a matter of meaning and behavior. Belief, then, is not the characteristic American problem, but the scope of spirituality, the extent to which our understanding and behavior are guided by our belief, surely is.

I am talking, of course, about the process of secularization. For secularization does not mean specifically the loss of faith, but the isolation of faith and religion from the rest of life. It signals the compartmentalization of life into various segments and the removal of religious norms from our everyday activities. In general, there is evidence of secularization not only in the limited extent to which Catholics' personal faith influences their public behavior, but in the ways in which the church itself measures its own performance.

The church in its social services and educational enterprise has largely adopted the criteria of performance belonging to academic and professional disciplines, public opinion, or governmental bodies. Don't we measure the effectiveness of our hospitals primarily by the standards of the medical profession and by reimbursement guidelines? Hasn't there been a considerable shift in the measures by which we judge our schools, adopting values and curricula that allow them to compete according to the criteria established for public school achievement? Hasn't a considerable amount of the social ministry of the church, at both the parish and diocesan level, moved the church into housing and welfare projects that have little explicit relationship to the building up of the church community? There are many reasons for these shifts, not the least being funding that prohibits explicit connections between these services and the church community. These apparent necessities notwithstanding, we have changed and been changed in ways not always faithful to our own priorities.

Secularization is not simply a process that has affected the culture "out there"; it is a process that has affected church culture as well. Thus, church efforts to address precisely our challenge of faith must be directed not so much at shoring up doctrine and orthodoxy, however important these may be, but at reestablishing the link between faith and life, or, as I have suggested above, at reconstructing Catholic spirituality.

SPIRITUALITY AND COMMUNITY

Spirituality depends on *community*. This is true theologically and sociologically, for we believe that God acts in and through the community of the church, and research findings make clear that living according to our faith depends on the support of a community. The work of Reverend Andrew Greeley and others indicates that support of one's spouse and family of origin, or of some other important community, is almost essential for active faith and participation in the church. Other studies further indicate that some communal support is necessary for maintaining a way of life that is distinct from that of the larger culture. Sociologist Peter Berger has described this as the establishment of a plausibility structure, that is, a way of thinking and acting, shared among a group of people, that enables people to maintain a minority position with confidence in the face of contrary cultural pressures.

If spirituality is a problem for us, it may well be partly because community has become a problem. To what extent has the Catholic community undergone erosion? How much do Catholic Americans retain a communal approach to their faith? To what extent have they adopted the individualist ethos of the American culture?

Considerable evidence suggests erosion of church community. Most obviously, we have lost about one-third of American Catholics from regular participation in the Sunday Eucharist. But in addition, many American Catholics have adopted a pick-and-choose attitude about church teaching, selectively adopting their own rules for personal and social behavior. Today's American Catholics clearly have a more voluntary approach than their parents to the way and degree they will participate in church life, whether this is a matter of church teaching, of parish membership, or of the level of participation in parish life. It has been a long time since we could assume that American Catholics would uncritically accept the teachings or the authority of the church, or demonstrate an unquestioning sense of loyalty and responsibility to the church community at any level, including the parish.

Furthermore, we should note that preachers may be as selective as parishioners about church teaching. Some seem to avoid preaching on sexual ethics, while others avoid social ethics. In short, within church structures as well as outside of them, among parishioners and pastors, with regard to teaching and behavior, extensive evidence indicates that American Catholicism has acquired a less communal cast than it once had. Surely, many of those shared factors, such as immigrant status, low income, and discrimination, that fostered an intense community life have dwindled. Now, American Catholics have become part of other communities that have acquired significance for them, communities associated with their middle-class status and income level, with the neighborhoods in which they live, or with their vocational or avocational interests. The church is no longer needed as an enclosed, protective, and exclusive community.

What I am saying is not new: these movements and tendencies have been experienced by people at every level of the church for some years now. In fact, individual pastoral efforts, renewal programs, and actions taken by the leadership of the church are an attempt to counter these trends, to restore a greater sense of church community.

In my view, there are among the current efforts five basic approaches to restoring church community. These are: (1) traditionalism, (2) sectarianism of the left and the right, (3) intimacy, (4) association, and (5) solidarity. Let us look at each in turn.

THE TRADITIONALIST RESPONSE

The traditionalist response to lack of community is a return to the past. This may take the form of proposing a return to the Baltimore catechism, to the Tridentine Mass, to the pious devotions of the past, to earlier forms of church discipline, even if these have lost their religious significance. Traditionalists want to push the priest back into the rectory and sacristy; religious women into their cloisters; lay people into the pews; and the church back into the past. This is an exercise in nostalgia, understandable perhaps, but nostalgia nonetheless. The tradition enshrined in this exercise is not the foundational tradition of the church, but the experience of the immediate past. This view canonizes a particular period in church history and endows it with a special authority that no other period, including the earliest days of the church, would enjoy were this position to be adopted.

Faced with a lack of effective spirituality and of church community, the traditionalist wants to restore rather narrow and rigid rules of church life. Orthodoxy is reduced to the narrow Integrism described by Archbishop John Quinn in *America* (September 21, 1985). Ministry again becomes a clerical preserve. Rules and regulations for receiving the sacraments begin to multiply. Participative structures such as parish councils, built so carefully since Vatican II, are reduced in their importance.

THE SECTARIAN RESPONSE: RIGHT & LEFT

Another approach to restoring spirituality and community is to adopt the view that the church must inevitably be a relatively small band of the elect. Acknowledging that God works in many ways throughout the world, the sectarian concludes that the church can no longer be a church for the masses. Those who are members of the church are special disciples of the Lord, giving testimony to the meaning of the gospel in lives of intense commitment.

Those on the left can find the theological context for their position in Karl Rahner's characterization of the church as a remnant in diaspora. This remnant, this band of disciples, is to be a prophetic and religious elite. Conversion must be a condition of full membership and perhaps only adults can really be members of the church. These disciples engage in symbolic actions (demonstrations, fasts, and the like), rather than in the give-and-take of political life, so as to call the world to justice and peace. This is the pacifist position with respect to the nuclear question: the Catholic Worker position with respect to property and money; these witnesses will risk their own freedom and lives to preserve life and promote justice. Though this is a powerful position, it is one that runs parallel to the normative Catholic style of spirituality and community.

The sectarian of the right also thinks that conversion is a condition for commitment. But for the sectarian right this conversion leads to the testimony of praise rather than the testimony of prophecy. This is the community of the Spirit, the spirituality of the charismatic renewal. Interior renewal is the key; social structures come and go and can never be an adequate expression of the communion of saints. The point is to live as much as possible the new life of the Spirit rather than try to change the world. This kind of community may be experienced in intense renewal weekends or in prayer groups.

Faced with all the seductions of today's world and with the difficulty of living by the gospel, the sectarian approach underscores both the importance of a deep personal relationship with God and the countercultural claims of discipleship. The simple message of the gospel, interpreted with the aid of recent scholarship or simply in the sincerity of one's own heart, must become a personal guide to life, a source of confidence amid confusion, a word to be held up against the nations.

No parish will embody either of these types of the sectarian style of community, but some in the parish will operate with this as the ultimate model of community. Both of these are the community of the special movement that must inevitably be compromised in any parish. They leave little room for the half-hearted or faint-hearted.

COMMUNITY AS INTIMACY

The third response to the problem of community comes from those who would try to restore relationships within the church on intimate terms. This is the community of the encounter weekend, a notion of community fostered by groups like marriage encounter, teen encounter, and renewal programs that primarily focus on emotional relationships among the participants. This community is nourished by sentimental music and themes for the celebration of the liturgy. The intimacy proposed is an emotional intimacy, though surely of emotions related to what we hold dear—love, family, forgiveness, and other needs.

Feelings and immediate experience are given greater significance than knowledge and long-term action. At stake is the extent to which the individual comes to feel strong relationships with others and not the ways in which the community engages in common action. A similar notion of community can be found in certain programs of priestly renewal and staff development. Some priest renewal programs, though not specifically proposing intimacy, put a premium on fraternal relationships among priests and with the bishop, rather than on common mission or the components of common work. Similarly, some staff development programs, through intimacy in prayer and social life, strive to build a community as the basis for the relationship among the staff.

This notion of the intimate community responds to the fragmentation of our time and the anonymity of urban culture by trying to restore intimate personal relationships among people. So, too, within the parish: small communities can be developed, which see as their function mutual nourishment and support, rather than reflection and action. In all these many ways intimacy becomes the goal and form of community.

The intimate community breaks through feelings of alienation. It is very accepting of people, reluctant to let teachings divide the church. The language of preaching is affective; the content of teaching is expressive; the tone of liturgy is sentimental; the process of renewal is reconciliation; the bonds of community are emotional.

Such intimacy usually requires social compatibility: close relationships are hard to achieve and maintain with people very much different from ourselves. Furthermore, true intimacy can be achieved only with a few others, and intimations of intimacy beyond that may not only offer little real support, but foster illusions of a support that is not there when we need it.

ASSOCIATION

A fourth approach to the problem of community is actually to give up the effort to create community altogether and to settle for the parish or church as an association. An association is made up of groups of people who find their respective, and not necessarily shared needs met by participation in some of the association's many activities. A parish is a good association if it offers a variety of useful activities for its diverse members without trying to bind them together in a common faith, a common understanding, or a common action. Thus, the associational parish offers a very good senior citizen program to the elderly whether they participate in the worship or not; housing programs and social service referral programs for the neighborhood; a good youth program; a prayer group for those who want it; and any number of other activities, depending on popular demand. Emphasis here is on providing what people want and need. Delivery of services becomes prominent, and multiplicity of activity is necessary. This is the situation of many parishes whose schools have increasingly become a service for those who wish to pay for it (Catholic or not). Clearly, many of these parish services are of enormous value for those who benefit from them. Many of these activities and services are undertaken not only with religious conviction but within a religious context. Nonetheless, the fundamental direction taken here leads the parish to forsake the attempt to bind people together in a community and to maintain thin threads of connection by respecting the diversity of interest among the parishioners.

The association style is nonjudgmental in preaching; undemanding in its sacrament programs; at its best, enterprising in meeting needs and attracting people. It offers efficient services and is impatient with all the passions of traditionalists or sectarians and all the personal involvement required for intimacy. This is "civilized" religion.

COMMUNITY AS SOLIDARITY

The final position is the effort to create a community of solidarity. Harvard law professor, Roberto M. Unger, defines solidarity as "community moving beyond the circle of intimacy." This speaks to the inclusiveness of community. A similar appeal to inclusiveness is voiced by Parker Palmer in his book *A Company of Strangers*. Palmer reminds us that Jesus did not come to bind us together with those with whom we are already intimate, or with whom we already share close ties. On the contrary, he came to bind us together with strangers, those who are not "of our own." Thus Jesus' constant positioning of the Samaritan, of the stranger, in the center of the community's concern and interest.

A community of solidarity is an inclusive community. It is also a community that sees its faith as a basis for action. By "community of faith" it does not mean small-group personal sharing of belief that can be so helpful to individuals. Instead, it means solidarity in common tradition, theology, and commitment. Here is a group of people whose idea of community allows them to stand together, publicly expressing and demonstrating the significance of their beliefs for public policy, corporate life, local community issues, and family life. This community always links its beliefs and its actions; thus, Sunday liturgy becomes its central act. This inclusive event puts a premium on the action of God in the human community—action that sanctifies our daily actions and makes it possible for us to transcend our own limitations. A community that stresses solidarity puts a high premium on respecting tradition, on linking the past with the future, on building structures for participation and action, on assuring a strong theological foundation for the positions it adopts, and on recognizing the importance of authority for any enduring and authentic community.

In practice, the achievement of solidarity depends on the *quality* of ministry. If a parish is to be at once "catholic" or inclusive, and "holy" or clear about the demands of the gospel, all its efforts must be well done. It is easy enough to be as inclusive as the associational parish, without fostering some clear and common mission. On the other hand, the mission of the sectarian approach is clear, but that approach is inevitably exclusive. The challenge is to remain open to all while representing commitment to discipleship.

It is the quality of all of its ministry that will enable a parish to foster solidarity among its members. Hymns with strong rhythms and good theology, rather than those with complicated meters and sentimental appeals are necessary. Preaching based on good theology, wisdom about life in the world, and personal conviction (the body language of the preacher) is essential. Art and decoration that elicits and allows a broad range of truly religious responses is crucial. Opportunities for joint action (processions, liturgies, social action, feasts) that require little discussion are critical to such a community. The more words needed, the more homogeneous the congregation must be: the more they must share a common "language" with all that that includes.

The parish that fosters solidarity among diverse groups of people through the quality of its activities will still have to complement these efforts by fostering smaller, more homogenous groups within the parish. For besides the experience of Catholic solidarity, most people also need opportunities for prayerful reflection and discussion with people like themselves. For the total parish it is actions, the action of liturgy and ministry, that unify and speak better than words; for subcommunities within the parish, there has to be room for words.

The need for a strong community, well grounded in the quality of its worship, teaching, and action seems clear enough. Here hospitality to all meets the challenge to discipleship. The danger in such an approach is to equate the community of the church with the communion of saints or to neglect the constant conversion necessary for enduring commitment.

TYPICAL EXPRESSIONS

No parish fully embodies any one of these approaches to community. Parishes and their various activities reflect some combination of approaches. Nonetheless, in the mind and behavior of the pastor and other parish leaders, probably one of these approaches represents the ideal, even if this ideal must be adjusted to reality.

Since there are no perfect exemplars of any of these approaches, it is probably helpful to indicate the kinds of activities that illustrate each.

Among the traditionalists, the Tridentine Mass and the Baltimore catechism appropriately fix roles in the church, stress order, hierarchy-and-obedience, and the unique language necessary for Catholic identity. The church discipline of confession before First Communion is a consoling assurance of the relationship between authority and grace. The criteria for a good Catholic school emphasize authority (pope, bishops, commandments, and so forth) more than Jesus, gospel, personal faith. There is great clarity in this approach. The ambiguities of scriptural studies are shunned, trustees picked by the pastor play a more prominent role than councils chosen by parishioners, and sisters in religious garb keep relationships clear.

Confirmation is the central symbol of the sectarian approach to church community, whether of right or left. The principal action is the movement of the Spirit, the principal response is conversion, conversion demonstrated in either works of service (the left) or praise of God (the right). Actions that foster and express such conversion are crucial: weekend renewals, prayer groups, demonstrations—peak episodes of one kind or another. Sincerity and intensity are the criteria for action. And the individual is the centerpiece. Because this approach is not primarily doctrinal, sacramental, or institutional, it tends to be quite ecumenical; Christians of various denominations can come together in these communities.

Marriage is the central sacrament, the model for all the other sacraments, in the intimacy approach. Personal, emotional, intimate relationships are the goal. Small groups, where people can find personal support, are important. Personal contact, knowing everyone's name, feeling close to God and one another are important. Home liturgies, small parishes, much personal sharing, whether in religious education programs or parish councils, is *de rigueur*. The parish as "family" is the image. The parish staff itself expends considerable effort building "community" among themselves. Many efforts are made to foster personal contact in liturgy. The rhythm of music is three-quarter time, the lyrics are as affectionate as were the devotional lyrics of the past.

If any sacramental event typifies the "associational" approach, it may be the funeral Mass—where strangers assemble little is required of the congregation and good service is provided at an important moment. But the good "associational" parish is more active than that might imply. It runs many programs, few of them markedly religious, but all of them of service to people. One institutional expression is the school, if its enrollment has become significantly non-Catholic, but another is preaching that may have settled into nonsectarian humanism—much talk of community and responsibility, little appeal to faith or sharpness of moral judgment. At its best, the homily sounds "human" and is cleverly phrased—nothing offensive.

The Sunday liturgy, well done, the kind that attracts people from neighboring parishes, is the symbol of solidarity. This is the liturgy where celebrant and staff are clearly hosts to the faith and worship of the entire congregation. The preaching shows both serious reflection on the Scriptures and awareness of the concerns of life that people bring to their faith. The worshipping congregation is regularly called to action in their individual lives, as well as in the collective life of the parish. They are encouraged to take action for their personal development as well as for the development of society. In fact, the worship clearly indicates that the church is neither an escape from life nor the preserve of the righteous. The church is empowerment in union with Jesus to go more deeply into the challenges of today's life as partner in the process of creation. The action of the parish will then ensure attention to those who are weak and needy, but it will also engage the talents of those who are strong and creative.

Sacramental preparation programs will present the wonder of God's grace and the demands people face if they are to celebrate the rites with integrity, but they will do so without simply multiplying the hurdles that people must jump.

The church of solidarity will be attracted to the Young Christian Student movement rather than to weekend encounters. And it will find that while Marriage Encounter is helpful, something like the old Christian Family Movement is of more enduring value. In other words, although "therapeutic" services are valuable in the parish, the parish has the opportunity to move beyond therapy to spirituality.

The church of solidarity puts its trust in sound structures—of theology, of good liturgy, of social ministry, and of parish council—rather than in authoritarianism, purity of principle, intensity of commitment, feelings of belonging. Similarly, it is respectful of the power of cultural and social structures and anxious to affect both. Thus it keeps seeking ways to appeal to ideals and to foster personal community, but relies on structures that ensure faithfulness. Symbols are important, all of them: the sacraments, creeds, traditions and sacramentals, the altar, the church, the cross, Marian devotions, fasting, anointing, and the like. This church respects the power of symbols; it avoids either burying this power or manipulating it through endless words. When time-conditioned symbols have lost their power and simply become signs, the church can let them go. Finally, this approach is reflected even in the finances of church and parish. The use of stewardship is related to solidarity, for this kind of parish tries to avoid the trend toward fee-for-service that is developing in the association-like parish or the resort to bingo that has become so prevalent. The parish community should together pay for what is important to the whole community.

MAKING CHOICES

It has been my proposal that the great American Catholic challenge is the challenge of spirituality and that strong spirituality requires a strong community. Recognizing that Catholic community has undergone serious erosion, many in the church are trying to restore it. Different approaches are attempted. In parish after parish, diocese after diocese, actions are being taken to foster church community, actions that respectively reflect various approaches to community. In choosing one or another approach, we determine the shape of tomorrow's church. I am clearly urging one approach to community, that of solidarity, admittedly more elusive and demanding than the alternatives. For the alternatives, each in its own way, represent reductionism—a determination to minimize complexity and ambiguity. It is this more elusive and demanding approach that is more faithful to our tradition and pertinent to our situation. It calls for an adult church, where lay people, indeed all, are treated as adults. It is, I believe, in fact, a commitment to the principles of Vatican II that will ensure that we remain faithful to this project and persist in this fellowship.

Timothy E. O'Connell, Ph.D.

A Theology of Sin

It is clear that the notion of sin has fallen on hard times. Whether the reality of sin is any less present on the contemporary scene is debatable, but there seems little doubt that the language of sin is far less in evidence. In fact, it seems that people go to great lengths to avoid using the word "sin" or referring to its reality. They are embarrassed to introduce that perspective. Why is that?

In this essay I hope to provide an answer to that question. And I hope to suggest the ways in which it remains both appropriate and essential for us to talk about sin. I will begin with a very general comment on the reality and the idea of sin. Then I will sketch out in some detail three understandings of sin that were part of the older tradition of moral theology in the Catholic Church. I will indicate the reasons for these understandings, and the problems that were connected with them. Several contemporary developments in philosophy and the social sciences will set a basis on which a contemporary theology of sin can then be built.

GOD-TALK

"Is it a sin for me to be an atheist?" This is the sort of question that, at first blush, appears quite plausible but upon reflection is utterly absurd. After all, if I am an atheist and if I am accurate in my atheism, then who will punish me for my sin? And if I truly see myself as an atheist, what am I doing asking a question about sin? What meaning can the word have for me?

This line of reflection is intended to show clearly that sin is "God-talk." It is an example of religious language, of language that makes sense only in a world rooted in God. Apart from God, in the absence of God, sin is literally meaningless. Sin is not synonymous with moral or ethical evil. It is quite different. Even atheists can be unethical, but only believers can sin. Indeed, sin is something that arises from their awareness of God, from their conviction that they live in the presence of God.

We can go further than this. Sin is a reality that follows from the relationship between God and human persons. Sin, whatever its precise meaning may be, points at a world where things are somehow not what God wants them to be. It implies that God is present and that he cares. And it asserts that despite this care, something about our world is wrong. So to talk of sin is paradoxically to make an act of faith in God.

SCRIPTURE

This sense of God's presence to the world and to humanity is quite evident in the scriptural references to sin. And there are many such references. Indeed, in some ways, one could describe the Bible as a book about sin, or at least as a book about what God does about sin. Other articles in this issue present the biblical evidence in great detail. Let me only add a few comments that are especially pertinent to our reflections.

In some of the earliest strata of the biblical material sin

means nothing more than "missing the mark," making a mistake. Even unintentional mistakes could be considered sins, since even they were not in accord with God's will for the world. But since the human challenge to free response is so central to the theology of covenant, to the self-understanding that Israel had, it was not long before the idea of sin was further nuanced. "Sin" came to be understood as a free offense against God, a free refusal to do what He wanted.

And what was that will of God? It was love of himself and of the neighbor. In the first instance love of God himself, and so all sins are ultimately subspecies of the paradigmatic sin, idolatry. Sometimes the idolatry is straightforward, as in the case of the golden calf (Ex. 32:1–6; Deut. 9:7–21). Other times it is the idolatry of self: pride, self-sufficiency, obstinacy (e.g. Deut. 32:18; Is. 10:13–19; Ezek. 28:2). But in either case idolatry. And in the second instance the will of God was love of neighbor, and so sin is the refusal to live out that love. Of course Israel was not always sophisticated in their understanding of "neighbor;" often they had quite an exclusivist understanding, where foreigners were easily ignored. But they did at least realize that God called them at the same time to worship of himself and to service of fellow human persons.

In our time this emphasis upon concern for neighbor is very much in evidence, so it does not require much comment. Perhaps what deserves highlighting is the theme already mentioned: that sin was always understood religiously and that God and neighbor were consequently viewed together and not in isolation. Consider the case of David's sin, where he arranges for the death of Uriah and takes his wife Bathsheba. In our modern perspective (reacting against a prior ignoring of our obligations to the neighbor) we would emphasize that David has sinned against Uriah and Bathsheba. But what does he say? "I have sinned against Yahweh" (II Sam. 12:13). The offense against the neighbor is at the same time an offense against God, because the believer is aware of the presence of God to the life that is shared with the neighbor.

This unified perspective is nowhere so clearly affirmed as in the New Testament story of the Prodigal Son. For there the repentant son says not once but twice that his apology will be phrased: "Father, I have sinned against God and against you" (Lk. 15:18 & 21). Always God is found in those acts where the believer refuses to love the neighbor and in so doing refuses to respond faithfully to the love that comes from God.

In the Bible, then, we have found two conceptions of sin. The more ancient sees sin as any mistake, any contradiction of the divine plan for life. The more developed sees sin as the free human refusal to participate in that plan. Yet a third conception should also be mentioned here.

Near the beginning of John's Gospel, the author has John the Baptist, in pointing out Jesus, announce: "There is the lamb of God who takes away the sin of the world" (Jn. 1:29). Note that he speaks of sin, not sins, singular, not plural. The Baptist is not pointing out the one who will forgive our many sins, failings, and faults. He is announcing the one who will deal with the sinful situation in our world, who will heal the world's brokenness, illumine its darkness, bridge its chasms of isolation. He will deal with the sin-of-the-world, *hae hamartia tou cosmou*, and in that way will make it possible for us to overcome our tendency to sins of our own.

In formulating things in this way, John the Evangelist is focussing on a very profound, almost metaphysical understanding of sin, an understanding that is different from the two already mentioned, that does not deny them but that does complement and enrich and complete them with its own truth. It is an understanding of sin not merely as some thoughtless mistake nor even as some conscious act, but as a tragic cosmic situation: humankind alienated from God, from one another, and ultimately even from itself.

TRADITIONAL VISION

If we find these diverse understandings of sin in the Bible, it is not surprising that we also find variety in the theological conceptions developed through the centuries. All the more is this to be expected when we focus on the fact that "sin" is the believer's word for things not right in our world. As our vision of the world changes, as our presumption of how things should be changes, and most of all as our understanding of ourselves as human persons changes, so our understanding of sin will change. Thus, our next task will be to review some traditional visions of sin, to try to understand why these visions were formulated and what perspective on life and humanity they presumed. This will lead us simultaneously to a respect for that tradition and to an awareness of its ultimate inadequacy. And it will, I hope, provide us with a basis for a renewed, enriched, and illuminating understanding for our own time.

Essentially, I want to suggest that the word "sin" can point to three different realities. What is characteristic of the traditional understanding, the understanding that the church lived out of for centuries, was the way in which those three realities were organized. And what has now changed is the way in which those three realities are organized, so that today the word "sin" still refers to three realities but they are understood quite differently.

What is "sin"? "A sin is an action by which I refuse to do what I believe God wants me to do, and thereby injure my neighbor." This definition seems fairly reasonable. It is the kind of definition one could encounter most anywhere. But did you notice the way in which the answer modified the question? The question asked about "sin." The answer described "a sin." That is, the answer understood sin not as a reality but as an event, an act. And typically so. In the traditional view, the root understanding of sin, the very paradigm of sin, was that it is an act. Sin was something people do. At times, this act was understood very trivially, as if sins could even be committed by accident. At other times it was understood with considerable sophistication, when attention was paid to the impediments to human freedom, the requirements of a genuine evaluative understanding, and the mystery of genuine human decision. No matter, in all cases sin was understood as an act. Indeed the tradition could speak of "actual sins."

The tradition did not limit its understanding of sin to actual sin, however. It did affirm the existence of a quite different reality, original sin. Let me call that "sin as a fact," sin not as something we do, but as something we are subject to. But how was original sin understood? At least in the popular mind, original sin could be defined as "exactly like actual sin, only you didn't do it. But you might as well have, for you are guilty nonetheless!" That is, original sin was understood as a variation on the paradigm of actual sin. Original sin was somehow both like and unlike actual sin. And precisely because original sin was so understood, most Catholics today find it an embarrassment. They either do not believe in original sin, or they choose to avoid the question. Not only do they view the biblical images of apple tree, serpent and garden as quaint; they view the very reality of original sin as quaint. They can accept the reality of actual sin for they accept the truth of human responsibility, but they cannot accept the fact that we should be punished for the actual sins of another. That is unjust; and if that is what original sin is, then they cannot accept original sin.

In the tradition, there was yet a third type of sin. It spoke of the "state of mortal sin," that situation which arose from the act of mortal sin. It described a situation in which a person was abidingly cut off from God, out of the state of grace, and liable to hell. It described sin as the quality of a person in that situation, so that the person could be described as being "in sin."

But this understanding of sin, too, was viewed as derivative, not basic. It depended on the concept of actual sin for its meaning. After all, the Council of Trent specifically taught that Catholics must confess their mortal sins by species and number. It was insufficient for Catholics to announce "Bless me, Father, I am a sinner;" they must go on to describe the actual sins from which this situation arose. This is very curious! It is as if one announced that a friend was dead, only to be questioned about the precise location of the bullet holes. What is more important: being dead or how one got there? The tradition seemed to suggest that the acts were more important than the resulting state.

In summary then, Catholic tradition asserted three meanings for the word "sin." I call them sin as fact, sin as an act, and sin as a state. What is really significant is that the overall understanding was constructed around the second of those perspectives. It was sin as an act that was taken as the paradigm. Sin as a fact and sin as a state were defined in terms of, and made dependent upon, sin as an act. And, as I have implied in this description, that had regrettable effects. The overall view of the Catholic tradition can therefore be conceived in the following way:

FACT ◄———————————ACT———————————► STATE

TWO DIMENSIONS

Much of that has changed. But what has changed? The understanding of sin, to be sure. But as we saw earlier, our understanding of sin is really a function of our understanding of ourselves as human persons and as believers. It is that self-understanding that has changed.

In medieval philosophy, the description of the human person was premised on the fact that the human person is an *agent*. The human act was the fundamental category in terms of which the overall anthropology was developed. Human beings were identified with their acts in such a way that total description of human actions equalled description of the human person. It was an anthropology that could be described as "two-dimensional." Just as a piece of paper, having length and width but not depth, presents itself to us as immediate, evident, transparent and obvious, so this traditional anthropology described human beings in such terms.

Readers who studied medieval philosophy in college may remember the topic of Rational Psychology. We were introduced to concepts such as impressed species, agent intellect, and the like: a very intricate view of the human person, but at the same time a very shallow one. It was as if the human person were a large jigsaw puzzle composed of many pieces fitted together in a complex manner, but with all the pieces neatly next to each other—none above or below, none thicker or thinner. The intricacy was all two-dimensional. And the result was that the person, like the puzzle, was somehow simultaneously complex yet ultimately trivial.

Note that it was medieval philosophy that described the human person in this way. That description was not an article of faith, it was not intrinsic to the Christian gospel. And yet since our theology of sin is rooted in our understanding of ourselves, that anthropology could not avoid being absorbed into the proclamation of the faith. When that occurred, it was absorbed in its weakness as well as in its strength, and that same trivial complexity, or complex triviality, became a characteristic of the theology of sin. Still, inasmuch as the anthropology was not part of the faith, changing it does not involve changing the faith. And therein lies the hope of the future.

CHANGE OF VISION

For change it did. The last hundred years have seen a tremendous advance in human self-understanding, and this advance can fairly be summarized as the discovery of depth. It was the geometric third dimension that was added. It was the element of mystery, ambiguity, distance that was highlighted. Indeed, almost immediately the term "depth" was used to describe this advance. Rational Psychology was supplanted by Depth Psychology under the leadership of Sigmund Freud. In the writings of the German philosophers who developed this perspective, the term *grund* (depth) was much in evidence. Heidegger, Husserl, von Hildebrand, and later Rahner and the Fuchs often spoke of *Grunderkenntis* (deep awareness), *Grundfreiheit* (deep freedom) and the like. In the popular mind, this whole approach eventually became identified with the term *Grundentscheidung* (deep decision), which was translated *option fondamentale* or fundamental option.

But the core of this approach is found not in any item of terminology but in the conviction that the human person is three-dimensional, characterized by rich and mysterious depths. Human actions emerge from an abiding core of the human person and find their ultimate significance in that person. The most important question to ask of a human person is not "What did you do?" but "Who are you?"

This introduction of the third dimension, as it occurred over the last century, had obvious effects on our understanding of ourselves as human persons and on our understanding of sin. In recent years, however, another development has further affected those understandings.

Science fiction writers like to speak of the "fourth dimension." They like to remind us of time as a dimension within which we live. In life we deal not only with the three dimensions of space—up and down, back and forth, here and there, near and far; we deal also with the fourth dimension of time—before and after, soon and late, recent and ancient. And they are not alone in pursuing this insight. Process philosophers, particularly in the English-speaking world, have grown increasingly sensitive to the dimension of time, with its emphasis on movement, development and change. One thinks of figures such as Whitehead, Hartshorne and Cobb. Continental existentialists such as Sartre developed analogous ideas. And together, they remind us that in talking about human beings, we are in some sense talking not about nouns, but about verbs. We are talking about human be-ings. Or, if you will, we are talking about human becomings. There is in us the element of change, of incompleteness, of a "not-yet" which is everpresent in our consciousness. And as this temporality affects our perception of ourselves, it also affects who we are and how we live. We live in a four-dimensional world. And so perhaps the most relevant question of all is not "Who are you?" but "Where are you going?"

This sense of temporality is not nearly so well incorporated into our cultural self-concept as is the third dimension. It is of more recent vintage. Change has come upon us so abruptly, and accelerates at such a significant rate that it leaves us quite frightened. Books such as Toeffler's *Future Shock* speak to that fear of change. But it is here. We do live in a four-dimensional universe and the presence of the fourth dimension is becoming increasingly significant.

SIN TODAY: A FACT

Much earlier we said that our understanding of sin is greatly influenced by our understanding of ourselves. So now the question confronts us: how shall we understand sin in our four-dimensional world? If the understandings of sin that appear in the catechisms, understandings premised on our two-dimensional world, seem silly and irrelevant, what shall be our alternative? Can we use this very traditional term in a way that will illuminate our own experience? Can we understand sin in a manner that makes it both real and important? I believe that we can. Let me now outline an understanding of sin that seems to me to meet those criteria. Let us return to the three traditional aspects of sin—fact, act and state—and let me try to re-order all of them and refocus each of them in turn.

I start with sin as a fact. Why? One reason is that it is generally good practice to begin with facts! Another, more significant reason is because our experience of sin starts with sin as a fact. Picture the moment of birth. The physician or midwife holds up the newborn baby, slaps it smartly on the behind. And in response the baby gives forth a cry. What a powerfully symbolic exchange! The baby enters the human world, and what is its first experience? It is attacked! It is treated roughly, insensitively, almost brutally! Of course, we know that this action is in the baby's best interest. Still, the gesture is far from affectionate. And how does the baby respond? It protests. It screams out its displeasure, its anger, its fear, its surprise. It is as if the baby hoped to be born into heaven, and in the first instant it discovers that it has landed in the wrong place. This is not heaven. This is not the kingdom. This is not a place where all is well. And having discovered that, the baby gives forth a cry, a protest.

As time goes on, the same insight is re-encountered, and in much more profound ways. Over and over again, expectations are disappointed, plans are unfulfilled, desires are contradicted. The infant makes a sound by which it announces its hunger—and its diaper is changed. The three-year-old cries out in the terror of a nightmare—and the babysitter has the TV turned too loud to hear. The first-grader attempts to share the experience of starting school—and is not understood. Over and over again, the young child discovers that this is not the best of all possible worlds. It is not the world we would like to inhabit. And, if God is indeed good, then it is not the world he meant us to inhabit.

It is a sinful world. The baby does not yet know whose fault this sin is, but that does not make it any less real. The sin is a fact, and the baby is its victim. Sin here is not something the baby does, but something the baby discovers, experiences, encounters. But it is sin. Indeed, it is original, the *original* sin. It is sin in its most basic and elemental sense, sin as a situation, sin as a reality, sin as a curse under which we all stand.

But is this tragic dimension of life really sin? After all, we defined "sin" as a religious concept, as a term meaningful only to believers. And all human persons, believer and unbeliever alike, encounter the tragic. So how can the two be the same?

It is true that all human beings experience this dark side of life, but it is also true that all human cultures have found this dark side sufficiently perplexing as to deserve an explanation. The ancient Persians, for example, explained it by positing the existence of two gods, one good and the other evil. The two gods are in mortal combat with neither clearly the victor. We are simply caught in the middle, experiencing sometimes good and other times ill. Not an unreasonable explanation! The French philosopher, Albert Camus, found an explanation in his assertion that the world is absurd, that the world is intrinsically evil, and that part of its evil is to have the sometimes appearance of good. For Camus the only logical response to life is suicide, and therefore he proposes survival as a final frantic act of human independence.

EXPLAINING THE FACT

The Judaeo-Christian tradition likewise experiences the evil of life and feels the need to provide an explanation. Characteristically, it proposes its explanation in the form of a story.

Once upon a time, it says, there were a man and a woman, intensely happy, utterly at peace. They lived in a place where all their needs were met and all their desires satisfied. So comfortable was their setting, both physically and emotionally, that they did not even experience the need for clothing.

In this veritable garden of delight, there was, however, one tree whose fruit they were not to taste. (If you ask why this tree is forbidden, the storyteller will quite rightly tell you not to interrupt the tale. After all, no story is perfect!) But they disobeyed and ate the fruit. Admittedly, it was not altogether their fault; they were tempted by some other-worldly force who took the form of a snake. And it was even less the fault of the man (for whom the storyteller evidently has special sympathy). But even he ate the fruit. Both of them violated the order that had constituted and supported their paradise. They had disrupted that order. (Note that "order" means both command and structure.) Obviously they know it, and are not proud of themselves. Suddenly they feel a need to hide, from God behind trees and from each other behind clothes. They have made their world one of dis-order, a place of subterfuge and deception, a place of domination and dissimulation. They have made it a place where things are not right. They have made it a place of sin.

What is the point of the story then? It is very simple. We do not really know why things are often so bad in our world. We do not have any "scientific" explanation. There is no item of history that will explain our predicament. Still we believe in God. Almost against the data of our experience we believe in God. And so we will not blame him. If blame must be placed somewhere, we will place it upon ourselves. We will accept responsibility for the darkness that inhabits our world. We will accept the guilt. And since the tragic has always been part of our experience, we will assert and presume that the first disruptive act occurred at the very beginning of our human history. None of us is guiltless. All of us—and not God—are responsible for the mess we are in. In yet another sense, this sin is original, for it comes from the very beginning.

So evil is a fact. That is a sad truth, and it must surely cause us all pain. But at the same time, it is a somehow dignified truth. We are sin's victims, and our pain is not our fault. If we must suffer, then at least we can enjoy the compensation of appropriate self-pity. That is, if sin is merely a fact. . . .

AN ACT

But it is not. Granted that Adam and Eve did the destructive and disobedient deed, so have you and so have I. Granted that they said "no" to life, so have we. Granted that they indulged in self-serving deception, so have we. Granted that they have tried to dominate life when they ought to have harmonized with it, so have we. Granted that they have introduced sin into the world, so indeed have we.

Above and beyond sin as a fact, there also exists sin as an act. The deeds that we have done, the acts that we have perpetrated are not always grand acts, often they are small and trivial. Still, we in our own unique ways have made things worse. If sin is a fact today, it is partly our fault too. And not just today, in the full bloom of our adulthood. As we moved out of our childhood we did the deed. Perhaps even beginning at the age of nine or ten, at the very "age of reason," we knowingly did what we knew would make it worse. In a simple and childish way of course, but little by little we grasped the fact that our behavior could make it better or worse. And at times, from selfishness or fear or anger or spite or fatigue, we chose to make it worse. In that moment, we encountered and experienced and indeed perpetrated sin as an act. No longer was it sufficient to say "It's a shame and I need help." Now it became necessary to say "I was wrong and I need forgiveness."

A DIRECTION

As we moved into adulthood, however, we passed another turning point. It is difficult to say just when or how, but we discovered the mystery of our freedom.

I can remember, as a college student, staring into the mirror, looking into my own eyes, sensing the depths and the mysteries that lay behind those strange organs. For the first time I realized in a genuine and convincing way that I was free. I was not on a leash; no one controlled me. I had the power to say "yes" or "no," to affirm or reject whatever was presented. I was not a dog or cat. I was a human person, and I was free. That freedom was a frightening thing. I almost wished it didn't exist. But it did, and that made all the difference.

I had the power to choose how I would stand towards life. I had the power to choose the posture I would assume, the attitude I would enflesh, the direction I would take. I had the power to choose to stand on the side of good, to resist evil, to combat the fact of sin, to struggle that life might be better and not worse. Or I had the power to stand on the side of sin, to accept it and embrace it, to let the fact of sin define my life and shape it, to let go of the dream of a better world and settle for a cozy spot in the broken world that we know, to take sin as given, and let it shape my life. Far more frightening than any simple act of sin, I had the power to make sin my very state of life. And so, in that awesome moment when I discovered the full meaning of human freedom, I also discovered the possibility and therefore, in some sense, the reality of the state of sin.

Or perhaps the word "state" sounds too definitive. Perhaps it suggests more clarity and finality than we actually experience in life. For we do live in a four-dimensional world where we are much more becoming than being. So perhaps the word should be "direction." I discovered that sin could be the direction of my life, that my path could be away from the dream as well as toward it, that ambiguity could be allowed to progressively deepen into death as well as move toward the clarity of new life. I discovered that I could shape the direction of my life: that is a human insight. And I understood the alternative directions as sanctity and sin, union with God and isolation from him, fidelity and idolatry: that is the conviction of Christian faith.

What is sin, then? It is all three of these: a fact, an act, and a direction. But it is all three, precisely in that order. We begin with original sin, the most basic and fundamental meaning of the word. We grow into the possibility and the reality of actual sin, an expression of our human freedom of choice. And we finally face the possibility of a sinful life-direction, sin in its ultimate most profound and fearsome, most characteristically human form. In the end, the deepest question each of us adults faces is the question of where we will point our lives, the question of direction. In some sense everything else leads up to this and is important because of how it relates to this. Sin as a direction-possibility and its blessed alternative of a direction pointed toward God: these alternatives are, in the end, what life is all about.

So what does "sin" mean? It means three things. And they should be ordered as follows:

FACT ⟶ ACT ⟶ DIRECTION

MORTAL AND VENIAL

Catholics who have been raised in the traditional understanding of sin will find it difficult to avoid a question. No matter how much they may like the overall vision of sin proposed here, they will wonder how it relates, or if it relates, to the various terms they learned as children. And in particular they will wonder about the terms "mortal" and "venial." Do these terms have meaning any more? Are they useful or appropriate? It is obvious that they used to be employed in a way that focussed almost exclusively on individual acts. But that is not surprising, given that the entire understanding of sin had a similar focus. But must they have this focus? Or can they be reconceived in such a way as to be helpful and meaningful in a four-dimensional world?

I think so. Indeed, I suspect that, if we simply take these words at face value, we will find them almost self-evident in their importance. Take the word "mortal." What does it mean? Deadly, utterly destructive, producing annihilation. Apart from the world of religion, in ordinary conversation, we may speak of a "mortal blow," "the curse of mortality," "wounds that turned out to be mortal," and so on. And take the word "venial." What does it mean? In both religious and legal contexts it refers to things that are pardonable, light, ordinary, etc. Current usage does not often find this word in non-moral contexts. But even apart from the religious focus on God one can speak of a "venial fault," a "venial matter," and the like.

With these understandings, then, we can return to our vision of sin and sense the connection. After all, we view sin as something awry with our world and with our relationship with God. But how bad is our situation? Is it hopeless (mortal) or resolvable (venial)? What about our relationship with God? Is it, like a marriage that has been abused too often, simply hopeless and dead? Or is it wounded but still alive, needing remedial attention but still capable of responding to that attention? What about our actions? Are they deadly in their effects (mortal)? Or are they simply ordinary (venial) faults? Would our destructive deeds be better described as deadly or daily? Mortal or venial?

"Was it a mortal sin?" That is, I think, a meaningful question. It asks whether an act or series of acts has been hopelessly destructive. And some acts do have that effect. Relationships are killed, blessings are thrown away, things of beauty are destroyed. And sometimes there is nothing the agent can do to restore the prior state of things. Perhaps an undeserved gift can inject hope into the situation; perhaps a grace can come. But nothing else will do the trick. So it is meaningful to speak of "mortal sin." But notice that what makes the sin mortal is not some arbitrary stipulation of a human authority. Rather what makes it a mortal sin is the objective and intrinsic fact that the sin is mortal! That is, its intrinsic destructiveness is what makes a sin mortal. The deed either was hopelessly destructive or it was not. If so, it can be rightly termed "mortal." If not, then it was in fact "venial."

So again we hear the question: Was it a mortal sin? My answer is simple: I don't know. You tell me. Is your relationship with God and neighbor still alive? Are you in fact still trying to love and serve, albeit with weakness and failing? If so, then evidently the sin was not mortal but merely venial. If not, if there is really nothing left, if you have given up, then it is evident your sin was mortal. In either case we are speaking not about some legal definition of particular acts, but about the intrinsic effects of behavior, and of their underlying human decisions, upon relationships with God and neighbor.

CONCLUSIONS

Having responded to that predictable question about the traditional terms, we are now in a position to bring this essay to a close. And by way of doing that, I wish to list several significant conclusions which seem to follow from what has been said here.

First, I think it is clear that sin is a real thing, a substantial and fearsome reality. But it is also clear that as such, sin is much less something we do than it is something in which we find ourselves. It is the situation we inhabit, the air we breathe, the glasses we wear. Of course, it is not the only situation, air, glasses; "where sin abounded, grace did more abound" (Rom. 5:20). There is the good news, too, of God's free gift in Jesus. About that the next issue of *Chicago Studies* will have much to say. But for now it is enough to affirm the pernicious reality that goes by the name of sin.

Second, it follows that in raising questions about sin, the locating of fault and blame is far from the highest priority. Because of our overwhelming emphasis upon individual acts (and because of a close relationship of Catholic moral theology and canon law) our past history tended to obsess over the issue of culpability. Whose fault is it? If the objective is to assign blame so that punishment may be justly assigned, then this is an important question. But if the objective is to facilitate salvation and healing, forgiveness and hope, then the question becomes unimportant. If a house has been burglarized, who cares which family member left the door unlocked? Far more important to take steps to retrieve the stolen merchandise! So this understanding of sin has the surprising effect of separating reflections on sin from conversations on culpability. We care less and less about *who* sinned, and more and more about what sin—and salvation—really are.

It is a very healthy thing, too, to separate the question of sin from the obsession with culpability. For in our four-dimensional world we realize how problematic it is to assign that culpability. The old two-dimensional textbooks said that Catholics were to confess their actual sins, those committed with knowledge and freedom. And many of us, in our attempt to satisfy that requirement, have been embarrassed at our confusion. Was I really free? Did I truly comprehend the meaning of what I did? Questions such as these had the effect of making us feel very foolish; we were not only evil, we were dumb and evil! But now we realize that people quite commonly have these doubts. The three-dimensional mystery of the human person, to say nothing of fourth-dimensional mutability and process, makes it difficult if not impossible to be certain about culpability.

And who cares? Even if I did not freely choose to say the bitter things that have scarred my marriage, the relationship remains wounded. Even if I was not precisely "guilty" of actual sin, I find myself trapped by the burden of sin as a fact. So in either case, I stand in need of redemption. If my sin was free, then perhaps my need can be termed "forgiveness." If I am more the victim of this sin, then perhaps it should be called "healing." But in either case I need a gift of new possibility and new life, a gift which I cannot create for myself and which I can only hope will come as wondrous and gratuitous grace.

Which brings us to a direct comment on the function of the Sacrament of Reconciliation. More will be said about this in a future issue of *Chicago Studies*. But we should not overlook one obvious conclusion of these reflections. Reconciliation is intended to respond to the reality of sin. But what sort of sin? In the past it was presumed that Reconciliation primarily responded to actual sin. I would suggest that it responds to all three sorts of sin. Where a person has held to a destructive life-direction, Reconciliation may be the affirmation and celebration of a genuine conversion achieved through grace and ratified in the sacramental encounter. Where behavior has made things worse without actually destroying a positive life-direction and a relationship with God and neighbor, the sacrament may serve to facilitate recommitment by proclaiming the already-offered forgiveness of God. Where life has presented one with burden and scar, with failure and frustration, with hopelessness and shame, the sacrament comes as healing balm, tangibly presented love, revitalized relationship, deeper possibility, and new life happening right before our eyes. And when, perhaps most typically, we experience ourselves as in the midst of a strange mixture of all these, when we know ourselves to be trapped by sin, when we suspect that we have made it worse even if we cannot quote chapter and verse, when we are troubled by the ambiguity of our life direction, then the Sacrament of Reconciliation offers a redeeming response to that whole very human complexity.

In doing that the Sacrament paradoxically affirms the reality of sin. Indeed, in its gesture and word, its experience and context it evocatively says what I have taken many words to describe. And it proclaims what I take to be the ultimate Christian truth: the mess we are in is real. But God is more real. And in his love for us we have a hope that will not fail.

Karl Rahner

Why Am I a Christian Today?

I shall try to report what I am trying to say and be when I say: "I would like to be a Christian." One has to say here, "I would like to be." In the Christian view, one must in the end leave it to God to decide whether one really is—in theory and, above all, in practice—what one claims to be and automatically is in social life and in the Church on the surface of everyday life.

I would like to be a person who is free and can hope, who understands and shows by his actions that he himself is at the mercy of his freedom, a freedom which throughout life is creating itself and making him finally what he should be according to his original pattern of human nature, a person who is faithful, who loves, who is responsible. I am well aware that such words can very easily sound very lofty and theoretical, that they create a feeling that real life is being shrouded in a haze of fine words, but also that in their meaning they are far from "clear." We can ignore the first difficulty because no one, not even the most primitive materialist, can do without ideals which, because they have not yet been reached, draw one on and keep one's life moving. As to the second difficulty, the vagueness of the "ideals" just mentioned, this must be admitted. All words which express or invoke the totality of human existence are "unclear": that is, they cannot be defined by being assigned a place in an intrinsically clear system of coordinates distinct from them. They are "unclear" because they point to the one, most real, absolutely single totality which we call "God." For us, however, this "unclarity" has an absolutely positive and irreplaceable function, and a person who does not accept this "unclarity" as a good and a promise drifts into trivial stupidity.

I am convinced that such a free history of real self-determination takes place in and through all the impenetrable details, and uncertainties, perplexities, inadequacies, all the starts that never reach a tangible goal, and all the internal and external determinisms which fill our lives and make them, even for ourselves, almost a meaningless accident. I am convinced that a human being's historical life moves in freedom toward a point of decision, that it contains this decision in itself, that life as a whole must be answered for and does not simply run away into a void in these details. Of course, this outlook on which my life is based, which is almost inescapable and yet required of me, is nothing but breathtaking optimism, so terrifying that everything in me trembles with the sheer audacity of it.

Yet I cannot give up this attitude, cannot let it decay into the triviality of the everyday or the cowardice of scepticism. Of course philosophers and other theorists of human life can talk forever about the meaning of freedom, responsibility, love, selflessness, and so forth. Nor do I find such terms clear and transparent. Nevertheless they have a meaning and guide choices in the thousand and one trivia of life. It may seem that such words can be analysed psychoanalytically, biologically and sociologically and revealed as an avoidable or unavoidable superstructure on much more primitive things, which alone can count as true reality. I also constantly discover cases in which, to my consolation or my horror, such detailed analyses are in fact correct. And yet because in such attempts at analysis as elsewhere it is always the same responsible subject which is at work, and is responsible even for this destruction of its own subjectivity because it is the subjectivity that does the work, in the end, on the whole, such attempts at destruction are in my view false.

I am not trying to escape from myself and have no desire to escape from my responsible freedom as a true subject. Will this being left to oneself end in my case in a final protest or a final acceptance? Since I exist and an acceptance is so firmly planted in me and my freedom, my acceptance seems to me in one sense so obvious an implication of the ground of reality that I often feel that all protests against one's own existence in its full particularity are no more than passing incidents in a fundamentally universal acceptance of oneself and the whole of one's existence. On the other hand I cannot escape the knowledge that a subject's freedom cannot be directed simply to this or that particularity alone, but existence as such, and that therefore the temptation to straightforward rejection, to a total protest (which is the essence of true sin), always exists and can become a reality in the triviality of a banal existence.

I accept myself. I accept myself without protest with all the accidents of my biological and historical existence, even though I have the right and duty to change and improve those elements in it which I feel oppressive. It is this very critical desire to change my existence in all its dimensions which is the form and the proof of the fact that in the end I really accept this existence. But for all the hope of really changing something, this existence (my own and that of others, for which I also feel responsible) remains opaque, burdensome, will not dissolve into controllable transparency; it remains short and full of pains and problems, subject to death, to which all generations remain exposed.

I accept this existence, accept it in hope. I accept it in the one hope which includes and supports everything, which one can never know that one really has (or only pretends to have because at a particular moment one feels marvellous). This hope, whose inner light is its only justification, is the hope that the incomprehensibility of existence (for all the obvious beauty it also contains) will one day be revealed in its ultimate meaning and will be this finally and blissfully. It is a total hope, which I cannot replace with a vague mixture of a little hope and un-admitted despair, though this may always also be present in the deepest core of existence when the foreground of my life seems to be occupied by nothing but meaninglessness and de-spair. This all-embracing and unconditional hope is what I want to have. I declare my allegiance to it; it is my supreme possibility and what I must answer for as my real task in life. Who will convince me that this is utopia, that such a hope is false and cowardly, worse than if I let myself fall into a radical scepticism which is theoretically possible, but in the reality of life where we take responsibility and love is impossible to maintain? This ultimate basic trust in the complete and com-prehensive meaning of existence is not a free-floating ideology; it not only supports everything else, but is also supported by all the other experiences of life. It includes (at least partial) ex-perience of meaning, light, joy, love and faithfulness, which make an absolute claim.

These specific experiences which support ultimate hope just as they are supported by it will have to be discussed later. For the present, I take it for granted that we are above the dull naiveté which thinks (as even sophisticated scientists some-times do) that matter is more real than mind or spirit, which floats over matter as no more than a sort of exhalation or side effect of physical constructions. These "materialists" do not see that they cannot come into contact with this matter except through mind, or they are totally unable to say what matter as such really and fundamentally is.

This free fundamental act of existence, which can only be described haltingly and of course does not exist only where it is explicitly talked about, moves towards what or, better, the person, we call God. I know that this word is obscure, by definition the most obscure word there can be, the word which it is genuinely impossible to include among the other words of human language as one more word. I know that what is meant by the word may be present in a person's life even if its name is never spoken by the person. (Anonymous theists do exist because in the totality of reality God is not a particular entity like Australia or a blackbird, which one really doesn't need to know anything about, but supports everything, is the origin of everything, permeates everything and therefore exists and rules anonymously but genuinely as the unexpressed condition of possibility for all knowledge and all freedom wherever mind is at work.) I know that today what we mean by God is very difficult to imagine by means of the image of a great architect of the world (which was still acceptable in the period of the Enlightenment). I know that the word "God" has been used to do any number of terrible and stupid things. I know that it is very easy to keep on finding, in oneself and in others, stupid misunderstandings which do their mischief under cover of the word "God." And yet I say that the ultimate basis of my hope in the act of unconditional acceptance of the meaningfulness of my existence is promised to me by God. This does not make him the projection of my hope into a void for in the instant that I envisage God as my projection, "God" becomes meaningless and ineffective for me. Equally, I can no more abandon the basis of my hope than abandon the hope or identify it with my powerless, finite self, which has to hope, no more make myself God than I can simply think of this God as outside me and one thing alongside others. God must be what is most real and what embraces all things in its support for him to be at once the basis and goal of the unbounded and unconditional hope which becomes a basic acceptance in trust of existence.

On the other hand, this God is incomprehensible mystery. This hope (in which reason and freedom are still united) transcends any possible explanation because every detail which can be understood and included as an element in the equation of life is and always remains influenced and threatened by others which have not been included. Even in everyday life we experience the unboundedness of our transcendence of what is nevertheless not subject to our transcendence.

In addition, human transcendence in knowledge and freedom also shows this. It can neither be made to stop at a particular point nor derive power from any "nothingness" (because "nothing" can do nothing), and moves towards mystery as such inasmuch as by its own power it is completely unable to fill the infinite sphere of consciousness. But the miracle of existence is not so much that there is this mystery (who can really deny it except by obstinately refusing to take an interest in it?), but that we can and may become involved with it without being tossed back in that very instant into our own nothingness (to the point where atheism becomes the only form of recognition worthy of God).

The act of accepting existence in trust and hope is therefore, if it does not misinterpret itself, the act of letting oneself sink trustfully into the incomprehensible mystery. Therefore my Christianity, if it is not to misinterpret itself, is my letting myself sink into the incomprehensible mystery. It is therefore anything but an "explanation" of the world and my existence, much more an instruction not to regard any experience, any understanding (however good and illuminating they may be) as final, as intelligible in themselves.

Even less than other people do Christians have "final" answers, which they can endorse with a "solves everything" label. Christians cannot include their God as a specific understood element in the equations of their lives, but only accept him as the incomprehensible mystery, in silence and adoration, as the beginning and end of their hope and so as their only ultimate and universal salvation.

The movement of finite mind towards God in such a way that God becomes the content and the goal of this movement and not just the initiator of a movement which in the end remains far from him in the finite must be supported by God himself. Because Christians know that this fundamental trust of theirs, because it is really absolute and desires God himself, is supported by God himself, they call this most intimate movement of their existence towards God by the power of God "grace," "the Holy Spirit," and express this single movement towards the immediate presence of God in faith, hope and love.

Christians believe that anyone who is faithful to the dictates of his or her conscience is following this intimate movement in God towards God. They believe that this movement takes place even if a person does not recognise it for what it is, and has been unable to see its historical manifestation in Jesus Christ, even in the descriptions of an explicitly Christian faith. Christians fear in their own case (and therefore in the case of others) that in the final balance of their lives they may freely say No to this deepest movement of their existence in an open or concealed unbelief or lack of hope. However, at the same time they hope for all others and so also for themselves that this movement may find its way through all the darkness and superficiality of life to its final "eternal" goal. Christians accept this ultimate threat to themselves from themselves (to freedom from freedom, which can say no to God). They keep on overcoming it in the hope that the human race's history of freedom, which is in turn contained by the freedom of the incomprehensible mystery and by the power of his love, will on balance have a happy outcome through God. It makes no difference to this that no theoretical statements can be made about the salvation of individuals—in other words, that in the present absolute hope is the ultimate.

All that has been said so far forms for me, as a Christian, a mysterious synthesis with the encounter with Jesus of Nazareth. In this synthesis primal hope and knowledge of Jesus form a circle which is in the end unbreakable and give each other mutual support and justification before the intellectual conscience of a person who wants to be honest—but with an intellectual honesty which includes what we Christians call "humility." Through the mediation of the message of Christianity and the Church in the gospel of Jesus, and also supported by that ultimate hope in grace, the Christian encounters Jesus. The experience of this synthesis between ultimate primal trust in grace and the encounter with Jesus is naturally somewhat different in the lives of different people, and there is a difference in particular between those who throughout their conscious lives have been Christians and those whose explicit encounter with Jesus for their salvation took place only at a later stage in their lives. However, since the grace which moves all human beings is the grace of Jesus Christ even if the person who receives grace is not consciously aware of this, and since all love of neighbour is, by Jesus' own statement, love for him even if a person is not consciously aware of it, this synthesis (at least as an offer made to freedom) is present in every human being. As far as this synthesis is concerned, therefore, the distinction between Christians and non-Christians (a distinction the importance of which should be neither underestimated nor overestimated) relates, not to its presence, but to its conscious realisation in explicit faith. So in this synthesis whom does a Christian recognise Jesus as?

This experience in which Jesus becomes for a particular person the event of the unique and qualitatively unsurpassable and irreversible approach of God, is always affected by the totality of its elements as a single entity even if each of the elements is not necessarily immediately present explicitly and clearly in conscious awareness. There is Jesus, a human being who loves, who is faithful unto death, in whom all of human existence, life, speech and action, is open to the mystery which he calls his Father and to which he surrenders in confidence even when all is lost. For him the immeasurable dark abyss of his life is the Father's protecting hand. And so he holds fast to love for human beings and also to his one hope even when everything seems to be being destroyed in death, when it no longer seems possible to love God and human beings. But in Jesus all this was supported and crowned by the conviction that with him, his word and his person the "kingdom of God" was made finally and irreversibly present. Christians believe that in Jesus God himself was triumphantly promising himself directly in love and forgiveness to human beings. In Jesus God, on his own initiative, was bringing about and also proclaiming his victory in the human history of freedom, and so of course creating a new and ultimate radical situation of choice for the person who hears this message.

In Christianity this experience of Jesus includes the assurance that this is a man in whom reality does not lag behind the demands of human nature; despite the scepticism produced by the rest of our experience of human beings we can here really rely on a human being. This does not mean that we have to have a stylised picture of Jesus as a superman. He had his limitations, even in his teaching and its presentation, because this is an inevitable part of being a real human being. But he was the person he was supposed to be, in life and in death. His disciples, who witnessed his downfall on Good Friday without illusions, discovered in themselves, as something given by him, a certainty that life was not destroyed, that death in reality was his victory, that he was taken into the protection of the mystery of God, that he "rose." Resurrection here of course does not mean a return into our spatio-temporal and biological reality, but the definitive rescue of the whole human being ("in body and soul") in God. Because this resurrection is being accepted by the mystery which, in its incomprehensibility, is called God, how it happened is impossible to imagine. However, where our absolute hope and the experience of this life and death meet we can no longer think in terms of Jesus' destruction without also denying our own absolute hope, without, whether we admit it or not, allowing ourselves to fall in despair into bottomless emptiness and ultimate nullity.

When, in our own hope for ourselves, we try to find somewhere in the history of the human race a person of whom we can dare to believe that here the hope that embraces all the dimensions of our existence is fulfilled and that this fulfilment itself makes itself known to us, that is, appears in history, this search can find no identifiable figure without the apostolic witness to Jesus. In the first place at least, amazing as it may seem, we simply can find no one who, according to the testimony of their disciples, made this claim. (If we also accept this claim as the guarantee of our own salvation, it then becomes even more unusual.) If, through the witness of the apostles, we have experienced the risen Christ, that experience gives us then the power and the courage to say from the centre of our own existence, "He is risen." The fundamental structure of human hope and its historical experience form a unity: he is the one who has been accepted by God. The question which human beings constitute for the limitlessness of incomprehensibility has been answered by God in Jesus.

Here human existence has finally achieved happiness in the victory achieved from both sides, the victory of grace and of freedom. Here the sceptical doubts about human beings in their uselessness and sin have been left behind. Jesus regarded himself in life and word as the irrevocable coming of God's kingdom, God's victory in human freedom achieved by the power of God, and his self-understanding, which derived from the unbreakable unity of his unconditional solidarity with God and with the world, is confirmed by what we call his resurrection. He is now both the question and the answer present in human life. He is the ultimate answer which cannot be bettered, because every other conceivable question for human beings is made superfluous by death and in him this all-consuming question has been answered if he is the risen one and irrevocably promises us the incomprehensible boundlessness of God himself, alongside which there is nothing else which could be question or answer. He is the word of God to us, the answer to the one question which we ourselves are, a question no longer about a particular detail, but the universal question, about God.

From this position, the statements of traditional ecclesiology and theology about Jesus Christ can be recapitulated and at the same time protected against misunderstandings. We can say what is meant by his "metaphysical divine sonship," by the hypostatic union of the eternal word of God, by the complete and unimpaired human reality in Jesus, by the communication of idioms. This Christology, which is more than fifteen hundred years old and even today for the most part shared by all the main Christian churches, is still valid and will continue to be so, because it expresses, remorselessly and correctly, what the Christian faith experiences in Jesus, God's irrevocable promise of himself to the world, which is historically accessible in its irrevocability.

On the other hand, it is possible for these official Christological formulas of the Christian churches to be misunderstood and then rightly rejected. They do not simply need repeating to be immediately understood; and the orthodox believer, while he may explain them, may still admit that what they say can also be said in other ways. Anyone who says in the orthodox sense that Jesus is God has stated the Christian truth, provided that he correctly understands this statement, which cannot be taken for granted. This also implies the converse, that anyone who accepts Jesus as the insurpassable word of God to himself or herself, as the final confirmation of their own hope, is a Christian even if he or she cannot reproduce, or can reproduce only with difficulty, these traditional Christological formulas, which derive from a conceptual framework which it is hard for us to recover.

The cross and the resurrection belong together in any authentic faith in Jesus. The cross means the no longer obscured requirement that human beings must surrender completely before the mystery of existence, which human beings can no longer bring under their control because they are finite and sinful. The resurrection means the content of the absolute hope that in this surrender there takes place the forgiving and blissful and final acceptance of a human being by this mystery, that when we let go completely we do not fall. The cross and resurrection of Jesus together mean that precisely this letting go without falling took place in an exemplary way through God's act in Jesus and that we too are irrevocably promised this possibility (including that of being able to let go, which is the most difficult task of our lives) in Jesus.

Here, in Jesus, we have the "absolutely particular." We need only to rely on this particular person lovingly and absolutely. (In the end the interposition of time is no more an obstacle to this than that of a body. We only have to take a chance.) Then we have everything. True, we have to die together with him, but no one can escape this fate. We should not try to squeeze past death until others—emphatically not ourselves—can no longer notice whether we accept our own death. So why not die with Jesus, saying in unison with him, "My God, why have you abandoned me?" and "Into your hands I commend my spirit"?

Only here does all the metaphysics about human beings become real. And it is no longer so important what the meta-

physics is or might be like "in itself." By the time it has arrived
at Jesus, it contains very little, and therefore everything. Because it treats reaching death as reaching life, and there we
have the answer to the question, all or nothing! Not in talking
about death, but in death, his and ours. Not until this moment,
which for oneself is still to come, has one finally embraced
Christianity.

Nevertheless, even beforehand we can prepare to be open
to this event. This training for dying does not destroy the
splendour of the life we lead now. Let those who can and want
to enjoy this glorious life. But let them enjoy it with an eye on
death. Only in death does everything acquire its ultimate importance and so become the "light burden." Christianity is for
me the simplest way because it embodies the single totality of
existence, plunges this totality calmly and hopefully with the
dying Jesus into God's incomprehensibility and leaves all the
details of life to us as they are, but without giving us a formula.

Nevertheless the simplest is also the most difficult. It is
grace, the grace offered to all, which can be accepted and (this
is Christian hope) is accepted, even where absolute hope has
still not explicitly found the person it is looking for as its em-
bodiment, Jesus of Nazareth. Perhaps it is ordained that many
"find" him more easily by looking for him in anonymous hope
without being able to call him by his historical name. If the
conscious personal history of the human race forms a unity,
everything in it is important for all and for that reason the original sacrament which is Jesus Christ has been established from
the beginning above all the periods and spaces of this one history, but over it as over a history in which necessarily not
everything can be at the same historical distance from everything else or have the same explicit closeness. Nevertheless,
anyone who has met Jesus with sufficient clarity must acknowledge him because otherwise he or she would be denying
his or her own hope.

If the resurrection of Jesus is mystery victoriously promising itself to us by the power of God as the mystery of our definitive life, it is certain and understandable that his resurrection would not exist if Jesus did not also rise in the belief in his eternal validity. It is for that reason that there exists the community of people who believe in him as the one who was crucified and rose from the dead. This community is called a Church all the more because those who believe in Jesus Christ, simply because of their shared reference to the one Jesus just cannot simply be religious individualists. Nor can this faith in Jesus be transmitted without active witness, which again ultimately requires a social structure in the community of faith which gathers round Jesus.

For this and many other reasons Christianity means Church. Human beings are social beings always driven even by the history of their ultimate freedom from a socially constituted community and toward one. Even the most radical religious individualist is still related to the Church by language, holy scripture, tradition, and so on even if he or she wants to make himself or herself totally independent of it. Truth, too, is connected with an open and yet critical relationship to society and therefore to institutions, though this does not mean that an individual's "own" truth can be something arbitrary. Truth which is not constantly seeking to communicate itself to others in unity and love, and which is not constantly given to the individual by a community, is not truth, because in religion truth is the consciousness of the person who gives himself or herself to others in love.

Nor can this truth in community escape the solidity inherent in the social nature of a community. The various Christian churches and denominations may not attach exactly the same value to the Church, but throughout Christianity there are institutions, and therefore in principle there is a desire for the Church. Where individual freedom and uniqueness (which are essential to a Christian) exist as the individual's immediate relation to God, and yet because of them religious groups and a Church are necessary, there will always be the permanent tension, which constantly takes different forms and must always be resolved afresh, between Christian freedom and the Christian need for the Church. This tension cannot be resolved either by an ecclesiastical totalitarianism (a genuine danger easily underestimated by ecclesiastics) or by a Christian anarchism, nor can there ever be such specific rules for dealing with it in particular cases that a solution could be merely an administrative matter of applying the rules. In the end it is only in hope that the individual Christian can endure this tension in patience, in the hope that one day the eternal kingdom of love will exist and not the Church. Nevertheless the recognition more or less everywhere in the Christian world of baptism as the rite of initiation into the Christian community in the confession of the divine Trinity is a universal admission in principle that membership in the Church is an essential feature of Christianity.

I do not want to say much here about what in the Christian world is the bitter topic of the divisions between the Christian churches, this problem which has produced the most terrible events in Christian history, religious wars between Christians. Today this question, which has existed throughout almost the whole history of Christianity, exists perhaps primarily as the question whether and in what way the Christian religious conscience has to make a distinction of religious significance between the different Christian denominations and churches. In the past the question did not take this form. Hitherto (and quite properly, on their terms) all the Christian denominations were convinced that the diversity of creeds and the ecclesial institutions which held them were not simply purely accidental and ultimately unimportant variations of the one Christian faith, but that they raised a genuine religious question for the conscience of each individual. It was held that true Christianity, which alone led to salvation, was to be found only in one or other of the denominations and churches. Today, whether we like it or not, the situation in this respect has certainly become more difficult for the average Christian. On many issues at least, it is no longer so easy to say whether the various Christian creeds are really in direct contradiction or whether they are all (or many of them) simply expressions of the same Christian truth and reality within different conceptual frameworks and with different linguistic resources and different, historically conditioned, emphases, and would therefore certainly all find a place in the one Church.

Christians throughout the world have come to realise that the diversity of church laws, rights, customs and spiritualities can be much greater than that which European Christendom was previously used to. It has at least become clear in principle that one Church does not mean the same canon law in all its detail. The historical accidents, which in themselves have nothing to do with the unity of faith and the unity of the Church and yet have played a very important part in the division, are well known.

Everywhere there is a growing understanding of the need for ecumenism. In such a situation it is certainly no longer so easy to regard one of the Christian confessions and churches, to the exclusion of all the others, as the only legitimate one and the only route to salvation. There has of course been progress in this difficult situation, even where (as in the Roman Catholic Church) there is not yet a willingness to recognise all the churches with their different creeds and institutions as in principle equal in status. The title "Church" is given on all sides, the universal validity of baptism is stressed, there is a recognition of the genuine religious value of many doctrines, institutions, and forms of spirituality in the various churches, rejoicing at the identity of holy scripture throughout the Chris-

tian world, and so on. However, these very attempts at ecumenical rapprochement have made it much more difficult in
practice, at least for Catholic Christians, to still allow their
Church the unique status which, even at the Second Vatican
Council, it claimed for itself as opposed to all the other Christian churches.

Today there are also all the difficulties of historical knowledge which affect the precise connection between even the
most primitive stage of the Church and the historical Jesus and
also the impossibility (at least for the average Christian) of de-
ciding rationally which developments in subsequent church
history are legitimate and which are illegitimate (or at least not
binding in faith)—and there certainly have been both. In this
situation even Catholic Christians have to distinguish between
the content and absoluteness of their assent in faith to their
Church, if they can give such assent, which is in principle possible and required, and the arguments from fundamental theology which justify this assent but are in themselves external
to it. The two are not the same, as every traditional fundamental theology knows. The true assent of faith accepts the actual Church as it understands itself.

On the other hand, as regards fundamental theology and
the external justification for this assent, the average Catholic
will answer yes to a double question and thus legitimise his or
her relationship in faith to the Roman Catholic Church. A
Catholic will ask whether he or she can find in this Church the
liberating spirit of Jesus, his truth, without at the same time
encountering obstacles in the shape of the Church itself or its
doctrine or an absolutely binding practice. A Catholic will ask
whether he or she, despite and through all historical and unavoidable change, can find in this Church the clearest and
strongest possible connection in historical continuity with the
beginnings of the Church and so with Jesus.

An affirmative answer to this double question seems to

me, a born Catholic, to give me the right and duty to maintain an unqualified relationship with my Church, a relationship which naturally, by its nature, includes a critical attitude to it as the locus of evangelical freedom. How a non-Catholic can come to the Catholic Church, something which is in principle possible, is a different question and one which cannot be explored further here.

Every true Christian naturally suffers because of the social and historical structure of the Church. In its empirical reality the Church always lags behind its essence. It proclaims a message by which its own empirical reality is always called in question. The Church is also always the Church of sinners, whose members by their actions deny what they profess. In fact the Church cannot in this connection rely totally on the argument that it is made up of human beings and therefore, like every other historical community or association, reveals human nature. The Church's role is to be *par excellence* the place in which the power of grace demonstrates its victory over the depths of malice and narrowness in human beings.

Of course the Church can point to people in whom this power of grace is really made manifest, but are such people that much easier to see in the Church than outside it? How is one expected to prove that without becoming pharisaical and arrogant when one really honestly looks "outside" the Church for such people? A difficult question. Quite enough terrible and base things have happened in the history of the Church. There is so much that is terrible and base that the only helpful answer is this: where else would we go if we left the Church? Would we then be more faithful to the liberating spirit of Jesus if, egotistical sinners that we are, we distanced ourselves as the "pure" from this poor Church? We can do our part to remove its meanness only if we help to bear the burden of this wretchedness (for which all of us too bear some guilt), if we try to live in the Church as Christians, if we help to bear the responsibility of constantly changing it from inside. The Church in all denominations must always be the Church of the "reformation."

If we believe we can discover some element of genuine Christianity in ourselves and understand what it really means, how then can we refuse to graft it unselfishly into this community of sinners? Are they not in fact, through the power of the spirit of Jesus, moving through all the wretchedness of history towards that fulfilment promised by the death and resurrection of Jesus to all of us and not just to a small élite among the human race?

Christians have always known, in theory at least, that they can only know, make real and credible their relationship of hope and love to the incomprehensible mystery of their lives in unconditional love for their neighbour, which is the only way we can really break out of the hell of our egotism. This love for others in all the varied forms which it can take is by no means so straightforward, even without being distorted into a method of covert egotism; it is the liberating grace of God. Where this love is real, the spirit of Jesus is at work, even if it is not named, as Matthew 25 clearly teaches us. We can only say in trembling: Let us hope that the grace of God is working this miracle somewhere in ourselves! Everything depends on this, absolutely everything.

Of course in a period such as ours it has to be realised that this love of neighbour cannot possibly be itself if it lends grace and dignity merely to the private relations of individuals. Today it must also be practised particularly (though not only) as the responsibility of every person and every Christian for the social domain as such. It must take the form of justice and peace because in the end justice cannot be sought by a compromise of merely rational calculation, but only by the occurrence often enough in society and history of the absurd miracle of selfless love.

And the other way around, this miracle is concealed in sober calculations of justice. Social and political responsibilities have a particular form for the individual Christian, individual Christian groups and the Church as such. The Church must make its love of neighbour credible through its commitment to action in society and against it. There is a horrifying amount of injustice, violence, alienation and war in the world and all this injustice adopts the disguise of inevitability, cold reason and legitimate interest. Because sinful Christians in a sinful Church are beneficiaries of this injustice, whether they know and admit it or not, the critical function of the Church in society cannot have as its true and own responsibility the defense of a socio-political status quo. If it gives the average person the impression that it is a support of a conservative system, if it wants to be on good terms with everyone instead of like Jesus, preferring the poor and rootless, if it receives more sympathy from the socially secure and the rich than from the poor and from the oppressed, then there is something wrong with this Church.

The Church must carry out its critical commitment in society under the guidance of the spirit which has been given to it, the spirit of Jesus, and in the hope of eternal life. The memory of the death and resurrection of Jesus gives the Church a critical distance from society which allows it not to treat as absolute (explicitly or covertly) either the future already achieved or the nearest feasible future. If the Church were to develop into a merely "humanitarian concern" it would be betraying its responsibility because its task is to proclaim to human beings the ultimate seriousness and incomprehensible dignity of this love for human beings. But even today the greater danger seems to be that love of neighbour, and our neighbours today are mainly secular society, is not taken sufficiently seriously by Christians. And yet this is the only place where the God whom the Christians are looking for can be found, with Jesus, not even he dissolved the incomprehensible mystery, but accepted it in faith and love by refusing to make a choice between love of God and love of human beings.

Christianity and the churches are slowly acquiring new and much more complex relationships with the non-Christian world religions than they had in the past, when these religions were outside the cultural orbit of Christianity. Christianity cannot withdraw the claim to have heard and to preach the universal and unrepeatable word of grace in Jesus, who was crucified and rose from the dead. But Christianity does not for that reason deny that the Spirit of God is carrying out its liberating work throughout history in the middle of human limitations and culpable confusion, the Spirit in whom Jesus surrendered himself to God in death.

The non-Christian world religions also bear witness in their own way to this spirit and not merely to human limitations. Many of their provisional and important experiences may be included as elements of an answer in the all-embracing answer which is Jesus because the history of the Christian message is by no means yet at an end. Nor can Christianity treat atheism, which today has become a mass-phenomenon on a world scale, simply as a manifestation of rejection on the part of human beings who refuse to submit to the incomprehensible mystery of God, rather also as an element in the history of the experience of God in which God is seen in an ever more radical way as the mystery to be adored, to which we give ourselves in hope.

Both in my life and in my thinking I keep finding myself in situations of confusion which cannot be "cleared up." At first even I feel that one just has to carry on, even if one doesn't know where it's all leading. I feel that one must just keep quiet when one can't speak clearly, that carrying on in ordinary honesty is the only appropriate attitude for human beings, and the most that can be expected of us. But then I find I cannot avoid or keep silent about the question of what underlies this carrying on. What I find when I ask that question is the hope which accepts no limits as final. This hope concentrates all our experience into two words, "mystery" and "death." "Mystery" means confusion in hope, but "death" orders us not to disguise the confusion, but to endure it. I look at Jesus on the cross and know that I am spared nothing. I place myself (I hope) in his death and so hope that this shared death is the dawn of the blessed mystery. I must interpret death, and interpreting it as final emptiness and darkness has no more justification. But in this hope, even in all the darkness and disappointment, life already begins to emerge in its beauty and everything becomes promise. I find that being a Christian is the simplest task, the utterly simple and therefore heavy-light burden, as the Gospel calls it. When we carry it, it carries us. The longer one lives the heavier and the lighter it becomes. At the end we are left with mystery, but it is the mystery of Jesus. One can despair or become impatient, tired, sceptical and bitter because time goes by and the mystery still does not dawn as happiness, but it is better to wait in patience for the day that knows no ending.

Sandra M. Schneiders, I.H.M.

Theology and Spirituality:
Strangers, Rivals, or Partners?

The attempt to describe or define the contemporary academic discipline of spirituality so as to discern its relationship with theology involves us in two distinct but related questions. The first has to do with the *subject matter* of spirituality, with that which is the object of study of the discipline. In other words, our first question is "What is spirituality?" as a human phenomenon? What are people speaking about when they talk about spirituality? The second question has to do with the kind of *academic discipline* which studies whatever it is that spirituality is.

Perhaps a good starting point for arriving at a working definition of spirituality as human phenomenon is to say what spirituality is *not*.

First, as noted earlier, and in contradistinction to what we have seen to be the case historically, spirituality is no longer an exclusively Roman Catholic phenomenon. In fact, it is not even an exclusively Christian phenomenon. People speak intelligibly of Buddhist, Native American, or African spirituality. Some would maintain that spirituality is not even necessarily theistic or religious.

Second, spirituality today is neither dogmatic nor prescriptive. It does not consist in the application to concrete life of principles derived from theology. Spirituality is understood as the unique and personal response of individuals to all that calls them to integrity and transcendence.

Third, spirituality is not concerned with "perfection" but with growth, and consequently it is not the concern of a select few but of everyone who experiences him or herself drawn toward the fullness of humanity.

Fourth, spirituality is not concerned solely with the "interior life" as distinguished from or in opposition to bodily, social, political, or secular life. On the contrary, spirituality has something to do with the integration of all aspects of human life and experience.

In short, people speaking of spirituality today are talking about something quite different from that which was under discussion in the volumes of Tanquerey and Pourrat. No doubt the subject matter of earlier usages of the term would be included in the subject matter of today's term but the latter is much broader in every sense of the term.

However, stating what spirituality is not is much easier than saying what it *is* and this precisely because the boundaries of the term have expanded so much. Jon Alexander, in a recent article, after surveying the definitions of spirituality offered by such writers as Carolyn Osiek, Raymundo Panikkar, Hans Urs von Balthasar, John Macquarrie, and Shirley Guthrie, concluded that the term is being used today in an experiential and generic sense.[1] While I have some reservations about the accuracy of the second characterization I am in complete agreement that, whatever the term means today, it denotes experience. The question is, what kind of experience is spirituality?

THE SUBJECT MATTER OF THE DISCIPLINE

Perhaps a useful way to begin our investigation of this question is to list a few of the definitions of spirituality offered by modern authors, Catholic and Protestant:

Panikkar: "one typical way of handling the human condition"[2]

Macquarrie: "fundamentally spirituality has to do with *becoming a person in the fullest sense*"[3]

Wakefield: "a word . . . to describe those attitudes, beliefs, practices which animate people's lives and help them to reach out towards super-sensible realities"[4]

Hardy: "spirituality is that attitude, that frame of mind which breaks the human person out of the isolating self. As it does that, it directs him or her to another in relationship to whom one's growth takes root and sustenance"[5]

Williams: "And if 'spirituality' can be given any coherent meaning, perhaps it is to be understood in terms of this task: each believer making his or her own that engagement with the questioning at the heart of faith which is so evident in the classical documents of Christian belief"[6]

Duquoc: "the lived unity of human existence in faith."[7]

All of these definitions, no matter how vague and general they may sound, suggest that spirituality has something to do with the unification of life by reference to something beyond the individual person. While striving, perhaps in an exaggerated way, to avoid Christian exclusiveness and denominational narrowness, virtually everyone talking about spirituality today is talking about self-transcendence which gives integrity and meaning to the whole of life and to life in its wholeness by situating and orienting the person within the horizon of ultimacy in some ongoing and transforming way.

At this point we can perhaps be aided by that distinction made in the Middle Ages between the philosophical and the religious meanings of the term "spirituality." The *philosophical meaning* is based on the distinction between the material and the spiritual, the spiritual being understood as that capacity for self-transcendence through knowledge and love which characterizes the human being as a person. Thus, in the philosophical sense of the term, all humans are essentially "spiritual" and spirituality would be the actualization of that dimension of selfhood, that capacity for self-transcendence, in and through the establishment of personal relationships. The *religious meaning* of spirituality is based on the conception of what constitutes the proper and highest actualization of the human capacity for self-transcendence in personal relationship, namely, relationship with God. Spirituality, then, in its religious or theological sense, refers to the relationship between the individual and God pursued in the life of faith, hope, and love. The *Christian meaning* is a particular specification of the religious meaning. We might define Christian spirituality as that particular actualization of the capacity for self-transcendence that is constituted by the substantial gift of the Holy Spirit establishing a life-giving relationship with God in Christ within the believing community. Thus, Christian spirituality is trinitarian, christological, and ecclesial religious experience.

In short, spirituality refers to the experience of consciously striving to integrate one's life in terms not of isolation and self-absorption but of self-transcendence toward the ultimate value one perceives. If the ultimate value is the Transcendent itself, the Deity, the spirituality is explicitly religious. But the avoidance of specifically religious language in many discussions of spirituality is an attempt to recognize that there are people whose lives are lived consciously within the horizon of ultimate concern but who do not recognize that ultimate value as God. In this sense, I do not think that the avoidance of specifically theological language necessarily involves the effort to develop a "generic" definition of spirituality. There is no such thing as generic spirituality or spirituality in general. Every spirituality is necessarily historically concrete and therefore involves some thematically explicit commitments, some actual and distinct symbol system, some traditional language, in short, a theoretical-linguistic framework which is integral to it and without which it cannot be meaningfully discussed at all. But by focusing on the common experience of *integrating self-transcendence within the horizon of ultimacy* one keeps open the possibility of dialogue among people of very different world views.

Among Christians, however, it seems to me that we could simplify the discussion by agreeing that the referent of the term "spirituality" is *Christian religious experience as such*. What this means is that spirituality, for Christians, is *Christian* and therefore theological considerations are relevant at every point; it is also *religious*, which means that it is affective as well as cognitive, social as well as personal, God-centered and other-directed all at the same time; and it is *experience*, which means that whatever enters into the actual living of this ongoing integrating self-transcendence is relevant, whether it be mystical, theological, ethical, psychological, political, or physical. The Transcendent who is the horizon, the focus, and the energizing source of Christian spirituality is an Other who is personal, living, and loving and is fully revealed in a human being, Jesus of

Nazareth. This cannot fail to have a profound and distinguishing effect on the shape and dynamics of Christian spirituality but it is not impossible for Christians to recognize that within other religious, cultural, and historical frameworks analogous experiences of ultimate value have given rise to analogous life-integrating dynamics which can legitimately be called spiritualities.

THE DISCIPLINE WHICH STUDIES SPIRITUALITY

If spirituality is understood as we have suggested, certain notes will characterize the emerging discipline which purports to study spirituality. First, this discipline will be *descriptive and analytic* rather than prescriptive and evaluative. Whether the researcher is studying mysticism, the relation of prayer to social justice involvement, discernment of spirits, ritual, feminist religious experience, God images or any of the hundreds of other topics which are attracting the attention of students of spirituality today, the first task will be to try to understand the phenomenon on its own terms, that is, as it is or was actually experienced by Christians.

This leads immediately to the second characteristic, namely, the *interdisciplinary approach* of spirituality. Very diverse phenomena fall within the purview of spirituality and each of these presents a variety of facets. At times the appropriate methods will be historical, at other times aesthetic, at others psychological, sociological, or anthropological. And, of course, the biblical and theological questions will always need to be raised. But the time is gone when a single discipline, namely, theology, can be considered to supply the sole or even the determining approach to a given research project in the field of spirituality.

Third, spirituality seems irrevocably committed to an *ecu-*

menical and even cross-cultural approach. This greatly complicates the work of the specialist in Christian spirituality but we
live in a global village which is both irreducibly pluralistic and
intimately interrelated. Part of understanding any significant
phenomenon is seeing how it fits into the larger picture, and
for those in spirituality the larger picture is the human quest
for meaning and integration of which the Christian quest is one
actualization.

Fourth, spirituality is *inclusive or holistic* in its approach. It
is not the "interior man" who seeks integration in holiness of
life but the whole person, body and spirit, mind and will and
emotions, individual and social, masculine and feminine. It is
not only our activities but also our passivities which must be
integrated, not only our achievements but also our sufferings,
not only our prayer but also our struggles for justice. Again,
the holistic approach makes the study of spirituality infinitely
more complex than its nineteenth-century forebear but it is no
longer possible for us to fragment the human person into parts
and faculties, into inner and outer, into personal and social. We
are all of these things at once and much of the spiritual task
consists precisely in bringing this rich multi-facetedness into
unity. What spirituality as life process must bring together
spirituality as academic discipline must not split asunder.

Fifth, spirituality seems to be a necessarily *"participant"*
discipline. The researcher must know the spiritual quest by personal experience if he or she is to be able to understand the phenomena of spirituality. One might be studying a spirituality
quite different from one's own, but without analogous experience it is difficult to imagine how the student could come to
comprehend the activities and passivities of the spiritual life.
The purely disinterested phenomenological approach seems,
in the very nature of the case, to be inappropriate if not impossible for spirituality.

Sixth, and as has already been suggested, spirituality

studies not principles to be applied nor general classes or typical cases but *concrete individuals:* persons, works, events. Consequently, the student of spirituality is necessarily involved in what Ricoeur has called the "science of the individual" in which interpretation plays the key role and validation of interpretation through a dialectic of explanation and understanding rather than verification of repeatable scientific results is the objective.[8] There can, then, be no avoiding of the truth questions about revelation, theology, creed, code, and cult. These questions can be suppressed when talking about spirituality in general, but not when the actual practice of the discipline is underway.

Seventh, spirituality, like psychology, will always have a *triple objective* that cannot be neatly simplified. One studies spirituality to understand spirituality; but one also studies it in order to foster one's own spirituality; and finally, one studies it in order to foster the spirituality of others. The relative importance of each of these objectives varies from student to student and from one research project to another but it is not really possible to answer once and for all the question about whether spirituality is a theoretical or a practical discipline, an objective or a subjective pursuit. It is all of these, although the emphasis varies at different moments in each project.

A final point regarding the discipline of spirituality will bring this description to a close. Spirituality is, at this point, an immature discipline. No doubt it is well past the initial stage of an emerging field during which there is little more than a felt affinity among certain scholars who sense a common interest but who are all engaged in unrelated research the results of which cannot be cumulative because they lack common vocabulary, common categories, and even organs of publication. But spirituality has not reached the point at which it is equipped with the kind of generalized theory which would constitute it a fully developed discipline recognizable as such in the halls of the academy. It is in that intermediate stage which is as awkward, but as exciting, as adolescence. People in the field today recognize each other; vocabulary is developing; the primary resources and research tools are becoming available; research and publications are increasing in quantity and quality; meetings are bringing scholars together; good students are entering the field, and, almost as important, are finding good positions when they finish their studies. The question of methodology is becoming urgent and that would seem to indicate that maturity is rapidly approaching. It is partly the issue of methodology which raised the question with which this essay is concerned: what is the relationship between spirituality and theology?

RELATIONSHIP OF SPIRITUALITY
TO THEOLOGY

On the basis of the foregoing we are in a position to suggest at least a tentative answer to the question with which we began: what is the relationship between spirituality and theology. For our purposes, I am presupposing that we are talking about Christian spirituality and Christian theology. It should be clear by now that this question actually has two foci which must be considered separately. We must inquire, first, into the relationship between theology and spirituality as lived Christian experience, and, second, into the relationship between spirituality as an academic discipline and theology which is also an academic discipline.

LIVED SPIRITUALITY AND THEOLOGY

As the history of the Church makes abundantly clear, spirituality as lived religious experience is prior to theology, both ontologically and psychologically. The New Testament itself bears witness to this fact. Christians, because of the experience they had with the historical Jesus and especially because of the resurrection experience, began to reflect theologically, in light of both Old Testament revelation and available philosophical frameworks, on his identity and mission. Later experience of conflicting interpretations of the Christ-event led to theological refinements, while subsequent experience of Christians interacting with diverse historical-cultural circumstances raised new problems and suggested new answers which required to be integrated into the already elaborated synthesis. Over the span of centuries the intellectual edifice of Christian theology came into being and reached a peak of integration and clarity in the thirteenth century.

The medieval synthesis held well until the middle of the twentieth century when the world-shattering events of two world wars, the technological revolution, liberation movements of all kinds, an explosion of knowledge, and rapid developments in philosophy, the humanities, the personality and social sciences brought its comprehensive hold on the Christian mind and imagination to an end. Theology today is both critical and pluralistic and it seems unlikely that it will settle into a new "perennial" form any time in the foreseeable future. But this thumbnail sketch suffices to illustrate our point, namely, that it is spirituality, that is, Christian experience of living the faith in various times, places, cultures and in the midst of various issues, problems, and triumphs that generates theology, not, as the nineteenth-century theologians thought, theology which generates spirituality.

However, by that curious dialectic observable in other fields as well, once theology has arisen in response to and as an explicit articulation of Christian religious experience, it comes to have both the ability and the responsibility to criticize spirituality. Just as it is literature which generates literary criticism but the latter which then operates to sift the good from the bad, to analyze and explicate the good, and even to stimulate artists in their work, so theology generated by spirituality is the primary evaluator and critic of spirituality. It is theology which renders judgment on the adequacy of a particular spirituality to the Gospel and Tradition; theology which challenges partial or one-sided approaches; theology which defends the prophetic and charismatic; theology which finally helps the believer to understand his or her experience and by understanding to appropriate it more deeply and live it more fully. It must never be forgotten that, despite this important role, theology is a servant of Christian experience, not its master. Just as the biblical scholar must never presume to fetter the Word of God with the human bonds of exegesis, so the theologian must not presume to manufacture or to control the work of the Spirit in the churches. But without the service of the biblical scholar much in scripture would remain unintelligible, and without the service of the theologian spirituality could degenerate into enthusiastic chaos, dangerous aberrations, or anemia.

It must also be kept in mind that, while theology is the most important single discipline at the service of spirituality, it is by no means the only one. The spiritual life, as has been said, embraces the whole of human experience within the horizon of ultimate concern. Consequently, the personality sciences, the social sciences, literary and aesthetic disciplines, history, comparative religion, and a variety of other fields of study are important to the understanding and to the living of Christian religious experience.

THE ACADEMIC DISCIPLINES OF SPIRITUALITY AND THEOLOGY

The second question, that of the place of this new field of study, Christian spirituality, in the academic world is receiving a good deal of attention today, and necessarily so. Does this field, because of its interdisciplinary, humanistic, and cross-cultural character, belong in the university; or, because of its necessarily concrete confessional character, in the theological school; or, because of its orientation toward practice, in the ministerial school? And even if it is placed in the theology department should it be accorded autonomous status as a distinct discipline, an equal partner alongside biblical studies and systematic theology, or should it be diffused among the older disciplines as the proper horizon for or a focus of interest in the study of all theology?

First of all, we must clarify the term "theology" as it is used in the academy. Often "theology" is used as an umbrella term for all of the sacred sciences, that is, for all religious studies carried out in the context of explicit reference to revelation and explicitly affirmed confessional commitment. Thus, under the heading of theology one finds systematic theology including foundational theology, theology of God, ecclesiology, christology, and eschatology; moral theology including both general and special, personal and social ethics; and, finally, church history and biblical studies. A theology department or school might also include practical and/or mixed disciplines such as religious education, pastoral counseling, liturgy, homiletics, and ministry.

When theology is understood in this manner the discipline of Christian spirituality belongs under the heading of theology as one field of revelation-related, confessionally committed scholarly endeavor, namely, the field that studies Christian religious experience as such in an interdisciplinary way. As in other theological disciplines today the edges of the field are often "soft." Several of the once-designated "secular" disciplines are an integral part of the studies carried out in the field of spirituality. But this does not cancel the central fact that the essential work of spirituality as a field of study is theological in this broad sense of the term.

However, there is a second and narrower understanding of theology. In this second sense theology denotes systematic theology and moral theology, the two major fields which have, since the Middle Ages, organized the scientific study of the faith. Taken in this restricted sense, theology does not include biblical studies, church history, or the practical and mixed disciplines. And by the same token it also does not include spirituality. This amounts to a denial of the classical position that spirituality is a dependent of dogmatic theology and/or a subdivision of moral theology. Although spirituality as the lived experience of the faith is indeed the horizon within which all theological work must be done since theology arises from and is oriented toward that lived experience of the Christian community, spirituality as an academic discipline has its own subjects of study, its own methods and approaches, and its own objectives, just as do biblical studies, church history, and the practical theological disciplines.

It suffices to list the subjects of some recent doctoral dissertations in spirituality to be convinced that the subject matter of spirituality is distinct from, however intimately related to, that of systematic and moral theology. Subjects such as mysticism, prayer, discernment, spiritual friendship, spiritual direction, the relation of prayer to social justice, schools of spirituality, the spirituality of certain great figures, the relation of analogous spiritual phenomena and/or practices across confessional or cultural boundaries, the body/spirit dialectic in the spiritual life, the patterns and dynamics of spiritual growth, the interaction of culture and faith in the development of the spiritual life, the meaning of sanctity, the relationship of psychological maturity to spiritual development, biblical spirituality, liturgical spirituality, the distinctiveness of feminine religious experience, and the like are all subjects the study of which has an important theological moment but which cannot be adequately investigated as purely theological problems in the narrower sense of the term "theology."

Because of the very nature of the phenomena which spirituality studies its methods and approaches are irreducibly pluralistic and thoroughly interdisciplinary. Most research projects in spirituality will involve biblical, historical, theological, social, psychological, aesthetic, and comparative approaches. The use of these disciplines will be governed by the methods appropriate to these disciplines themselves but the underlying and guiding philosophical presuppositions are usually hermeneutical since the fundamental problem in spirituality is always that of interpretation of particulars in order to understand the experience which comes to expression therein.

Finally, the objectives of the discipline of spirituality are distinct and peculiar to the field. As has been mentioned, the objectives are always simultaneously theoretical and practical in a way analogous to the objectives of psychology or art. The objective is not so much double as dual, the theoretical and practical dimensions being in a constant dialectical relationship throughout the study. It may well be that spirituality as a discipline will have to address in a self-conscious way, in the not too distant future, the question of what effect this dual character has on the nature and quality of research in the field. Students in the field of spirituality neither want to nor can be "objective" in the sense of personally uninvolved in their subject matter (if, indeed, any researcher is purely "objective" in any field!). There is no "factoring out" of personal questions and ultimate self-implication in results. In this sense, the field resembles the arts more than the sciences. It is certainly a humanistic rather than an exact or "hard" science. In any case, there seems to me to be little question that the objectives of the study of spirituality are distinct from, although not unrelated to, those of the classical theological disciplines.

CONCLUSION

By a long and tortuous path we have come to a tentative response to our original question: what is the relationship between spirituality and theology? We have traced the trajectory of a long and troubled relationship which began serenely in a peaceful unity. But, as so often happens, the two partners in the relationship matured, each at a different rate of speed and in different ways. This resulted in a domination, within the relationship, of spirituality by theology. But in recent decades this well-behaved and subordinate partner has emerged as an autonomous dialogue partner demanding independence for the sake of mature interdependence. Some will say, not entirely without basis, that spirituality, freed from its subordination to theology, is wandering abroad in strange places and experimenting with strange relationships. Some think the solution is to restore the order of the theological household by either reasserting theology's proper headship or expelling the wanderer from the house altogether. Those who know the field of spirituality are certain that neither solution is appropriate. Spirituality has grown up and is here to stay. It must make its own alliances, and its own mistakes, but it belongs in the household of theology in the broad sense of that term. It is no longer a mindless subordinate controlled by theology nor a pedestaled idol, lovely to look at but useless in discussion. Spirituality is that field-encompassing field[9] which studies Christian religious experience as such. And there is, when all is said and done, almost nothing whose study is more important than spirituality for us who are called to integrate our lives in self-transcending faith, hope, and love through and in the Spirit of Jesus the Christ.

NOTES

[1]Alexander, "What do Recent Writers Mean?" pp. 251–52.

[2]Raymundo Panikkar, *The Trinity and the Religious Experience of Man: Icon-Person-Mystery* (Maryknoll, NY: Orbis, 1973), p. 9.

[3]John Macquarrie, *Paths in Spirituality* (New York: Harper & Row, 1972), p. 40.

[4]Gordon Wakefield, "Spirituality," *Westminster Dictionary of Christian Spirituality*, ed. G. Wakefield (Philadelphia: Westminster, 1983), p. 361.

[5]Richard P. Hardy, "Christian Spirituality Today: Notes on its Meaning," *Spiritual Life* 28 (1982), 154.

[6]Rowan Williams, *Christian Spirituality: A Theological History from the New Testament to Luther and St. John of the Cross* (Atlanta: John Knox, 1979), p. 1.

[7]Christian Duquoc, "Theology and Culture: Religious Culture, Critical Spirit, the Humility of Faith, and Ecclesiastical Obedience," tr. J. R. Foster, in *Concilium* 19 (New York: Paulist, 1966), 89.

[8]See Paul Ricoeur, *Interpretation Theory: Discourse and the Surplus of Meaning* (Fort Worth: Texas Christian University Press, 1976), p. 79.

[9]See, on the nature of the field-encompassing field, Van A. Harvey, *The Historian and the Believer: The Morality of Historical Knowledge and Christian Belief* (Philadelphia: Westminster, 1966), pp. 38–67, esp. 54–59.

A Commitment
to the Future

326. Because Jesus' command to love our neighbor is universal, we hold that the life of each person on this globe is sacred. This commits us to bringing about a just economic order where all, without exception, will be treated with dignity and to working in collaboration with those who share this vision. The world is complex and this may often tempt us to seek simple and self-centered solutions; but as a community of disciples we are called to a new hope and to a new vision that we must live without fear and without oversimplification. Not only must we learn more about our moral responsibility for the larger economic issues that touch the daily life of each and every person on this planet, but we also want to help shape the Church as a model of social and economic justice. Thus, this chapter deals with the Christian vocation in the world today, the special challenges to the Church at this moment of history, ways in which the themes of this letter should be followed up, and a call to the kind of commitment that will be needed to reshape the future.

A. THE CHRISTIAN VOCATION IN THE WORLD TODAY

327. This letter has addressed many matters commonly regarded as secular, for example, employment rates, income

levels, and international economic relationships. Yet, the affairs of the world, including economic ones, cannot be separated from the spiritual hunger of the human heart. We have presented the biblical vision of humanity and the Church's moral and religious tradition as a framework for asking the deeper questions about the meaning of economic life and for actively responding to them. But words alone are not enough. The Christian perspective on the meaning of economic life must transform the lives of individuals, families, in fact, our whole culture. The Gospel confers on each Christian the vocation to love God and neighbor in ways that bear fruit in the life of society. That vocation consists above all in a change of heart: a conversion expressed in praise of God and in concrete deeds of justice and service.

1. Conversion

328. The transformation of social structures begins with and is always accompanied by a conversion of the heart.[1] As disciples of Christ each of us is called to a deep personal conversion and to "action on behalf of justice and participation in the transformation of the world."[2] By faith and baptism we are fashioned into a "new creature"; we are filled with the Holy Spirit and a new love that compels us to seek out a new profound relationship with God, with the human family, and with all created things.[3] Renouncing self-centered desires, bearing one's daily cross, and imitating Christ's compassion, all involve a personal struggle to control greed and selfishness, a personal commitment to reverence one's own human dignity and the dignity of others by avoiding self-indulgence and those attachments that make us insensitive to the conditions of others and that erode social solidarity. Christ warned us against attachments to material things, against total self-reliance, against the idolatry of accumulating material goods and seeking safety in

them. We must take these teachings seriously and in their light examine how each of us lives and acts towards others. But personal conversion is not gained once and for all. It is a process that goes on through our entire life. Conversion, moreover, takes place in the context of a larger faith community: through baptism into the Church, through common prayer, and through our activity with others on behalf of justice.

2. Worship and Prayer

329. Challenging U.S. economic life with the Christian vision calls for a deeper awareness of the integral connection between worship and the world of work. Worship and common prayer are the wellsprings that give life to any reflection on economic problems and that continually call the participants to greater fidelity to discipleship. To worship and pray to the God of the universe is to acknowledge that the healing love of God extends to all persons and to every part of existence, including work, leisure, money, economic and political power and their use, and to all those practical policies that either lead to justice or impede it. Therefore, when Christians come together in prayer, they make a commitment to carry God's love into all these areas of life.

330. The unity of work and worship finds expression in a unique way in the Eucharist. As people of a new covenant, the faithful hear God's challenging word proclaimed to them—a message of hope to the poor and oppressed—and they call upon the Holy Spirit to unite all into one body of Christ. For the Eucharist to be a living promise of the fullness of God's Kingdom, the faithful must commit themselves to living as redeemed people with the same care and love for all people that Jesus showed. The body of Christ which worshipers receive in Communion is also a reminder of the reconciling power of his death on the Cross. It empowers them to work to heal the bro-

kenness of society and human relationships and to grow in a spirit of self-giving for others.

331. The liturgy teaches us to have grateful hearts: to thank God for the gift of life, the gift of this earth, and the gift of all people. It turns our hearts from self-seeking to a spirituality that sees the signs of true discipleship in our sharing of goods and working for justice. By uniting us in prayer with all the people of God, with the rich and the poor, with those near and dear, and with those in distant lands, liturgy challenges our way of living and refines our values. Together in the community of worship, we are encouraged to use the goods of this earth for the benefit of all. In worship and in deeds for justice, the Church becomes a "sacrament," a visible sign of that unity in justice and peace that God wills for the whole of humanity.[4]

3. Call to Holiness in the World

332. Holiness is not limited to the sanctuary or to moments of private prayer; it is a call to direct our whole heart and life toward God and according to God's plan for this world. For the laity holiness is achieved in the midst of the world, in family, in community, in friendships, in work, in leisure, in citizenship. Through their competency and by their activity, lay men and women have the vocation to bring the light of the Gospel to economic affairs, "so that the world may be filled with the Spirit of Christ and may more effectively attain its destiny in justice, in love, and in peace."[5]

333. But as disciples of Christ we must constantly ask ourselves how deeply the biblical and ethical vision of justice and love permeates our thinking. How thoroughly does it influence our way of life? We may hide behind the complexity of the issues or dismiss the significance of our personal contribution; in fact, each one has a role to play, because every day each one makes economic decisions. Some, by reason of their

work or their position in society, have a vocation to be involved in a more decisive way in those decisions that affect the economic well-being of others. They must be encouraged and sustained by all in their search for greater justice.

334. At times we will be called upon to say no to the cultural manifestations that emphasize values and aims that are selfish, wasteful, and opposed to the Scriptures. Together we must reflect on our personal and family decisions and curb unnecessary wants in order to meet the needs of others. There are many questions we must keep asking ourselves: Are we becomming ever more wasteful in a "throw-away" society? Are we able to distinguish between our true needs and those thrust on us by advertising and a society that values consumption more than saving? All of us could well ask ourselves whether as a Christian prophetic witness we are not called to adopt a simpler lifestyle, in the face of the excessive accumulation of material goods that characterizes an affluent society.

335. Husbands and wives, in particular, should weigh their needs carefully and establish a proper priority of values as they discuss the questions of both parents working outside the home and the responsibilities of raising children with proper care and attention. At times we will be called as individuals, as families, as parishes, as Church, to identify more closely with the poor in their struggle for participation and to close the gap of understanding between them and the affluent. By sharing the perspectives of those who are suffering, we can come to understand economic and social problems in a deeper way, thus leading us to seek more durable solutions.

336. In the workplace the laity are often called to make tough decisions with little information about the consequences that such decisions have on the economic lives of others. Such times call for collaborative dialogue together with prayerful reflection on Scripture and ethical norms. The same can be said of the need to elaborate policies that will reflect sound ethical

principles and that can become a part of our political and social system. Since this is a part of the lay vocation and its call to holiness, the laity must seek to instill a moral and ethical dimension into the public debate on these issues and help enunciate the ethical questions that must be faced. To weigh political options according to criteria that go beyond efficiency and expediency requires prayer, reflection, and dialogue on all the ethical norms involved. Holiness for the laity will involve all the sacrifices needed to lead such a life of prayer and reflection within a worshiping and supporting faith community. In this way the laity will bridge the gap that so easily arises between the moral principles that guide the personal life of the Christian and the considerations that govern decisions in society in the political forum and in the marketplace.

4. Leisure

337. Some of the difficulty in bringing Christian faith to economic life in the United States today results from the obstacles to establishing a balance of labor and leisure in daily life. Tedious and boring work leads some to look for fulfillment only during time off the job. Others have become "workaholics," people who work compulsively and without reflection on the deeper meaning of life and their actions. The quality and pace of work should be more human in scale enabling people to experience the dignity and value of their work and giving them time for other duties and obligations. This balance is vitally important for sustaining the social, political, educational, and cultural structures of society. The family, in particular, requires such balance. Without leisure there is too little time for nurturing marriages, for developing parent-child relationships, and for fulfilling commitments to other important groups: the extended family, the community of friends, the parish, the neighborhood, schools, and political organizations.

Why is it one hears so little today about shortening the work week, especially if both parents are working? Such a change would give them more time for each other, for their children, and for their other social and political responsibilities.

338. Leisure is connected to the whole of one's value system and influenced by the general culture one lives in. It can be trivialized into boredom and laziness, or end in nothing but a desire for greater consumption and waste. For disciples of Christ, the use of leisure may demand being countercultural. The Christian tradition sees in leisure, time to build family and societal relationships and an opportunity for communal prayer and worship, for relaxed contemplation and enjoyment of God's creation, and for the cultivation of the arts which help fill the human longing for wholeness. Most of all, we must be convinced that economic decisions affect our use of leisure and that such decisions are also to be based on moral and ethical considerations. In this area of leisure we must be on our guard against being swept along by a lack of cultural values and by the changing fads of an affluent society. In the creation narrative God worked six days to create the world and rested on the seventh (Gn 2:1–4). We must take that image seriously and learn how to harmonize action and rest, work and leisure, so that both contribute to building up the person as well as the family and community.

B. CHALLENGES TO THE CHURCH

339. The Church is all the people of God, gathered in smaller faith communities, guided and served by a pope and a hierarchy of bishops, ministered to by priests, deacons, religious, and laity, through visible institutions and agencies. Church is, thus, primarily a communion of people bonded by the Spirit with Christ as their Head, sustaining one another in

love, and acting as a sign or sacrament in the world. By its nature it is people called to a transcendent end; but, it is also a visible social institution functioning in this world. According to their calling, members participate in the mission and work of the Church and share, to varying degrees, the responsibility for its institutions and agencies.[6]

At this moment in history, it is particularly important to emphasize the responsibilities of the whole Church for education and family life.

1. Education

340. We have already emphasized the commitment to quality education that is necessary if the poor are to take their rightful place in the economic structures of our society. We have called the Church to remember its own obligation in this regard and we have endorsed support for improvements in public education.

341. The educational mission of the Church is not only to the poor but to all its members. We reiterate our 1972 statement: "Through education, the Church seeks to prepare its members to proclaim the Good News and to translate this proclamation into action. Since the Christian vocation is a call to transform oneself and society with God's help, the educational efforts of the Church must encompass the twin purposes of personal sanctification and social reform in the light of Christian values."[7] Through her educational mission the Church seeks: to integrate knowledge about this world with revelation about God; to understand God's relationship to the human race and its ultimate destiny in the Kingdom of God; to build up human communities of justice and peace; and to teach the value of all creation. By inculcating these values the educational system of the Church contributes to society and to social justice. Economic questions are, thus, seen as a part of a

larger vision of the human person and the human family, the value of this created earth, and the duties and responsibilities that all have toward each other and toward this universe.

342. For these reasons the Church must incorporate into all levels of her educational system the teaching of social justice and the biblical and ethical principles that support it. We call on our universities, in particular, to make Catholic social teaching, and the social encyclicals of the popes a part of their curriculum, especially for those whose vocation will call them to an active role in U.S. economic and political decision making. Faith and technological progress are not opposed one to another, but this progress must not be channeled and directed by greed, self-indulgence, or novelty for its own sake, but by values that respect human dignity and foster social solidarity.

343. The Church has always held that the first task and responsibility for education lies in the hands of parents: they have the right to choose freely the schools or other means necessary to educate their children in the faith.[8] The Church also has consistently held that public authorities must ensure that public subsidies for the education of children are allocated so that parents can freely choose to exercise this right without incurring unjust burdens. This parental right should not be taken from them. We call again for equitable sharing in public benefits for those parents who choose private and religious schools for their children. Such help should be available especially for low-income parents. Though many of these parents sacrifice a great deal for their children's education, others are effectively deprived of the possibility of exercising this right.

2. Supporting the Family

344. Economic life has a profound effect on all social structures and particularly on the family. A breakdown of fam-

ily life often brings with it hardship and poverty. Divorce, failure to provide support to mothers and children, abandonment of children, pregnancies out of wedlock, all contribute to the amount of poverty among us. Though these breakdowns of marriage and the family are more visible among the poor, they do not affect only that one segment of our society. In fact, one could argue that many of these breakdowns come from the false values found among the more affluent—values which ultimately pervade the whole of society.

345. More studies are needed to probe the possible connections between affluence and family and marital breakdowns. The constant seeking for self-gratification and the exaggerated individualism of our age, spurred on by false values often seen in advertising and on television, contribute to the lack of firm commitment in marriage and to destructive notions of responsibility and personal growth.[9]

346. With good reason, the Church has traditionally held that the family is the basic building block of any society. In fighting against economic arrangements that weaken the family, the Church contributes to the well-being of society. The same must be said of the Church's teaching on responsible human sexuality and its relationship to marriage and family. Economic arrangements must support the family and promote its solidity.

3. The Church as Economic Actor

347. Although all members of the Church are economic actors every day in their individual lives, they also play an economic role united together as Church. On the parish and diocesan level, through its agencies and institutions, the Church employs many people; it has investments; it has extensive properties for worship and mission. *All the moral principles that govern the just operation of any economic endeavor apply to the Church*

and its agencies and institutions; indeed the Church should be exemplary. The Synod of Bishops in 1971 worded this challenge most aptly: "While the Church is bound to give witness to justice, she recognizes that anyone who ventures to speak to people about justice must first be just in their eyes. Hence, we must undertake an examination of the modes of acting and of the possessions and lifestyle found within the Church herself."[10]

348. Catholics in the United States can be justly proud of their accomplishments in building and maintaining churches and chapels, and an extensive system of schools, hospitals, and charitable institutions. Through sacrifices and personal labor our immigrant ancestors built these institutions. For many decades religious orders of women and men taught in our schools and worked in our hospitals with very little remuneration. Right now, we see the same spirit of generosity among the religious and lay people even as we seek to pay more adequate salaries.

349. We would be insincere were we to deny a need for renewal in the economic life of the Church itself and for renewed zeal on the part of the Church in examining its role in the larger context of reinforcing in U.S. society and culture those values that support economic justice.[11]

350. We select here five areas for special reflection: (1) wages and salaries, (2) rights of employees, (3) investments and property, (4) works of charity, and (5) working for economic justice.

351. We bishops commit ourselves to the principle that those who serve the Church—laity, clergy, and religious—should receive a sufficient livelihood and the social benefits provided by responsible employers in our nation. These obligations, however, cannot be met without the increased contributions of all the members of the Church. We call on all to recognize their responsibility to contribute monetarily to the support of those who carry out the public mission of the

Church. Sacrificial giving or tithing by all the People of God would provide the funds necessary to pay these adequate salaries for religious and lay people; the lack of funds is the usual underlying cause for the lack of adequate salaries. The obligation to sustain the Church's institutions—education and health care, social service agencies, religious education programs, care of the elderly, youth ministry, and the like—falls on all the members of the community because of their baptism; the obligation is not just on the users or on those who staff them. Increased resources are also needed for the support of elderly members of religious communities. These dedicated women and men have not always asked for or received the stipends and pensions that would have assured their future. It would be a breach of our obligations to them to let them or their communities face retirement without adequate funds.

352. Many volunteers provide services to the Church and its mission which cannot be measured in dollars and cents. These services are important to the life and vitality of the Church in the United States and carry on a practice that has marked the history of the Church in this country since its founding. In this tradition, we ask young people to make themselves available for a year or more of voluntary service before beginning their training for more specific vocations in life; we also recommend expanding voluntary service roles for retired persons; we encourage those who have accepted this challenge.

353. All church institutions must also fully recognize the rights of employees to organize and bargain collectively with the institution through whatever association or organization they freely choose.[12] In the light of new creative models of collaboration between labor and management described earlier in this letter, we challenge our church institutions to adopt new fruitful modes of cooperation. Although the Church has its own nature and mission that must be respected and fostered, we are pleased that many who are not of our faith, but who

share similar hopes and aspirations for the human family, work for us and with us in achieving this vision. In seeking greater justice in wages, we recognize the need to be alert particularly to the continuing discrimination against women throughout Church and society, especially reflected in both the inequities of salaries between women and men and in the concentration of women in jobs at the lower end of the wage scale.

354. Individual Christians who are shareholders and those responsible within church institutions that own stocks in U.S. corporations must see to it that the invested funds are used responsibly. Although it is a moral and legal fiduciary responsibility of the trustees to ensure an adequate return on investment for the support of the work of the Church, their stewardship embraces broader moral concerns. As part-owners, they must cooperate in shaping the policies of those companies through dialogue with management, through votes at corporate meetings, through the introduction of resolutions, and through participation in investment decisions. We praise the efforts of dioceses and other religious and ecumenical bodies that work together toward these goals. We also praise efforts to develop alternative investment policies, especially those which support enterprises that promote economic development in depressed communities and which help the Church respond to local and regional needs.[13] When the decision to divest seems unavoidable, it should be done after prudent examination and with a clear explanation of the motives.

355. The use of church property demands special attention today. Changing demographic patterns have left many parishes and institutions with empty or partially used buildings. The decline in the number of religious who are teaching in the schools and the reduction in the number of clergy often result in large residences with few occupants. In this regard, the Church must be sensitive to the image the possession of such large facilities often projects, namely, that it is wealthy

and extravagant in the use of its resources. This image can be overcome only by clear public accountability of its financial holdings, of its properties and their use, and of the services it renders to its members and to society at large. We support and encourage the creative use of these facilities by many parishes and dioceses to serve the needs of the poor.

356. The Church has a special call to be a servant of the poor, the sick, and the marginalized, thereby becoming a true sign of the Church's mission—a mission shared by every member of the Christian community. The Church now serves many such people through one of the largest private human services delivery systems in the country. The networks of agencies, institutions, and programs provide services to millions of persons of all faiths. Still we must be reminded that in our day our Christian concerns must increase and extend beyond our borders, because everyone in need is our neighbor. We must also be reminded that charity requires more than alleviating misery. It demands genuine love for the person in need. It should probe the meaning of suffering and provoke a response that seeks to remedy causes. True charity leads to advocacy.

357. Yet charity alone is not a corrective to all economic social ills. All citizens, working through various organizations of society and through government, bear the responsibility of caring for those who are in need. The Church, too, through all its members individually and through its agencies, must work to alleviate injustices that prevent some from participating fully in economic life. Our experience with the Campaign for Human Development confirms our judgment about the validity of self-help and empowerment of the poor. The campaign, which has received the positive support of American Catholics since it was launched in 1970, provides a model that we think sets a high standard for similar efforts. We bishops know of the many faithful in all walks of life who use their skills and their compassion to seek innovative ways to carry out the goals we

are proposing in this letter. As they do this, they *are* the Church acting for economic justice. At the same time, we hope they will join together with us and their priests to influence our society so that even more steps can be taken to alleviate injustices. Grassroots efforts by the poor themselves, helped by community support, are indispensable. The entire Christian community can learn much from the way our deprived brothers and sisters assist each other in their struggles.

358. In addition to being an economic actor, the Church is a significant cultural actor concerned about the deeper cultural roots of our economic problems. As we have proposed a new experiment in collaboration and participation in decision making by all those affected at all levels of U.S. society, so we also commit the Church to become a model of collaboration and participation.

C. THE ROAD AHEAD

359. The completion of a letter such as this one is but the beginning of a long process of education, discussion and action; its contents must be brought to all members of the Church and of society.

360. In this respect we mentioned the twofold aim of this pastoral letter: to help Catholics form their consciences on the moral dimensions of economic decision making and to articulate a moral perspective in the general societal and political debate that surrounds these questions. These two purposes help us to reflect on the different ways the institutions and ministers of the Church can assist the laity in their vocation in the world. Renewed emphasis on Catholic social teaching in our schools, colleges, and universities; special seminars with corporate officials, union leaders, legislators, bankers, and the like; the organization of small groups composed of people from different

ways of life to meditate together on the Gospel and ethical norms; speakers' bureaus; family programs; clearinghouses of available material; pulpit aids for priests; diocesan television and radio programs; research projects in our universities—all of these are appropriate means for continued discussion and action. Some of these are done best on the parish level, others by the state Catholic conferences, and others by the National Conference of Catholic Bishops. These same bodies can assist the laity in the many difficult decisions that deal with political options that affect economic decisions. Where many options are available, it must be the concern of all in such debates that we as Catholics do not become polarized. All must be challenged to show how the decisions they make and the policies they suggest flow from the ethical moral vision outlined here. As new problems arise, we hope through our continual reflection that we will be able to help refine Catholic social teaching and contribute to its further development.

361. We call upon our priests, in particular, to continue their study of these issues, so that they can proclaim the gospel message in a way that not only challenges the faithful but also sustains and encourages their vocation in and to the world. Priestly formation in our seminaries will also have to prepare candidates for this role.

362. We wish to emphasize the need to undertake research into many of the areas this document could not deal with in depth and to continue exploration of those we have dealt with. We encourage our Catholic universities, foundations, and other institutions to assist in these necessary projects. The following areas for further research are merely suggestive, not exhaustive: the impact of arms production and large military spending on the domestic economy and on culture; arms production and sales as they relate to Third World poverty; tax reforms to express the preferential option for the poor; the rights of women and minorities in the work force; the development of communications tech-

nology and its global influences; robotics, automation, and reduction of defense industries as they will affect employment; the economy and the stability of the family; legitimate profit versus greed; securing economic rights; environmental and ecological questions; future roles of labor and unions; international financial institutions and Third World debt; our national deficit; world food problems; "full employment" and its implementation; plant closings and dealing with the human costs of an evolving economy; cooperatives and new modes of sharing; welfare reform and national eligibility standards; income support systems; concentration of land ownership; assistance to Third World nations; migration and its effects; population policies and development; the effects of increased inequality of incomes in society.

D. COMMITMENT TO A KINGDOM OF LOVE AND JUSTICE

363. Confronted by this economic complexity and seeking clarity for the future, we can rightly ask ourselves one single question: How does our economic system affect the lives of people—*all* people? Part of the American dream has been to make this world a better place for people to live in; at this moment of history that dream must include everyone on this globe. Since we profess to be members of a "catholic" or universal Church, we all must raise our sights to a concern for the well-being of everyone in the world. Third World debt becomes our problem. Famine and starvation in sub-Saharan Africa become our concern. Rising military expenditures everywhere in the world become part of our fears for the future of this planet. We cannot be content if we see ecological neglect or the squandering of natural resources. In this letter we bishops have spoken often of economic interdependence; now is the moment when all of us must con-

front the reality of such economic bonding and its consequences
and see it as a moment of grace—a *kairos*—that can unite all of us
in a common community of the human family. We commit ourselves to this global vision.

364. We cannot be frightened by the magnitude and complexity of these problems. We must not be discouraged. In the
midst of this struggle, it is inevitable that we become aware of
greed, laziness, and envy. No utopia is possible on this earth;
but as believers in the redemptive love of God and as those who
have experienced God's forgiving mercy, we know that God's
providence is not and will not be lacking to us today.

365. The fulfillment of human needs, we know, is not the
final purpose of the creation of the human person. We have
been created to share in the divine life through a destiny that
goes far beyond our human capabilities and before which we
must in all humility stand in awe. Like Mary in proclaiming
her *Magnificat*, we marvel at the wonders God has done for us,
how God has raised up the poor and the lowly and promised
great things for them in the Kingdom. God now asks of us sacrifices and reflection on our reverence for human dignity—in
ourselves and in others—and on our service and discipleship,
so that the divine goal for the human family and this earth can
be fulfilled. Communion with God, sharing God's life, involves a mutual bonding with all on this globe. Jesus taught us
to love God and one another and that the concept of neighbor
is without limit. We know that we are called to be members of
a new covenant of love. We have to move from our devotion to
independence, through an understanding of interdependence,
to a commitment to human solidarity. That challenge must
find its realization in the kind of community we build among
us. Love implies concern for all—especially the poor—and a
continued search for those social and economic structures that
permit everyone to share in a community that is a part of a redeemed creation (Rom 8:21–23).

NOTES

[1]*Reconciliation and Penance*, 13.

[2]*Justice in the World*, 6.

[3]Medellin Documents: *Justice* (1968), 4.

[4]*Dogmatic Constitution on the Church*, 1; *Pastoral Constitution*, 42, 45; *Constitution on the Liturgy*, 26; *Decree on the Church's Missionary Activity*, 5; *Liturgy and Social Justice*, ed. by Mark Searle, (Collegeville, Minn.: Liturgical Press, 1980); National Conference of Catholic Bishops, *The Church at Prayer* (Washington, D.C.: USCC Office of Publishing and Promotion Services, 1983).

[5]*Dogmatic Constitution on the Church*, 36.

[6]*Justice in the World*, 41.

[7]National Conference of Catholic Bishops, *To Teach as Jesus Did*, A Pastoral Message on Education (Washington, D.C.: USCC Office of Publishing and Promotion Services, 1972), 7.

[8]Cf. Vatican Council II, *Declaration on Christian Education*, 3, 6. See also, *Charter of the Rights of the Family*, 5b; *Instruction on Christian Freedom and Liberation*, 94.

[9]Pope John Paul II, *On the Family* (Washington, D.C.: USCC Office of Publishing and Promotion Services, 1981), 6. See also Robert N. Bellah, Richard Madsen, William M. Sullivan, Ann Swidler, Steven M. Tipton, *Habits of the Heart: Individualism and Commitment in American Life* (Berkeley: University of California Press, 1985); *The Family Today and Tomorrow: The Church Addresses Her Future* (Boston, Mass.: The Pope John Center, 1985).

[10]*Justice in the World*, 40.

[11]*Dogmatic Constitution on the Church*, 8.

[12]National Conference of Catholic Bishops, *Health and Health Care* (Washington, D.C.: USCC Office of Publishing and Promotion Services, 1981), 50.

[13]See ch. IV of this pastoral letter.